EDGE OF THE

Michael Powell (1905–1990) was born i:
School, Canterbury and Dulwich Colle
Rex Ingram's MGM unit based near Nice ии 192) anu gaиcu слрсиспсс
in many departments before returning to England in 1928. Soon established as a prolific director of low-budget thrillers, he revealed his
ambition with *The Edge of the World* (1936), which led to a contract
with Alexander Korda's London Films, Powell's eventual involvement
with the spectacular *Thief of Bagdad* and the beginning of a twenty-
year partnership with the writer Emeric Pressburger on *The Spy in
Black* (1939).

Together they created some of the most daring and oblique contri-
butions to the war effort, including *49th Parallel* (1942), *The Life and
Death of Colonel Blimp* (1943), *A Canterbury Tale* (1944), *I Know Where
I'm Going!* (1945) and *A Matter of Life and Death* (1946). The Archers,
as Powell and Pressburger now signed their joint films, continued to
exploit Technicolor and their feeling for metaphysical melodrama with
the controversial *Black Narcissus* (1947) and *The Red Shoes* (1948), before
renewed crisis in the British film industry forced them into the compromised co-productions of *Gone to Earth* and *The Elusive Pimpernel* (both
1950). *The Tales of Hoffmann* (1951) marked the climax of their 'total
cinema' incorporating opera, ballet and stylized design, and it led to
three years of failed projects. After an updated *Fledermaus, Oh Rosa-
linda!!* (1955) and two war films, *The Battle of the River Plate* and *Ill
Met By Moonlight* (both 1956), they dissolved the partnership.

Powell continued to pursue his vision of a cinema drawing upon all
the other arts, but found scant backing, except in Spain (*Honeymoon*,
1959), West Germany (*Bluebeard's Castle*, 1964) and Australia (*Age of
Consent*, 1969). His later career was dominated by the scandal of *Peeping
Tom* (1960), a latter-day Gothic shocker which offended many, while
also inspiring a new generation of British and American film-makers.
Among the latter were Francis Coppola, who invited Powell to his
Zoetrope Studios in 1980 as a consultant, and Martin Scorsese, who
helped relaunch the uncut *Peeping Tom*. Powell's last decade saw
impressive restorations of his major films and tributes around the
world, his marriage to the distinguished editor Thelma Schoonmaker,
and the first volume of a major autobiography, *A Life in Movies* (1986).

THIS MAP is a present from the Men of Foula to the Joe Rock Film Unit, in memory of four months of comradeship, of sunshine and of cloud, of wind and of rain, of waiting and watching, of climbing and falling, from Hoevdi Burn to the Haa, from the North End to the Hametoun, not forgetting the Sneck of the Smallie, making our film *"The Edge of the World,"* June to October, 1936.

Walter Ratter + James Gray + Peter Gray + Andrew Manson

Andrew Umphray + James Henry + Willy Smith + Peter Manson

Peter Ratter + James Ratter + William Umphray + Thomas Umphray

Thomas Gray + Robert. W. Isbister + James Morrison
Peter Peterson + Robert Isbister June + George Isbister

Gaada Stack

Strem Ness

Kittiwakes Haa

Soberlie Hill 800 feet

Ruscar Head

Gone Over Stone

Camp 3

The Kame 1220 feet

Flick Lochs

North and South Harrier

Nebbifeld

The Sneug 1373 feet

Hamnafeld 1126 feet

Rosie's Loch

Taing Head

Wester Hoevdi

Base Camp

The Haa

Camp 2

The Ufshins

Townafeld

Mill Loch

Ham Voe

Baa Head

Wick of Mucklaberg

The Sneck

The Daal

War Memorial

Durga Ness

Camp 1

Hellibergs Wick

The Noup 730 feet

Foula

Grissgarth

South Ness

Rippack Stack

N

THE SOUVENIR MAP OF FOULA
(*see page 322*)

Edge of the World

MICHAEL POWELL

faber and faber

LONDON · BOSTON

This book
is dedicated affectionately
to all my friends
and enemies

First published in 1938
as *200,000 Feet on Foula*
by Faber and Faber Limited
3 Queen Square London WCIN 3AU
This new paperback edition
first published in 1990

Printed in Great Britain by
Richard Clay Ltd, Bungay, Suffolk

A CIP record for this book is
available from the British Library

ISBN 0–571–15306–2

CONTENTS

★

LIST OF ILLUSTRATIONS

★

INTRODUCTION:
RETURNING TO THE EDGE OF
THE WORLD

★

The gulls that bank around the mast
Insinuate that nothing we pass is past,
   That all our beginnings are long since begun.

Louis MacNeice, 'Passage Steamer'

Michael Powell's account of his seven-year struggle to make a film about the depopulation of the Scottish islands appeared, astonishingly, when he was only thirty-three and still quite unknown outside film-making circles. How he persuaded Faber and Faber in 1938 to put out *200,000 Feet on Foula*, as it was first cryptically titled, we may wonder.★ Why it should now be reissued is easier to explain. In the last fifteen years, Powell has been belatedly recognized as one of the British cinema's greatest, if least domesticated, talents. The publication of his first volume of autobiography, *A Life in Movies* in 1986, confirmed what some already knew: that his pen was as mighty, and mercurial, as his camera. His letters and diaries, if they are ever published, will earn him a greater reputation than any mere film-maker could expect in Britain – even one responsible for *The Life and Death of Colonel Blimp, A Matter of Life and Death* and *The Red Shoes*.

But all these, which followed from his meeting with Emeric Press-burger in the same year that the book appeared, still lay in the future. At that time Powell could only claim to have started in movies some-where near the top, albeit as a floor sweeper, with Rex Ingram's ex-MGM company in Nice in 1925, before restarting at what felt like the bottom back in England three years later at Elstree studios. From 1930, however, he had benefited from the peculiar conditions of British production to direct no less than twenty-three films in seven years, even if the majority of these played second fiddle to American films and all were produced in the teeth of tight schedules and budgets.

After this unusual apprenticeship, Powell was ready to stake his bid for independence with a film set far beyond studio walls and evoking a primitive grandeur very different from the shallow West End sophist-ication of other assignments of the same year, such as *Her Last Affaire* and *Crown v. Stevens*. He was well aware that the film, which had

★The original title refers to the amount of film shot on Foula.

involved so much dedication and effort, might very well suffer the same fate as many other low-budget British productions and soon disappear from public view, so a book would at least commemorate the venture.

Sure enough, *The Edge of the World* soon disappeared into archival limbo and has only been seen by other than scholars in recent years thanks to its imaginative resurrection as *Return to the Edge of the World* in 1978 for a BBC TV transmission. This enabled Powell to add a new prologue and epilogue to the now-shortened original film, making it a characteristic excursion into *Temps Perdus*.

The book, however, remains wholly innocent of hindsight, which makes it both delightful and invaluable: a portrait of the artist as a young zealot, bursting to tell his story and to make it compelling by whatever means. These were the qualities that marked all his films, including those of the Powell–Pressburger partnership, and here we can actually see the chemistry of chance, inspiration and labour at work. To read the passage that runs from Powell's rejection by Lord Dumfries, the owner of St Kilda, to his meeting with Alasdair Holbourn of the family that owned Foula (pp. 46–69) is to follow the workings of a born director's mind, swooping over ellipses from image to image. And on characterization, try the index entry for the same Alasdair Holbourn in his three Kiplingesque personae. What follows here by way of introduction sketches the circumstances, personal and industrial, that brought Powell to what he later called 'the turning point of my life in art'.

The British film industry to which young Micky Powell returned from France in 1928 was on the brink of a series of profound upheavals. London may have seemed cold after the Côte d'Azur, but there could scarcely have been a better time for an outsider to find a foothold.

Already underway was the complex process of adjusting to synchronized sound production, now proceeding at breakneck speed less than a year after the sensational American success of Warner's *The Jazz Singer* (1927). Britain lagged behind America, apprehensively waiting to see if sound would prove a passing fad and judge which technical system was best. But public interest ran high and between 1929, with only a third of releases having some form of sound-on-film, and the following year, when a majority did, it became clear that the balance had tipped decisively.

Films started as conventional 'silents' were converted in mid-production to meet the new demand for 'talkies'. Some merely had sound-effects and music added, with a minimum of actual dialogue scenes. Others, like Hitchcock's *Blackmail* (on which Powell did uncredited script work), were completed in two distinct versions. Harry Lachman, his first mentor in the Ingram unit who had then starred him in the short-lived *'Travelaughs'* series, became a technical supervisor at British International Pictures' Elstree studio and soon

Introduction

graduated to directing. His *Under the Greenwood Tree* came only four months after *Blackmail* as one of the first British full-length talkies.

Sound caused major changes throughout the industry. It meant expensive re-equipping of studios and cinemas, which increased the power of bankers and investors. The scale of investment dictated improving profitability and decreasing risk; hence the shift away from a (relatively) open market relationship between producers, distributors and exhibitors towards the 'vertical integration' of these functions in large conglomerate empires which would be a feature of the 1930s.

From the producers' and the public's viewpoint, new stars with singing and acting skills were at a premium, while the merely photogenic soon faded. New technical skills were needed and what amounted to a new grammar of cinema had to emerge through trial and error. Early sound recording equipment demanded highly controlled shooting conditions, with a minimum of extraneous noise and smooth floors for the cumbersome cameras, all of which encouraged studio use and soon led to the construction of the insulated 'sound stage'.

Scripts also became central to film production in a way they had never been during the silent era, when a mass of footage could be shaped in many different ways by ingenious title-writing. And where could ready-made scripts, complete with dialogue and appropriate actors, be found? In Britain the West End stage assumed the same importance as Broadway did for American sound cinema; and such was the demand that some theatre actors found themselves going straight from their West End appearances to one of the numerous studios circling London, where they would work through the night on a talkie.

The consequences of sound went far beyond a technical revolution. It accelerated an underlying trend towards American domination of the international cinema which had started during the First World War, and nowhere more so than in Britain which – nominally at least – spoke the same language. As Powell later noted in his autobiography, the sheer cost of converting to sound and the fact that the best equipment came from America, delivered an already weakened British industry even further into economic subservience.

There had been growing concern about the decline in British production since the early 1920s. By 1926, when only 5 per cent of films shown in Britain were indigenous productions, a reluctant government followed what was already a broad European strategy in the face of increasing American penetration which threatened the very existence of national production industries. The Cinematograph Films Act of 1927 introduced the 'quotas' that would echo through the following fifty years of British cinema history and give rise to the notorious category of 'quota pictures' – or, as they were known in the trade, 'quota quickies'.

Not that 'quota' production itself proved entirely barren. The recent reassessment of a neglected figure such as Bernard Vorhaus who worked within the same constraints as Powell underlines how much could be achieved by ingenious directors constantly seeking to demonstrate their skills even with inferior material – and also how little we know about what has been a despised period. Nothing of Powell's strictly quota picture output of 1931–4 was thought to have survived, until the National Film Archive recently found his third film, *Rynox*, dating from 1931 and three others from the same period. But a 'discovery' like Vorhaus's *The Ghost Camera* (1933), made for Julius Hagen at Twickenham as was Powell's extant *Lazybones* (1935), shows how much stylistic freedom at least the directors of such material had. Powell recalls his own pound-a-minute début, *Two Crowded Hours* (1931) as showing 'Continental' influence with its 'clever angles and quick cutting', culminating in a 'kaleidoscopic montage of images inspired by the Soviet cinema', achieved with the aid of an experienced editor.

While this admittedly artificial demand kept indigenous production going and helped train a new generation of directors and writers – at the same time serving as a talent-spotting resource for Hollywood – the British industry was in fact being reshaped by a new breed of producer and by the rising tide of European immigration. The Hungarian Alexander Korda broke the mould of British producers when he arrived in 1931 with both French and Hollywood credits and established London Films. His early commercial and critical success with *The Private Life of Henry VIII* (1933) set a standard to which many aspired, if few, including Korda himself, again achieved. Equally significant, though less exotic, was Michael Balcon's move from Gainsborough Pictures to head its Gaumont–British parent company. A short-lived alliance with the German UFA in 1932 strengthened Gaumont's continental connections; and the events of the following year added to the trickle of refugees already on its staff.

There were other ambitious producer-impresarios too, such as Basil Dean of Associated Talking Pictures and Herbert Wilcox of British and Dominion, mining different veins of appeal to the British audience. But it was Balcon, the force behind Hitchcock's thrillers and Saville's musicals and the cosmopolitan Korda, who commanded most respect. When Powell and his producer partner Jerry Jackson landed a contract with Gaumont–British in 1933 to make four topical thrillers, they felt they had at last escaped from the 'poverty row' of quota production – although it was in fact their reputation for stylish economy which had brought them to Balcon's attention.

Powell was now established with a modest but growing reputation for delivering contemporary thrillers. He worked for Warner's and Fox's British subsidiaries. Yet as a romantic at heart, who had already experienced the excitement of bravura international production at an impressionable age with Rex Ingram in Nice, he hankered after some grander statement and a different palette. The germ of *The Edge of the World*, as he recounts, came from a newspaper account of the evacuation of St Kilda. But the concept of a film shot in spectacular natural locations, which would have both an epic dimension and mythic resonance, was one which had survived from the silent era and was now undergoing transformation in many different contexts. In America, the Western already provided a popular vehicle for such preoccupations, while the New Deal was also stimulating celebrations as *The Plow That Broke the Plains*; the films of Dovzhenko and Eisenstein, although now superseded by new Soviet styles, were still influential in the west; and in France, Jean Epstein had turned his back on the fashionable avant-garde to celebrate the Breton people and landscape.

Its lineage can be traced from the protean figure of Robet Flaherty, explorer turned film-maker, who virtually invented this arch-romantic genre with his portrait of an Eskimo hunter, *Nanook of the North*, released in 1922. With this, the cinema triumphantly succeeded in realizing its potential to transport a largely urban audience to the remote frontiers of human existence and to involve it in an exotic, endangered way of life. The fact that Nanook himself died soon after the film's release, while his image 'lived on' in the film's circulation, recalled those predictions made after the first demonstration of the Lumière *cinématographe* that henceforth 'death will be no longer final'.

Travellers' tales, formerly accompanied by magic lantern slides, would never be the same again. And this vein of popular ethnography was taken up by others, notably Ernest Schoedsack and Merian Cooper with their *Grass* (1925, subtitled 'The Epic of a Lost Tribe') and *Chang* (1927). But it was Flaherty who remained most identified with it, as he turned to Polynesia for *Moana* (1926) and eventually to Ireland for *Man of Aran* (1934).

This latter was financed by Balcon's Gaumont–British, and Powell has recalled his year-long proximity to Flaherty in the GB cutting rooms, where he turned out four films in less time than the notoriously demanding Flaherty took to edit his Aran material. According to Powell, the Great Man's response to his proposed St Kilda story was emphatic:

> Facts are facts, you cannot beat Nature. You cannot beat Nature. You can't invent the evacuation of an island, you can't ignore the death of a people! Ya' should have been there when it happened! With half a dozen cameras.

Later research has shown that Flaherty was far from averse to 'inventing' what his noble primitives should be seen to do – and that for *Man of Aran* he effectively turned the clock back by teaching the islanders fishing techniques they had long abandoned.

Powell's account makes Flaherty sound more like a documentarist than he ever was – perhaps because their encounter took place at the very time when John Grierson and his young protégés at the Empire Marketing Board and GPO film units claimed Flaherty as their inspiration for a concept of 'documentary' that Powell mistrusted. Later he would cite the glorious improbability of the doomed-bomber open-ing of *A Matter of Life and Death* as a deliberate snook cocked at the now revered documentary movement. Truth for Powell – as, in a way, for Flaherty – lay not in the faithful record of externals, or the omniscient voice of the commentator (also guyed at the beginning of *A Matter of Life and Death*). It emerged from emotion, debate and conflict, which are the stuff of drama. A filmed record of the actual St Kilda evacuation would not necessarily have been more effective in conveying the significance of this watershed in a traditional way of life than a fictionalized drama filmed on a different, still-inhabited island. Cinema, after all, is illusion, although it is the illusion of reality.

For Powell in 1936, contemplating an endless prospect of more or less conventional thrillers amid the continuing uncertainties of British production, there was a stark choice: either secure backing for the St Kilda story or, like many of his colleagues, head for Hollywood. The only model for the kind of film he envisaged – *Turn of the Tide*, filmed in 1935 on location at Robin Hood's Bay – had made little headway in British distribution, despite a prize from the Venice Film Festival. However this failure reputedly stung its novice producer, the Methodist milling magnate J. Arthur Rank, into action and launched a career that would lead to near-domination of British cinema – and incidentally give Powell his greatest creative freedom in the period 1943–8.

Then he met Joe Rock, one of many expatriate Americans involved in British film-making at the time – there were estimated to be some 640 production companies registered in the decade up to 1937. And it was Rock, perhaps seeing the only hope for his threatened small com-pany in a bold gamble, who finally backed Powell's vision.

By the time some 200,000 feet of exposed film had been edited down to the film's original length of 7,300 feet and a special pre-release run arranged at the New Gallery in London, Rock Studios was already bankrupt, along with most of the myriad other small independents.

Amid scandal over producers' recklessness, loans were called in and even the flamboyant Korda imposed pay cuts on the instruction of his backers. Meanwhile, Rank took over as chairman of Pinewood Studios, where he had previously been a partner, and began to consolidate his production-distribution-exhibition empire. When the 1938 Film Act introduced a minimum budget level for quota qualification and allowed higher budget films to count as two for quota purposes, this exacer-bated an already fraught situation, and allowed the American compan-ies to further consolidate their indirect control of British production. Once again, Powell stood at the threshold of a new stage in his career in parlous times.

The *succès d'estime* of *The Edge of the World* had brought him to Korda's attention and led to a one-year contract, although the project he worked on, *Burmese Silver*, was dropped amid the retrenchment of 1938. But Powell clearly delighted in the cosmopolitan atmosphere of Korda's London Films and Denham studios. He notes with ill-

Introduction

concealed pride in his autobiography how Korda's Big Ben trademark was actually the same as that of his and Jackson's short-lived Westminster Films. Whatever Korda's shortcomings as a businessman, he undeniably had style – and he had the acumen to bring together two under-employed contract employees, Powell and the writer Emeric Pressburger, to create a vehicle for an equally under-employed star, Conrad Veidt. The outcome was *The Spy in Black* and the beginning of Powell and Pressburger's partnership as the 'Chesterbelloc' of British cinema, The Archers.

But what of *The Edge of the World* itself? The film was shortened for re-release at least twice and almost certainly has not been seen in its original version since the 1940s. It has perhaps been too easily incorporated into The Story of The Archers to note its own peculiar qualities. The classic review was by the well-known *Observer* critic C. A. Lejeune, who had followed Powell's career since his début. This review however appeared in *The School Master and Woman Teacher's Chronicle* on 23 September 1937 during the New Gallery run, and it is worth quoting at length.

> Comparison is inevitable between this film and *Man of Aran* and *Turn of the Tide*, that simple but moving little story of the Yorkshire lobster fishing. The same elemental things are the protagonists – the seaman's strength of limb, the parched earth, sickness, the fatalistic acceptance of death, and the curious, childish dread of speaking the word 'death'. The same clean, primitive honesty is in all of them. But *The Edge of the World*, I believe, is in every way the more successful picture. It is, in a degree that the other two are not, a picture-maker's picture. It is full of the tricks of the trade – double-exposures, ghost figures, narrative fade-outs, super-impositions of sound. But the tricks are discreetly done. They point up the emphasis of the story, never disfigure it.

Another, more sceptical, contemporary review in the *New Statesman* admitted that the film was 'artistic' and that 'the direction is admirable', but railed against the publicity given to the much-advertised production rigours by noting that 'it is not simple or unpretentious, and least of all is it realistic'.

These views are not of course incompatible; they merely confirm how relative is the accolade of 'realism'. *The Edge of the World* was indeed poised between two worlds, that of the romantic silent cinema which had originally seized Powell's imagination and the anticipation of a future cinema based on location shooting. But it lay closer to the 1920s in spirit. Many of the devices noted by Lejeune are precisely those once common in silent film, but already anachronistic in 1937 – such as the procession of superimposed 'ghosts' who make literal Andrew Gray's memory of the once-populated island in the film's prologue. Similarly the use of post-synchronized sound is highly selective, a series of accents and counterpoints to the image, rather than integrally naturalistic. Powell recalls how many of the Foula exteriors were shot in true silent-era style to the accompaniment of Smetana's 'Moldau' played on his portable gramophone.

Historians of cinema scan the early Powell films with an unanswerable question in mind: can they help better identify the 'Powell' of 'Powell and Pressburger'? As we look at *The Edge of the World* today, and indeed its 'revised edition' *Return to the Edge of the World*, we find the same fascination with embedding stories within stories, chinese box style, that marks The Archers' films. Think of *One of Our Aircraft Is Missing* or, of course, *The Life and Death of Colonel Blimp*, both of them exploiting the elementary fact that what we *see* in cinema is always in the present tense, whatever narrative signposting surrounds it. The break-up of the island community through external and internal pressures anticipates the collapse of the Himalayan convent in *Black Narcissus* (1947). But it was in *I Know Where I'm Going!* that Powell, aided by one of Pressburger's most personal scripts, redressed the pessimism of *The Edge of the World* and showed a Scottish island community facing up to the modern post-war world by rejecting what is alien and materialistic, and keeping faith with its ancient traditions as enshrined in myth.

All this came later – but in 1938, the un-English presumption of Powell's film *and* accompanying book attracted attention in many quarters and gave notice of impressive things to come. In particular, his stress on the co-operative nature of film-making found a welcome at the newly organized film union, the Association of Cinematograph Technicians. In a letter to the Board of Trade about the state of the industry, the ACT's secretary George Elvin quoted approvingly from *200,000 Feet on Foula*:

> To us in the film industry it is a vivid revelation of our own unexpressed feelings . . . We don't shout our admiration of our fellow technicians – perhaps we are at fault in that – but we feel and know that Powell is right when he says 'No one man ever made a film. He can inspire it. He can stamp his personality on it. But in the long run it is good team work that makes a good film.'

The Archers was to become the embodiment of that co-operative ideal, here so wonderfully anticipated and recorded in what is probably the most vivid book ever written about a film's making by its director.

Ian Christie

PREFACE

★

Two years ago, one person in a thousand had heard of Foula. To-day only one person in a thousand has not.

A year ago Foula had no communication with the mainland of Shetland; only last winter the island was completely isolated for seven weeks. To-day, there is a beam-wireless telephone installation and messages are received and transmitted five times a day.

To-day, there is no harbour for large boats on Foula, so that any commercial or tourist scheme is severely handicapped. To-morrow, let us hope, there will be that harbour.

In ten years' time, unknown, neglected and helpless, Foula would probably have become a desert island. To-day it is famous, a place of interest, its people have money in the bank. There is every hope that, in ten years' time, the island will be as independent as it has been for a thousand years.

In June 1936, when I took my company to the Shetlands to make the film, such a result was never in my head. Foula was only a means to an end, the ideal island for my purpose, which was to show dramatically how the Outer Isles of Scotland were slowly being depopulated. The rest of my company—actors, technicians, workmen—shared this view. But the island put its spell upon us all. In five months of work, shoulder to shoulder, the island folk got into our hearts. We came, we saw . . . were conquered.

Twice we were marooned, the last time seriously, cut off from fresh meat, vegetables, bread, worst of all, cigarettes. Though the wind blew a hundred miles an hour we went on shooting, while the world panicked outside and sent broadcast messages, aeroplanes and supply-ships to our rescue. Finally, during a lull in an October gale, we were pulled off our island by main force. Many of us were sorry to leave.

For the next six months we were busy editing the two hundred thousand feet of film exposed (whence the title of this book) down to seven thousand, the length of the finished film.

The Edge of the World differs from most films dealing with remote places of the earth in that its theme is told by means of a dramatic story, a conflict between two fathers and their sons. The chief parts were played by actors and the whole island took part in the film. It is essentially an exciting drama, not a series of beautiful and meaningless pictures.

Thanks to fan magazines, I suppose lots of people nowadays have a hazy idea of how film-makers go about spoiling celluloid, but few have any idea of the violent, mad, comic adventures that befall a film-promoter who is trying to get things started. Some of these are described in the first half of this book, for it happened that I was on this film from the word 'Go!' I had thought of the idea, written the story, sold it, promoted money to make it, written the scenario and dialogue, found the island, bossed the expedition, directed the film, shot the stills and acted a part in the picture. It seemed to me that nobody would ever have a better idea of how the wheels go round. That accounts for this book.

My thanks are due to the Rock Studios for permission to quote from my script and treatment of the story, and to use the negatives of my stills.

I must also thank Mrs. M. C. S. Holbourn and her sons, the present owners of Foula; especially Alasdair Holbourn, who was with us through the expedition and is still on Foula.

Also I thank Mr. A. G. Pringle for reading through the typescript and making many tactful suggestions.

January 1938   MICHAEL POWELL

PART I

'First the fish must be caught.'
—The White Queen

Chapter I

UNDER THIRTY-TWO FLAGS

★

'Ahoy! What ship is that?'

There was no reply, we had none ready.

('Where the devil is the megaphone, Wullie?')

The excitement of getting under way had betrayed us all. Vernon was skipper. Vernon should reply. But Vernon has a slight stammer when excited. On the bridge a megaphone gives him confidence. But the megaphone had vanished.

'Ahoy, there! Who are you?'

'Steam Yacht *V-Vedra* ... with f-film company aboard!'

('Wud this be it, sir?' 'No, you ass, look in the chartroom.')

A dry chuckle drifted across the water. The high slimy walls of Aberdeen docks were gliding past extraordinarily quickly. The deep voice of the harbour-master came again through the fog. In the darkness I could just make out a vague bridge-like structure and some dim figures watching us.

'Where bound, Captain?'

'LERWICK!'

Frantic search had at last produced the megaphone and the suddenly augmented voice of Captain Sewell nearly blew my ear off.

The answer was according to Board of Trade regulations but I felt I could improve on it. I seized the megaphone, bellowed: 'And the Isle of Foula!' and handed it back with

3

an apology for my mutinous behaviour. As the *Vedra* lifted to the first swells I think I heard a distant voice cry: 'Good luck.'

The day before had been the twenty-first of June, the longest day in the year, Midsummer Day. Nobody would have guessed it now. It was colder than it had any right to be and a thick sea-fog dripped off everything. Vernon rang for half-speed and the beat of the engines quickened. Lights appeared and disappeared in the channel. To a landsman it all appeared very dangerous but none of us liked to say so. Occasionally Vernon or White would vanish down the bridge ladder, dive into the chart-room, consult the chart, reappear and glare at the compass. Once a minute Wullie would pull an obscure piece of knotted wire which vanished through the roof of the wheel-house. Before you could say Heath Robinson, a shower of dirty water would descend on the starboard decks and the hoarse voice of the *Vedra* would bellow obediently. It was a novelty, but it soon wore off.

Our decks were covered with painfully hard shapes, swaddled in streaming black tarpaulins. Timber was piled high everywhere, a small motor tractor completely blocked the port side, huge packing-cases loomed. For two feverish days Vernon had been loading, swearing, and loading.

One by one we landlubbers left the decks and, nursing our bruises, gathered in the saloon. Normally a square, cosy deck-house, aft of the engine-room, it now looked like a scene in one of those superb but muddling American films where the whole cast is catching the Last Express from Shanghai or Madrid or Baskul and has crowded into the Left Luggage Office to talk it over. I counted noses. They were all there. Some of them were starting to look green as we rolled up the coast.

How the *Vedra* could roll! She rolled through gales, swells, flat calms. It was her natural gait, she knew no other. Nobody (except Vernon, who loved her dearly) ever got used to her, she was hated on sight by all who trod her dirty decks. And she rolled! All her good qualities —she had several—were lost sight of in that detestable habit. Also, she suffered (even her best friends told her) from 'B.O.'

She was a pilot boat out of Sunderland and from Sunderland was her first mate, Bill White, an old acquaintance of hers, who now stood peering through the streaming panes of the wheel-house. Beside him, Captain Vernon Sewell screwed his monocle firmly in his right eye and peered proudly at the splendid outsize binnacle which he had secretly purchased with his own money. He was outwardly unmoved but every button on his pea-jacket was strained to bursting. He gave me a curt nod as I reappeared on the bridge.

'Hullo, Micky, old man,' he said absently. I watched him thoughtfully. We were nosing blind through a tangle of mudbanks and fretful shipping; he had been on his feet for thirty-six hours and had the prospect of a sleepless night before him; his ship was a shambles, his cabin had two people asleep in it, but I knew, because I know Vernon, that he was struggling not to giggle out loud with the pure joy of his first steam command. Kipling would have appreciated Vernon: he has described him many times.

MacGinnis was equally at home. He stood at the wheel and was already dirtier than any of the *Vedra's* regular crew —a feat in itself. He had spent the afternoon in the engine-room. His black hair curled with the salt and in some mysterious way he had found the sea boots and stained jersey which he was to wear in the film. I thought of the dark, shy, untidy young actor with whom I had talked in London, rather nondescript except for the queer streak of poetry running through everything he said or did, and I knew more surely than ever that here was the one actor to play the part of 'Andrew' in my story.

There had been a good deal of noise aft while people

rummaged for a place to sleep. They were taking the mess and discomfort in a good-humoured way. The very sight of the *Vedra* alongside the quay at Aberdeen had been enough to frighten children. It was low tide when I met her for the first time and, sunk far beneath my feet, she looked about as big as a dinghy; her decks were a mess of shavings, wire and black paint (Vernon adored black paint, I can never remember when there was not a wet patch of black paint waiting for your coat-sleeve); derricks, steve-dores, engineers and just plain dirty men swarmed over her and Vernon put his head out of the wheel-house on a level with my boots and said:

'Hullo, Micky, old m-man. What do you think of her?'

I hadn't dared tell him but I found a new game in watch-ing the others arrive, on foot or by taxi, looking for the 'film company's private steam yacht', as the papers had des-cribed it. Fortunately for the success of the game there were two or three largish cargo boats lying near, as well as a beautiful white yacht moored out in the basin. This, of course, was everybody's first choice. It was grand to watch them approach the quay and make out the name of the yacht. Disappointed, their shining faces would turn to one towering hull after another. They would walk along. They would point. Then someone would at last look downwards. He would stiffen in horror. He would glance stealthily at the others. He would venture forward and see cases labelled 'Rock Studios'. He would look as I had looked, gulp as I had gulped. It had been great while it lasted.

A huge husky foghorn roared at us and a dim light flashed on our starboard bow. We were out on the high seas.

I was too restless to sleep. I was feeling a bit sick but even that could not kill my happiness. I wandered round the untidy boat. Len lay under the steam winch, rolled in a blanket. Above the saloon was a railed platform where, stretched between two canvas chairs, Sweeny defied gravity. John Laurie was under the saloon table. A heap was Bill Osborne. George and Hamish, the canny Edinburgh contingent, had found bunks in the mate's cabin. Monty was curled round the iron manhole on the bathroom floor. George Black was in the bath. Eric had bedded down aft in a mass of wire and wood shavings, soon to be the new radio cabin. I slid open the door of the chart-room and flashed a torch. Bill Martin and Tregellas lay gloriously under thirty-two flags, contents of the signal locker.

I went for'ard and leaned on the rail. Somewhere ahead of us in the fog the mail packet from Aberdeen to Lerwick was groping her way. The life and soul of the saloon passengers would be Finlay Currie. I could see the vigorous old trouper and hear his rich voice and his unfailing humour. Yes, Finlay was going to be one of my mainstays. With him was Maud, his wife, an unknown quantity. She was not going with us to the island but was to stay in Lerwick, the port of Shetland. With them on the steamer, too, was Mrs. Rutherford, my housekeeper, torn from Bloomsbury to be matron of Rock City. Five hours ago I knew, or at least I hoped, that Frankie and Belle had steamed out of King's Cross on the night train to Aberdeen. They would arrive in the morning, in time for the new Shetland air service to land them in Lerwick before any of us. Complete strangers to one another, for the next five months the two girls would have to sleep and eat and live together. I hoped they would like it.

The rest of my forces were scattered widely.

In Lerwick were waiting one tall, lean Irishman, Skeets Kelly, camera operator; one platinum blond, cynical-looking assistant cameraman, answering (sometimes) to the name of John Behr. I was to find them popular heroes, the only visible representatives of the glamorous film company, joyfully giving imaginative interviews to the local Press.

On Foula the three members of the advance guard would be drinking cups of strong tea in the Haa, with a peat fire blazing. John, as befits an old soldier, is sitting by it. He has made the tea, strong and sweet, and he has the largest cup. The hundred little lines on his face crinkle as he describes his adventures of that day. John is my chief assistant, cutter, continuity-girl and ambassador to the Isle of Foula. He has been visiting the crofts, getting their sympathy, trying to extract promises of men to work. To-day he has at last cornered Tom o' Gravins who, after two hours circumlocution, has admitted cautiously that he *might* find time to give a hand. John's soft voice carries on, chuckling at his own story, getting an answering chuckle from the other two, working at the square table by the kerosene lamp. The strong light gleams on Syd's spectacles and on his earnest cherubic face. He is consulting his little notebook (*The Carpenters' and Builders' Manual*) and lists of timber are by his side. Buddy has his own lists of stores and orders and he constantly exchanges a word or two with Syd. John pours himself another cup of tea.

It is only midnight, so outside the little house it is still day. In this season and latitude there is no real night at all, but a lamp is needed, for the windows are small and sunk two feet in the wall, against winter storms. Some fisherman, probably Andrew of Leirabach, passes the window on the way to his boat down in Ham Voe. Most place names in Shetland are Norse. 'Voe' is a large inlet, 'geo' is a small one.

At 32 Twageos Road (there *are* two, I have counted them) Bill Paton is looking out of his window across the sound to the island of Bressay. The tide is making and several fishing boats are passing silently down the wide channel. The lights of Lerwick Harbour twinkle in the dusk. Bill stretches himself and goes to bed, unconscious of his Destiny which is rolling up from the south.

At Elstree lights are burning in the managing director's

8

office. Joe Rock hangs up the telephone and turns to Gerry Blattner.

'Everything's O.K. They left Aberdeen on the tide.'

The news is expected, but he can't help smacking his lips over the colourful phrase, for Joe is a romantic and it is the romance of expeditions and of unusual films which appeals to him and has led him to back 'The Edge of the World'.

The *Vedra* rolled steadily northward. I drew a deep breath. All this was my doing. From Elstree to Foula, over eight hundred miles of land and sea, many people's lives were being transformed because, seven years ago, I had read a paragraph in a Sunday newspaper. A little interest item stuck in my head and became a story. Because of that idea twenty-four intelligent men, who had never been very far away from a pavement, were going to be dropped down among a primitive people on an extremely isolated island, there to live and work for five months. Their average age—if Finlay Currie and Kitty Kirwan won't mind standing down—was twenty-five.

Add to them two very attractive young women.

This might be described as my main problem. Of course, to make a successful film was our object, but my story was firm, I was sure of my cast and our greatest enemy, the weather, was at least an open fighter. No, my main problem was going to be social.

I thought it would be all right. I had picked them all myself, I am not easily surprised and, with two exceptions, I had worked with each one of them before. A belief in a common object is a very uniting thing and from what I had already seen of Foula there wouldn't be much of the devil left in anyone after a full day's work. This theory was soon disproved.

The *Vedra* gave a merciless lurch. John Laurie came hurriedly out of the saloon and made for the rail.

'Not to windward!' I called out, and he changed his course. A few minutes later he joined me.

'She must have a bottom like a punt,' he said bitterly.

'How are the others?'

'The lad Berry's bad.'

'Eric? I thought he was a good sailor?'

'Not on this boat.' He paused before going in. 'That other lad from Edinburgh—Hamish Sutherland—do you know what you've done there?'

'Made his fortune, I hope.'

'Michael, it's not financial—it's spiritual. We were talking, some of us, about the trip and he just sat there looking and listening, so I thought I would bring him into our talk. "You'll be pretty interested in all this?" I asks him. He gave us all a fright. His face turned crimson and he stuck out that great jaw of his and suddenly he burst out: "It's the dream of my life!" We were all so taken aback we just gaped. What do you say?'

'That I hope he will bite my other actors.'

'Spoken like a director. Good night.'

I returned to my dreaming. This was a far bigger job than any studio-made film. Soundproof walls tend to shut out the world. I was letting it in. £20,000 was to be spent not on sets and mysterious overheads, but on food, transport, shelter, carpenters, ship-chandlers, carriers, cliff-climbers, fishermen and crofters. The money would go directly from our hands to theirs, most of it in hard cash, value for money in return. I felt that it would be good value and would show in the finished film.

I looked back on the last three months. In the final paragraph of that classic thriller, *The Thirty-nine Steps*, the hero says, as he enlists: 'I had done my best service, I think, before I put on khaki.' I smiled as I remembered it. Then it made me think of Willie in *The Moon in the Yellow River*—'Och! I'm always on active sarvice'—(Niall was to imitate him for me later) and I laughed as I thought of what lay before me and behind me.

Chapter II

SEVEN YEARS HARD

★

I have always been fascinated by bare bones, but now that I return to the beginning of my own adventure I find I have a nervous horror of being tedious. Frankenstein would feel very much as I do. I can imagine him surrounded by reporters: 'Now please tell us, Mr. Frankenstein, how did you first get the idea of your Monster? Please give us an outline of your experiments!' I am sure that the inventor, shaken and astonished by triumph after a hundred failures, faced by the supreme fact of the fulfilment of his dream, would look back with weariness on his first struggles.

This parallel is more exact than I had at first imagined, for the Monster was not all that his creator intended, and what director is ever satisfied with his film? Like Frankenstein, I look upon my creation with mixed feelings.

In *The Observer* there is a regular feature called 'At Random'. It is a series of erudite paragraphs, edited with gentle humour. In June, 1930, one of these items was as follows:

'The evacuation of St. Kilda is proving a more difficult problem than was expected. It is not the men but the sheep:

' "The St. Kildan sheep are practically wild animals. They have run free and unhampered on their rocky island for a long period. They have never been sheared. The shepherds, with sheep dogs, who are now endeavouring to round them up, are having a difficult time. The sheep, unused to human beings and dogs, bite the dogs that are herding them. . . . The only practical method with most of the sheep is to throw them over the cliffs and pick them up out of the sea."

'Mr. Shaw once said that the sheep has many excellent military qualities, but we did not know that it was so military as all that.'

I tore the paragraph out and placed it in a file, then new, slender and clean, now old, bulging and weather-stained.

I was painfully ignorant. I did not know where St. Kilda was, I was hazy about the Hebrides, but I did realize that a tremendously dramatic thing was taking place here, a great story. I went down to the offices of the *Observer* and they courteously sent me on to *The Times*, who apparently had a correspondent on the island. I learnt a little from the files, but my next thrill was a page of photographs in the *Sphere*.

The island was there, rising sheer from the sea; the village, straggling along one side of the little street; the Lovers' Stone, a precipitous rock upon which St. Kildans used to stand to prove their manhood; a woman with the fulmar petrels she had snared; an iron lamp; a view of the great stacks, or pillars of rock that surround the coast. These pictures gave me a glimpse of a hard life and a barren land of which I knew nothing. 'As we in dreams behold the Hebrides': that was the moment when my story was conceived.

To the north-west of Scotland lie the Hebrides, a group of islands large and small, which, with the exception of Rona and St. Kilda, cluster together within easy reach of one another. Rona is in the north and has been abandoned many years. St. Kilda lies forty miles out into the Atlantic, west from North Uist, a lonely dot, a tiny pinhead on the maps.

But as that dot is approached, it is seen not to be one island, but seventeen. Some are only rocky stacks, covered with seabirds, but seven are big enough to be included in the Scottish survey. The main island was the only one ever constantly inhabited and its name was Hirta. On the others sheep were grazed and left to fend for themselves. Once a year the men of Hirta would visit them in calm weather, collect lambs and the wool; often a storm would maroon them for weeks at a time, until they won back at last to their homes. As I pictured this savage little group of islands, their great cliffs defying the Atlantic storms; as I realized they had at last conquered the men who had been so long their masters, I said to myself I would, one day, make a picture of that defeat.

It had to stay in the future for seven years.

At that time I had just been given my start as a director by Jerry Jackson, an irascible human dynamo of American manufacture, but with a human heart. I met him when I had been in England a year or so, after an apprenticeship served under Harry Lachman and Rex Ingram in the south of France. My short career had been colourful and unexpected. I quote here from Frank Scully's brilliant Press story of those days, if Frank won't mind stooging for me:

'Micky Powell, now only twenty-two years old, sighs like Alexander for more worlds to conquer. He has moved from mop-boy in a Rex Ingram production to stardom in three years.

'On holiday with his father he sought a job in Rex Ingram's Ciné Studios during the production of *Mare Nostrum*. He got the mop-boy job at four dollars a week. His first job was to wipe out Alice Terry's footsteps as she walked across the polished floor of the set.

'Since then he's been still photographer, publicity writer, interpreter, film-cutter, title writer, actor—in fact everything but night watchman.

'In a little while he began to attract attention by knocking over expensive sets, double-exposing important portraits, dropping glass plates and otherwise treating the serious side of studio life with unconscious humour.

' "Fire him!" said Ingram.

'He was fired, but reported again next morning.

' "That crazy loon is a born comedian," said Harry Lachman to Rex Ingram.

'Right there two minds started work on the same idea. Parts were written in for Powell in *The Magician* and *The Garden of Allah*.

'Now he is the star of a series of comedies that Lachman is making all over Europe, called "Travelaughs".

'All these honours heaped on him at such an early age must mean that henceforth life will be an anticlimax. Powell, however, isn't the sort to endure ennui for long. He is sure to find something new and exciting. Anyway at present he has signed a two-year contract with Lachman.'

Scully was right. Talkies were coming in and our deal with America was off. My two-year contract lasted six months. We had our own little studio in a mountain valley near Nice: oranges, grapes, and spaghetti were there for the asking but none of us were vegetarians. We closed up the studio, said good-bye to the sun and headed for the fogbelt. It was January and there was a deep fall of snow in England. Elstree was buried. I have never been so cold, before or since. The only shoes I had were sandals.

Various paths led me to the Blattner Studios at Elstree. They were a small plant, one of the oldest in England, and Ludwig Blattner had just bought them. He had brilliant ideas but too many of them. He was a promoter of genius. Even in those days (1928) he dreamed of colour, he had the first studio in England to be wired for sound. His general manager was Jerry Jackson. I was called in to recut a picture they had made. It took me ten days to cut it from 9,200 feet to 5,800. I collected £50 and went to France for a holiday. I heard later that Blattner had a fit when he saw the new version, recut it himself, kept on putting things back until it was almost the original length again. The picture had charm but not as much as that. Anyway I was paid on the nail, one of the last times that ever happened to me. More valuable than that, I had made a friend of Jerry.

1929 was a bad year. If I had kept a graph, like they do in Big Business, the line would have dived off the bottom of the chart. Jerry was in America. But he returned and sent for me. We started work on a small picture. It wasn't a good picture, but we ate.

I told Jerry about St. Kilda and he saw the possibilities. After all it cost him nothing. But he helped. He spoke to a British producer, who was in the money; he told him the idea, suggested he send a cameraman to cover the real evacuation. It couldn't cost much and would go into his film library for the present. The producer could not see it. At the time that annoyed me, but now I am thankful. Then I tried the news-reels. None of them were covering it, though it seems incredible they should have neglected a story like that. It was summer and I suppose they had not a man to spare from laying foundation stones. So that was all, for that time.

For the next few years Jerry and I worked together. We turned out a series of quota pictures, at first short four-reelers, then long features. We lost on the long pictures what we made on the short ones.

Well, things went from bad to worse and finally we had to go to work for Gaumont-British. They had an idea that smart young producers could turn out a series of small films, costing little money, in between the big ones, which cost a lot. Something went wrong with the idea, because the big films cost more than they were meant to and so the small films had to help pay for the big films and every time you took a breath it went on the overhead. Still we made *The Fire Raisers* and *Red Ensign* and *The Phantom Light* and we made good friends of Leslie Banks, Gordon Harker, and Ian Hunter. There was a little American I met there, too, who was doing a Russian story with Wainright. His name was Joe Rock and he liked my pictures so I liked him. He was short, brown, and muscular with a smile like a sun-ray treatment. I must admit I liked him anyway.

During this time I had returned again and again to the St. Kilda story. I had tried to sell the idea to many producers. None of them could see it with a microscope. But, as always happens, the more I told the idea the more the story grew. By this time I had read a good deal about the Islands and I brought a lot of local colour to my sales-talks. I don't know how it is with other people but I get some of my best ideas when I am telling somebody a new story. You can fool yourself on paper, writing away and thinking how clever you are, but in talking, when I reach a passage that is not quite true, or an incident that is dragged in by the heels, why, then I feel my voice quicken and a tendency creeps over me to say things like: 'Oh—and then there's the father'—a clear give-away. It is at those moments that I have to think fast and produce a watertight idea with which to plug the leak which threatens my whole ship. In this way the Story, as apart from the Idea, grew.

From the first, I saw it would have to be a simple one, merely a peg on which to hang necessary emotions and incidents. I took the simplest groundwork: two fathers and two sons. Each one took different sides. This gave conflict from the start in everything they said or did, like this:

FATHER I		FATHER II
(Diehard, refuses to leave the island)	*	(Far-seeing. Knows evacuation inevitable)
*		*
SON I		SON II
(Rebel, wants to work and marry outside island)	*	(Simple, strong, quite happy and in love with island girl)

With this pattern in mind, I only had to think continuously about it and talk a good deal. The scenes wrote themselves, though of course I had to think in pictures as well as dialogue.

16

Seven Years Hard

About this time I made a find in a second-hand book-shop. It was called *The Last Days of St. Kilda*. To my excitement I found that the author, A. A. MacGregor, had been *The Times* correspondent on the island at the time of the evacuation in 1930. When the people had petitioned the government to take them off Hirta and find them homes on the mainland, his interest had been aroused, for he was passionately fond of the Outer Isles and had never been to St. Kilda. He went to the island, shared their last summer with the inhabitants and interested himself in their fate. He found that they were to scatter among strangers; these men, who had never seen a tree in their lives, were to be put to work to learn the new trade of forestry.

The whole incident had made extraordinarily little im-pression at the time, except upon a few men who under-stood its importance. Yet, as MacGregor pointed out, the evacuation of St. Kilda was one of the most significant moves in the gradual depopulation of the Islands and High-lands of Scotland. When the last man left Hirta, Scotland had contracted another forty miles.

I devoured the book in one sitting. It was the most amaz-ing combination of industry, idealism, sympathy, and sheer wrong-headedness that I had ever read, but it was obvious that if I made the film on St. Kilda, I could not find a more suitable man to act as technical adviser. He spoke and sang Gaelic, which I intended to have in the film, he was a cliff climber, and an intelligent man. I wrote to him.

Eventually I got a reply from Chelsea, typed in small type, with a blue ink, on a flimsy slip of paper. He wrote with the abrupt, jerky style in which he talked. A film of the evacuation of St. Kilda would be an excellent idea, a very excellent idea. He agreed that he was just the man I needed. He was just off to do a travel book of Scotland. Then I was to let him know if I had something definite. He was mine faithfully, Alasdair Alpin MacGregor.

His letter amused and interested me. I could see he was

a handful: his book had made that plain too, for he was continually flying off on crusades which had nothing to do with his main narrative; this naturally gave the book sincerity, for the characteristic of your true crusader is an ability to start a holy war with half his face shaved and a stick snatched up in the hall as he shoots out of the front door.

When he returned later from Scotland he came to see me at the Gainsborough Studios at Islington. He found the studios without difficulty, which shows the sort of man he was, for a more God-forsaken spot would be difficult to find. They lie along the Regent's canal, through a maze of dreary slums. If you had a car, there was no place near at hand to park it, except in the street, where mob-rule reigned, administered by gangsters of eight to fourteen years of age. But tender years in Hoxton mean tough hides and hearts. You paid for 'protection', so much a week to the leaders: then no rude words, or ruder pictures, were drawn on your paint with a nail; no tintacks nestled in your tyre-covers; no little cherub was found gleefully relieving himself into your petrol tank. Or at least not often.

MacGregor was very lean, very brown, very dark, very clean-shaven, and his hair was wiry and stiff. I was astonished, for that was exactly how I had pictured him. I was pleased to see him at last and he withheld his opinion of me. He was greatly impressed with the studio. I hadn't much time to spare so I put him in a good position to watch and went back to work. He stayed some time then sought me out and said he must go. We shook hands again and he went. I liked him. There are not many visitors to a film studio who do not ask questions.

Time marched on, even then. One day at the end of 1935, I had just finished a picture at Warner Brothers for Jerry, who was now a swell producer, a big-shot, spoiling celluloid for Irving Asher at Teddington, when Chris Mann phoned me and said would I go and see Joe Rock about a picture. I went to Elstree, to the Rock Studios, but I knew them already. They were the old Blattner Studios; but Blattner was dead and his son Gerry was manager of the studio. Joe was still short, brown, muscular, and smiling, in spite of a terrible car accident which had nearly killed him that year on the Elstree by-pass. Stanley Haynes, my late assistant on *The Phantom Light*, was now his production manager, a good one, who would battle his own grandmother to a standstill on a cut-rate salary, if she was working for him. With a winning smile he knocked fifty pounds off my usual price and we made a deal for a film in January.

All these years I had been reading up lighthouses, shipbuilding, dam-construction, fire-assessing, plumbing, and housemaid's knee for various pictures, but any spare time I had was devoted to my pet subject, the Islands. I read Seton Gordon, Kearton, Martin, Boswell, and Johnson. By this time, of course, I had reduced my story to writing. I presented it in two parts. The first was a preface, intended to interest a producer in the unique setting and theme. The second part was a synopsis of the story. I called it *The Edge of the World*.

Chapter III

THINGS START MOVING

*

I had been inspired to write the lay-out of the Story and Idea by the comforting thought that I should then no longer have to sell it verbally to an unreceptive or hyper-critical audience. I handed it over to Chris Mann with the firm intention of letting him worry. But once a salesman, always an optimist: while I was working on this other picture for Joe I found somebody else to interest. Alec Rea and Paul Clift run several London theatres, and Paul is a friend of mine. We were neighbours in Gower Street and he sometimes came to dinner with Jane Millican, a delightful actress, a superb hostess, and an adversary respected and feared by every stall-keeper in the Caledonian Market. My housekeeper was Mrs. Rutherford, a valiant Irishwoman, of whom more later. She was fond of Jane and Paul and so was Hopalong Cassidy, my cat. So my dinners were nearly up to Jane's own standard and we all talked a great deal though I probably talked the most. Of course St. Kilda came into the conversation and Paul asked to read about it. He took away a copy of my story.

At about the same time, I told the idea to Joe. I did not know it but Joe has a craze for exterior pictures. (Perhaps I have cured him of it.) When he was working in Hollywood he planned pictures in China and Malaya, he made the trips himself, he had reams of material. The story of my lonely, haunted island hit him where he lived. He asked for a copy. I handed it over and thought no more about it.

20

Things Start Moving

Paul Clift is slender, kind and cautious. As far as can be discovered he has looked thirty-five ever since he was twenty and presumably always will. He rang me up and said:

'Micky, about that St. Kilda story of yours, I think it's extraordinarily good. Of course, I don't know anything about films, as you know, but it seems to me it would make an extraordinarily good film.'

I said: 'Thanks, Paul.'

He said: 'Do you know—of course I can't answer for Rea—but I think we might be interested in it, that is, of course, if everything else was satisfactory.'

I said: 'Let's meet and talk it over.'

I couldn't believe it. I knew of course that Clift and Rea were cautiously interested in films. I had warned them myself that, for an independent investor, there were only two possible kinds of picture: an expensive one, with most of the money spent on a real star; or a cheap one, with an unusual story like mine. That was why I had given him the story to read. But handing out copies had become a routine job, I expected nothing from it.

But it was true. We met. I told them the kind of terms we could expect to get from a firm of distributors. I told them the firm I thought of approaching, an English firm with a good reputation for square dealing. They knew them and approved. If I could get a deal close to the one I had outlined, they would put up the money to make the picture.

I walked out of the St. Martin's on air. St. Kilda here I come! I felt so sure of success that I walked right into a telephone box, spoke to John Seabourne and Vernon Sewell, sent MacGregor a telegram.

John Seabourne is an ex-Sergeant of the Royal Garrison Artillery, fifteen years' service, all through the War, military medal and Croix de Guerre, resigned to take a job at the old Gaumont Studios, first director of the *Gaumont*

Mirror screen magazine, editor-in-chief of the Nettlefold Studios at Walton-on-Thames, brilliant story-teller, my right hand all through the expedition, cutter, assistant, actor, dance director, ambassador, and friend. I wonder if there's another man as kind, as humorous, as gentle, and as unlucky.

If you met John in the flesh it wouldn't be long before you heard The Famous Story of Busty Hawkins and the Rocket Has Gone Up, Sir! Here it is, John speaking:

'It wasn't only Hawkins' size that was impressive, but his manner and his education. He was a superior man. When he was Orderly Sergeant, sitting there at his desk, even the Adjutant would think twice before he'd contradict him. Hawkins always spoke in a very polite, precise way and there was a gleam of sardonic humour that ran through everything he said, but it never came to the surface, merely made his superiors feel as if their buttons were undone. He took a fancy to me from the start. (I've told you about the time I didn't want to go to Malta.) He could see that I was a superior man, too.

'The times we had those days on garrison duty at Alderney. . . .'

(Here I would usually have to bring John back with a jerk to his story.)

'. . . the O.C. insisted that Surprise Night Attacks must be carried out in full. So, as dusk was falling, invading parties were detailed, His Majesty's Tug, *Sir Redvers Buller*, unwillingly co-operating. They were to grope round in the dark to a point opposite the fort, put off in boats with muffled oars and approach the land. When sighted, warning of their approach was to be given by igniting one explosive rocket, red, white, and blue stars, upon which Shore Operations would commence. If the invading party were able to land before the batteries got into action, then the surprise attack would be deemed successful, and vice versa.'

Things Start Moving

'Hawkins himself took charge of the rocket and chose me to assist him. It was as big as a small cannon. We had with us one issue of government fusees in a sort of bully-beef tin, which had to be opened with a key, like a sardine tin.

'It was very dark. I carried the rocket while Hawkins rolled along with the fusees. We were presently in position and while the rest peered out to sea, until their eyes ached, Hawkins and I prepared the rocket according to instructions on printed slip attached.

' "Rocket all ready, Hawkins?" called the Captain— Thompson, I think his name was.

'It was as dark as a bag but beside me Hawkins made a most tremendous formal salute, heels together, thumb in line with the seam of the trousers, right hand just not touching the peak of the cap, all quite invisible in the blackness, and roared reassuringly:

' "Rocket all Ready, sir!"

' "Remember, as soon as the alarm is given, light the fuse. Not a moment's delay!"

' "Very Good, sir! Do you hear that, bombardier?" The last remark was to me and I started to open the tin.

'At that moment the alarm was given. The Captain waited a moment, but two or three more shouts decided him. "Send the Rocket up, Hawkins!" he cried.

'Again Hawkins executed his tremendous salute in the dark.

' "Very Good, sir! Fusees, bombardier!"

'The key jammed and I gave it a twist with all my force. If you've ever opened a sardine tin you will know that it broke off in my hand, cutting my finger in the process. The swear word which I uttered told Hawkins what had happened and without a word of reproach that Man of Resource produced a folded newspaper from his pocket.

' "Matches, Seabourne," he hissed.

' "Hawkins!"

' "Coming, sir!" The paper flared up like a bonfire and we hastily jammed it against the rocket. If you have ever lit a firework you will know at once that it smouldered, hesitated, and went out, leaving a charred stump.

' "Why doesn't the Rocket Go Up, Hawkins?" bellowed the Captain.

'Again the wonderful salute.

' "Coming, sir! Touch paper is Damp, sir!"

'We made a bonfire round the rocket. We burnt our fingers. We shook the damn thing. Not a spark!

' "Hawkins, what the devil are you doing?"

'We could all hear now the sound of approaching oars. The Captain was dancing with rage. Hawkins was a wonderful man. His rich, calm voice never changed its tempo, while all around us men cursed and yelled.

' "Rocket refuses to Go Up, sir!"

' "Then leave it!" screamed the Captain. "Join the main body."

' "Very Good, sir! Shoulder Rocket, bombardier!"

'We set off at the double, and it did the trick! I suddenly heard an ominous fizzing. A spark had penetrated!

' "Look out, Hawkins!" I yelled.

'The next moment with a frightful bang the rocket exploded. I must have hurled it from me, for it tore over the sand-dunes about three feet from the ground, knocking both Hawkins and myself flat from the impact, and buried itself with another colossal report in the very dune on which Captain Thompson was dancing, instantly enveloping him in a splendid cloud of red, white, and blue stars, as per description on label.

'In the moment's pause before the batteries turned loose, Hawkins leapt to his feet, executed once more his wonderful salute and reported in a voice that could have been heard in Guernsey:

' "The Rocket has Gone Up, sir!" '

Things Start Moving

John and Vernon had always known of my plans and it was understood that they were part of the scheme. For some time Vernon had been making short documentary films. He was a most infernally adequate person. Whenever he wanted anything he built it himself. Camera, sound recorder, camera-crane, camera-truck, sets, trick shots; he made them all and took it quite as a matter of course. His hobby had always been motor-boats; at one time he built them. Our plan for St. Kilda was to buy a base ship and run it ourselves. No trouble then with charters, owners, and a skipper who refused to take a chance. At the thought of a steam command Vernon's eyes had stood out like hat pegs.

I warned John to stand by and asked Vernon and Mac-Gregor to dinner. I also sent MacGregor a copy of my story. I thought I had better get his approval of the general line, if we were going to work together.

I had already been pulling strings with the distributing company. I asked Chris to arrange an interview as soon as he could.

The other two came to dinner. MacGregor had told me he was a vegetarian, could he have something in that line. I broke the news to Mrs. Rutherford, who looked contemptuous, but produced an acceptable dish. We all ate fast and talked faster. MacGregor liked the story: he had no criticisms though he said he could give me a lot of detail when it came to actual production. Vernon was full of plans. I was very happy.

The next day Chris rang and said the sales manager of the distributing firm was expecting to see me. I was rather taken aback. I did not think a sales manager would like my idea. I knew them too well. Anything unusual, anything different, anything with no stars in it, in fact anything that requires selling is death to a sales manager. A sales manager's idea of heaven is to have nothing but Joan Crawfords, Fred Astaires, Gracie Fieldses. 'Then we know where we are,

25

old boy,' they explain. Anyway, perhaps this film salesman would be different.

He wasn't.

He had a tolerant smile right from the start. He had read the lay-out and I knew I was only wasting time but I went on trying to explain the greatness of the theme and the low cost compared to any studio production. He turned it down flat, this little salesman, still with a tolerant smile; and the words he used are so striking that I think they deserve to be recorded.

'Mr. Powell,' he said, 'I think you would make a very beautiful picture, a very artistic picture of that story. It's a fine idea but we don't want to have to sell it.'

I started to look for another firm and I was introduced to a young company. They had just started and were very keen. They read the story and liked it. They offered the same terms but of course they hadn't the standing of the other. I went to Clift. To my horror Rea had gone away on a cruise. He might approve the new deal but we could not go ahead with it till he came back in three weeks. By then it would be too late in the year.

Joe took a hand. He had mentioned the story once or twice but I had each time put him off, saying I had finance already arranged. He now sent for me and made a definite offer. He liked the idea and he liked me. If I would produce a finished scenario he would arrange a deal. It would be a different set-up. I could have the men I wanted but the administration would be in the hands of the studio. On the other hand, I should have all the resources of the studio at my back. I discussed it with the others and we accepted.

We should have to hurry. It was already May. I set to work on the scenario. Vernon dashed off to look for a suitable ship. MacGregor sent me a list of tinned vegetables and non-alcoholic beverages.

I concentrated on my job exclusively. A stenographer reported at my house at 9.30 every morning. We worked all day till six or seven; sometimes longer, wasn't it, Miss Brandon? But never after dinner. I dictated the action. Then while she transcribed I wrote the dialogue. Then I dictated it aloud, to get the feel of the lines. Then I prepared more action. In eight days exactly we were through.

I turned the script over to Joe and turned an ear to Vernon's troubles. They were looming rather large.

The previous November Vernon had invited me to accompany him on a North Sea trawler for two weeks, with the purpose of making a short documentary film. We were to shoot with his home-made equipment and bunk together in the captain's cabin under the wheel-house. I accepted with pleasure. Vernon had a lot to prepare so he left the provisioning to me. (On a trawler the hands find their own food, which is prepared by the cook.) I must have been in rather a vague mood for Vernon swears that there was no meat and twenty-four separate tins of butter. I fancy I had an idea about grease keeping out cold.

Anyway we arrived at Lowestoft with all our gear and spent the afternoon loading it into the *Boreas* (pronounced Bor-ease). I say 'into', because the only entrance and ventilator to the captain's cabin was through a small hatchway in the floor of the wheel-house and we just dropped everything in, followed by ourselves, and sorted things out. But at the hotel a telegram from Jerry summoned me back to start a film next week. It was a blow, but Vernon rose to it.

'Can't be helped,' he said. 'I'll wire Buddy.'

'Buddy?'

'Buddy Farr. He'll be up to-night.'

'But he may have other engagements.'

Vernon snorted. Late that evening Buddy magically appeared, ready for anything, with a blue sweater and looking as if he would stick at nothing, in a nice way.

Considerably impressed I enquired privately of Vernon what was this strange power over Buddy that he could call him to the vasty deep at a moment's notice. He dis-

missed the subject quite arbitrarily but I gathered that I
had unknowingly supplanted Buddy, who had been waiting, gnashing his teeth, like a hound on leash, in case I
should back out. I have a feeling to this day that Buddy
suspects me of sending myself that telegram, having once
seen our quarters on the *Boreas*.

This devoted friend of the unworthy Sewell not only
accompanied him on the trawler, being violently ill the
entire time, a fate which I should have no doubt shared,
but returned with him again at Christmas time and obligingly hurled himself into the North Sea in order to complete a sequence about a man overboard.

Such was Buddy; and Vernon's Svengali-like power
over him continued to the end.

It was with Buddy, then, that Vernon had been dashing
round the shipping agents. But his first ship was discovered
through a friend. I am sorry, but here I must digress once
more to discuss Vernon's multitudinous friends.

As the reader has already gathered Vernon had many
sound qualities and many gifts, but undoubtedly the greatest
was his remarkable ability for friendship. Never a town,
hamlet, ship or aeroplane but has its Sewell fan. At times
envious people have accused me of having an aunt in every
county. I admit I am rich in aunts but the name of Vernon's
friends is legion, for they are as the sands of the sea.

It was through a friend then that Vernon heard of a converted minelayer, lying restfully on the mud at Portsmouth.
When in commission, I gathered, she had been used for
bottle parties round the Isle of Wight. This was long ago.
But her engines were sound, she was a good size; if her
bottom was sound she might do, said Vernon. Her owner
supported her bottom. But Vernon told me privately that
if she was hauled off the mud she would very likely leave
it behind her. The only way was to put her on the slips. We
should have to pay for this and Joe was not quite ready to
go so far. The situation was ticklish. It was so late in the

year that the success of the expedition turned on finding a ship at once. Until the ship was found Joe would not commit himself. Drawing expenses was as easy as pulling wisdom teeth. But just then he got his copy of the script, read it and burst into superlatives. Vernon got the O.K., slipped her and found he could stick his boot through her bottom. The owner burst into tears.

So did Joe and Gerry Blattner. But by that time Vernon had disappeared, to Inverness-shire, Buddy reported. Apparently, while Vernon was in Portsmouth, Buddy and a shipping agent had discovered a snip. It was a trawler, converted into a yacht, ideal for our purpose, but which was lying on the shores of Loch Linnhe, in the woolly Highlands of Scotland. This romantic position seemed to me to reduce its qualities as a genuine snip, but by this time Vernon's safety valves were bubbling and he was off to Glasgow before anybody knew he had left Portsmouth.

I was making my own preparations and realized I should need friends in Scotland if I was to accomplish all I planned. I consulted my god-daughter, Jean Seymour-Ure, who promptly suggested her father. Philip Seymour-Ure had been a reporter on the *Scotsman* and he told me to write to Mr. J. W. Herries, the chief reporter. I did, and thereby came to meet the kindest and most unselfish friend and adviser that a man could have.

Vernon arrived at Glasgow to find the city enjoying what he described as 'some sort of comic holiday'. It was raining and not a car of any kind could be hired to take him to his destination. He did not embark on the madness of taking a local train; he went instead to Stirling where, I need hardly explain, he had friends. They rose to the occasion, as all Vernon's friends have to. They sheltered him, dried him, fed him and lent him an aged Daimler, with which he navigated through a howling rainstorm to the shores of Loch Linnhe. There the noble lord awaited him by appointment. I forgot to say that the owner of this boat was a lord, the first of two who appear in these pages; and, if I am accused of snobbery, I can only plead that, when dealing with yachts and private islands, noble lords are thick under foot. It was raining so steadily by this time that Vernon's account of this part of the saga has always been a little misty, but I think the owner was already on board his yacht, which lay well out in the loch. Huddled in a small boat, with his collar turned up more for convention than for any shelter it provided, Vernon was ferried out. His arrival aboard started unfavourably with a large part of the rail coming away in his hand. Vernon shook hands with the owner—Vernon is always very correct—then made a tour of inspection. He soon saw it was useless. The stringer plates, which hold the ship together, were like thin slices of Gruyère cheese. The whole ship was rotting. Vernon stalked sarcastically—Vernon can be witheringly sarcastic—about the ship. He snorted. He tore large lumps off the upper works of the yacht and hurled them overboard into the loch. The owner followed him weakly expostulating. The rain poured down like . . . like Highland rain. Splash! splash! went chunks of dry rot into the loch. The owner said that his father had gone for a cruise in the boat only the previous year.

'Then my dear m-man,' observed Vernon, 'he was exceedingly f-fortunate to return alive.' Splash! 'I advise you to clear off her at once, as I propose to do, before she s-sinks under us.' Splash!

Whether he ever returned the Daimler to Stirling I am not quite sure, but he was next day in Glasgow, talking to a friend he had unearthed. He omitted to telephone his bad news to the studio, fearing that Joe would call the whole thing off. But the friend knew a shipping agent, and a few hours later Vernon was racing southward to Sunderland, where the pilot boat *Vedra* had just been suspended from regular service in the estuary. It was love at first sight.

There was little question about her condition. She had

been doing active work until a week before, and was only
laid off as too expensive to run on pilot work. Vernon had
her inspected, photographed, and optioned in twenty-four
hours, wired the studio and arrived a few hours later himself. Six hundred and fifty pounds was her price and the
next day Joe okayed it.

Absolutely only one thing remained to be got: the permission of the present owner of St. Kilda. I knew that the
islands, owned by MacLeod of Dunvegan, had changed
hands. I had found out that Lord Dumfries was the new
owner, that he did not live there, nor any of his people, but
I had not yet approached him. It may be surprising that I
had neglected this, but I did not anticipate any great difficulty and wished to have everything ready. Now that all
my plans were set, now that I had my boat, my men, I
could mention dates and produce answers to any questions:
I was ready to meet Lord Dumfries.

Joe had already made enquiries for me. He was talking
over a business deal with a young man whose mother spoke
familiarly of Dumfries and expressed herself as only too
willing to act as ambassador. Rather incautiously I allowed
this. It is a good thing to get an introduction but only if
you know your sponsors. When Vernon arrived with his
news of the *Vedra*, Joe told his young friend to tell his
mother to ask permission. The answer was a point-blank
refusal from Lord Dumfries.

Panic reigned. I admit I could not believe it. I had
dreamed of the islands for so long that I felt as if I owned
them. I knew every name, every stack, every anchorage.
It was like being shut out of your own house. No reason
had been given and the refusal had been final.

But Vernon had a friend. His name was Niall Rankin.
He was rich, young, an enthusiastic cameraman and bird-
watcher. He was a personal friend of Lord Dumfries and
Vernon remembered now that Rankin had even been on
St. Kilda with its owner. Rankin was in town. Rankin was

traced to his home in St. John's Wood. Rankin had the whole story poured into his deafened ears. He only got about one word in ten but enough to gather that Vernon's happiness was at stake. It was enough. He sprang to the telephone and dialled TRU. But the noble lord was out. We waited on tenterhooks until, at dinner time, he returned. Niall Rankin pleaded our cause as if it were his own. Was he not a friend of Vernon's, one of that heroic band? Lord Dumfries lent an ear. He would have no objection to discussing the matter. Would Sunday morning at his house at Cumnock suit us? We would be there!

It was then Friday. We had been suffering extremes for so long that it was almost without an effort that we rose from blackest depression to rosy castles in the Hebrides. Rankin told us that his explanation had put quite a different complexion on the whole affair. We were confident our winning personalities would do the rest. We soon convinced Joe. Briefly we were going to obtain consent, go to Edinburgh and Glasgow and put everything in train, then Vernon would proceed to Sunderland, I myself return to the studio to collect a unit. It seemed almost too simple. That was Friday.

I decided to take my car. I knew enough about Scotland to be sure we should need it, if we were to move freely on Sunday. I looked up Cumnock. It lay in Ayr, seven miles from Mauchline, birthplace of Robert Burns. The best hotel was the 'Dumfries Arms'. The nearest big town was Kilmarnock, on the other side of Mauchline; the London train stopped there and it made an ideal rendezvous. As I read these names which I had always known so well from books, as well as others like Annan, Lochmaben and even Gretna Green, I got my first real thrill as I realized that to-morrow I would be crossing the Border and finding my way about those winding roads. A brief train journey by night to Glasgow and back had been my only taste of Scotland, an experience so transitory and hurried that I felt I could honestly say that this was my first visit to a land and a people that had always attracted me. It was in that moment that I knew I should be successful and, dimly within me, I felt that even if I failed with Lord Dumfries I would not return across the Border defeated.

When I left London early in the morning it was not as a hopeful ambassador, but as a general making the definite move which must result in victory.

Chapter IV

THE PAWKY WEE BODY

★

Why is it that express trains have their haughty movements mapped, timed, and charted by a body of experts, with everything printed in clear legible figures, only to have another expert sneak up and stick some ridiculous little letter of the alphabet into the time-table, which has the effect of cancelling everything that has been done?

Vernon, who will not let well alone, discovered that instead of Kilmarnock there was another station nearer Cumnock where the express stopped about 7 a.m. I reluctantly agreed to meet him there. Of course he had overlooked a 'd' or 'xf' or something and it did nothing of the kind.

The day before had been fine. I went by Market Harborough, for I wanted to see John Fothergill. He had deserted his London friends and taken 'The Three Swans', where rumour said he was creating an inn, the equal of 'The Spreadeagle' in good taste, good food and benevolent despotism. But what could that mean to the Faithful, bereft of an inspired host? Thame was forty-five miles away, Ascot only twenty; Market Harborough is eighty. . . . But the loss is too recent and too bitter.

I drove under an archway into a beautiful long stable yard, hung with the horns of stags. The doors were painted in gay colours. At first glance the place was signed 'Fothergill'. I went into the bar and bought some beer and wandered into the narrow passage with hatchways and windows at odd corners, and presently I heard my name spoken. For

34

about the first time since we met he didn't think I was
Anthony Powell. I wonder if he calls Anthony 'Michael'.
Probably not. I must meet Anthony Powell some day. I
inspected the beautiful dining-room and the priceless tables,
the bedrooms, the ballroom and, of course, the lavatory.
As usual, this last was giving him trouble. Apparently
hunting-men had unsteady aim for I saw displayed a courteous little notice: 'Will uncertain gentlemen please avoid
the floor?' John told me in his neat, tired voice that it had
been curiously misunderstood: 'Apparently they take the
adjective to reflect upon their breeding rather than their
habits. I have replaced the notice several times. No doubt,
it will sink in—the floor has already done so.'

He insisted that I lunch with them and entertained me
Fothergilly. Their private room looks, from bow windows,
on to the street of the town. The church is opposite. It is a
lovely place but I wished for Aladdin's lamp to move it
bodily fifty miles south-east.

I told him my purpose in going north. He had met
Dumfries once but had only a vague memory of him. He
knew his father. Apparently my adversary was quite a
young man. I worked out that he must be about thirty,
the same age as Vernon and myself. That gave me some
encouragement, though all the time I was supported by the
feeling I have described that I could not fail. There comes a
time, if you have been fighting long enough, when you
feel that now you are going to win, that every blow you
have given and received has been only a preparation for
this moment: then you go in and you win, or break your
heart; but I think that the people that get that feeling
usually win.

I said good-bye and promised to let John know the outcome. I had three hundred miles to go and seven hours to
do them in, unless I drove in the dark. At half-past nine
that evening the Auburn slid to a stop at the door of the
'Dumfries Arms'.

Better men than I have crossed the Border and described their feelings. Personally I felt more excited than I have ever felt, when crossing a frontier into a new country. It may have been imagination but soon everything began to look cleaner and simpler and sturdier and smaller. Cumnock itself was rather plain, but when I stopped to ask where the hotel was a small girl answered:

'Ye just passit it—up the brae.'

Those were the first Scottish words addressed to me by a Scot in Scotland. It was and remains a great occasion.

The 'Dumfries Arms' was not in the least put out by my late and unannounced arrival. I was shown my room (a tall, narrow one with a large bed) by a tiny, black-eyed, roly-poly little maid who bounded obediently to the cry of 'Jeanie!' and almost died of suppressed chuckles over my attempt to pronounce her name properly. High tea was announced ready for me and I was led amazed downstairs and up steps until we came out into a sitting-room, peopled with sleepy guests, where my meal was set out at one end of a vast table. Everybody beamed at me and I sat down to strong red tea from a huge teapot I could hardly lift, bannocks, jam, crumpets, bacon and eggs, oatcakes, potted meat, and home-baked bread.

It was not until after tea that I found out about the trains. I told Jeanie that I had to be up early to get to the station; she looked blank and did not think there was one. We both descended on the landlady, a decided person, who confirmed that they never stopped on Sunday. On the other hand there was a special train on Saturday night from Euston, which got to Kilmarnock about nine. No doubt my friend would be on that. No doubt, I thought, poor Vernon; and I went to bed, for I was tired.

I was therefore prepared next day for the frantic phone call which summoned me to Kilmarnock. Vernon was mortified. He was staring appalled at a Scottish town on the Sabbath, as viewed through the lace curtains of the grim

hotel in which he had taken shelter. All I remember are
steps, oilcloth, and linoleum, but it was not a cheerful
place. I took him away.

Our appointment was for eleven. I had made enquiries
and we found the house without much difficulty. It was
about three miles out of Cumnock and was very fine. My
impression is of a large, square, white house—early eigh-
teenth century, I suppose—standing in the middle of a flat
garden, all the trees drawn respectfully backwards, a drive
of loose pebbles encircling the building and spreading out
into a flat space in front, where a flight of steps, long, wide,
and shallow, mounted to double doors. The general effect
of the architecture was severe and rather confusing. It was
all so grand that it was very hard to tell the back from the
front, and we swung off to the left, deflected by a lopsided
piece of wire-netting which appeared to bar the right-hand
road, only to find ourselves receiving a blank stare from a
forbidding row of French windows, which looked loftily
past us to the distant hills. I backed and turned hastily.
Vernon was depressed by this social error and was generally
inclined to become twittery, so I impressed on him that his
role at first was to give class to our deputation, to let me
talk, with an occasional 'Hear, hear!' or 'Bis!' and on no
account to fiddle with his monocle until we were well
established.

At the place where the drive had forked we now took
the other road and pressed resolutely forward. An opening
in the wire-netting then appeared mysteriously, exactly
like the mouth of a hidden river in an adventure story. We
drew up at the foot of the steps and mounted them with
beating hearts. The steps would have been suitable for a
line of heralds, descending with measured tread in the early
Lubitsch manner; they might even have been child's play
to Border guests, bounding like hunted stags up to dinner,
with a broadsword in each hand; I found them tiresome.
Two paces to a step made me stub my toe. One pace forced

me to do the splits. Vernon stumbled grimly beside me.

I pulled a bell and as the first clang sounded distantly from a cavernous basement the door flew open, nearly precipitating me on my face. A young man faced us. He was fair and slender. His most prominent feature was a very fine, silky Guards moustache. He wore the kilt. It was the noble lord himself.

He saw facing him two normal young men of his own age, both with their mouths open; one fair and brainy-looking, the other darker, querulous, with a masterful nose.

Apparently our approach had been seen, our pardonable mistake watched with suspense, our shamefaced reappearance noted with relief, and our ascent of the steps awaited with such impatience that when I finally put a timid hand on the bell, our host must have fairly hurled himself on the door to admit us before we committed some other solecism.

Or perhaps he was just on his way out.

'I am Lord Dumfries,' he said quickly and rather shyly.

I introduced ourselves and we entered.

I had a brief glimpse of a large hall, around which the wings of the house were evidently built. It was paved with flagstones and was rather full of a medley of things. I caught an impression of a pile of wooden objects. I have forgotten what they were. (Vernon suggests wheelbarrows or toboggans.) Then our host led the way into a small drawing-room. The door was in a wall three feet thick. The room was panelled in white painted wood and each panel had individual carvings over it. The furniture was Chippendale and had been designed and made for the room. The fireplace was Adam—and very good Adam. I thought the panelling was his, too, but was told it was the work of Chippendale. Apparently the two craftsmen had worked together on the decoration of the whole house. The builder had been a local man and I wish I remembered his name for he was obviously quite as fine a craftsman in his own line. There was a steel grate in the fireplace with a fire laid in the neatest way I have ever seen, all the coal and wood packed up in thin white paper as clean as a grocer's parcel. With splendid unconcern Lord Dumfries put a match to this apparently permanent object, which turned into a cheerful blazing fire in less time than it takes to do the Indian rope trick. During these preliminaries we chatted. As I realized that these noble proportions and this splendid craftsmanship had been directed and inspired by the ancestors of Lord Dumfries, I was prepared to like their descendant.

In passing, this patronage of artists by great men, men who can say: 'Twenty years! What's twenty years, if it's good? Shoot the works, Chippendale!'—I repeat that this lavish and splendid support of men of genius, who would otherwise break their hearts with hack-work, is the most difficult thing for a communist to explain away.

I took the plunge and briefly explained who I was and how I had got the idea of making the film. Lord Dumfries was not impressed. We had a wall of prejudice to break down.

Fortunately Niall Rankin had done much to explain the situation and Dumfries soon began to see that this was not the amateur scheme which he had first imagined. The atmosphere became more genial. To make the matter clear to him I had tried to explain what a good thing it would be for the Islands. We were going to employ local labour, there would be camps to build, boats to hire. Unemployed men and women would be brought to St. Kilda to people the island once more. There would be work, well paid, all the summer.

It is easy to talk of generosity. Most of us, if we were told that we possessed the one thing necessary for a big scheme to proceed, would say: 'If they want it they will have to pay for it.' It is a matter of personal ethics, I think. Every man is entitled to his own opinion if he can justify it. Lord Dumfries talked about his birds.

His point was quite straightforward. He had bought St.

Kilda for a bird sanctuary. He was also interested in preserving the unique race of island sheep on Soay (which name means, in Gaelic, Isle of Sheep). He did not want all this disturbed. He had enlarged and improved the main house of the island. He had piped water from the fells above, installed a kitchen and bathroom. He planned to go for a month's stay in August and had invited guests. All this would be upset by our invasion. At this season the birds were nesting and rearing young. Every time we blew the siren on our ship, thousands of birds would rise startled, sending eggs and chicks hurtling off the ledges to their death.

All this was unanswerable and I sympathized with him. He talked well about his hobbies. Nobody said anything about money, as far as I can remember, yet suddenly there was hovering in the air a faint idea, I cannot call it a suggestion, an idea that something might be arranged, not here and now but later, perhaps next week, perhaps tomorrow.

I had told Joe that if there were any question of payment I would propose the payment of a hundred pounds or so into any charity the owner might name. It was evident that a hundred would not go very far. It always astonishes me how polite conversations can take place, without a contract or a figure being mentioned, yet with both parties at the end having a very clear idea of both.

'I must talk with my factor,' he said at last. 'I must see what he says. I will discuss it with him and my solicitor and I will let you know in a week's time."

'But, Lord Dumfries,' I protested, 'I can't wait as long as that. You said yourself it is already late in the year, we have wasted the two best months.'

'That is not my fault, you will agree.'

The truth, but hardly agreeable.

It was finally arranged to meet next day at the office of his solicitor in Glasgow. His parting words were sinister.

'It is my solicitor you must convince. I shall leave all this for him to decide.' Then, after a pause, but without undue emphasis: 'He's a pawky wee body.'

We were too downcast, as we passed once more through the hall, to take another look at the objects which had excited our curiosity on entering, and I shall never know if they were really toboggans or wheelbarrows. It seems unlikely.

We drove back to the 'Dumfries Arms' with furrowed brows. The engagement had been indecisive except that it had revealed our opponent's strong position and firm intention to maintain it. The first chill of doubt was spreading through us. But in both our minds, even before we compared notes, the doubt was purely a financial one. How would Rock react to paying a large sum for using the island? The answer was easy. He would hate it.

'Look here, Vernon,' I said suddenly across the lunch table, 'one thing is plain, he won't let us use St. Kilda without being paid and he won't do it for a song. There are his birds. . . .'

'Birds!' growled Vernon; for some reason, the statement about the *Vedra's* siren sowing death and destruction on the cliffs had been taken by him as a personal insult. 'I should like to know what happens when the *Dunara Castle* and other boats visit the island! What about the trawlers that shelter there? Don't talk to me about birds!'

This was all very well but got nowhere.

'He has the upper hand,' I said.

'Yes,' admitted Vernon, examining a bannock suspiciously.

'And so we can't bargain with him.'

'No,' agreed Vernon, inserting a portion of bannock into his mouth; 'but it won't be so bad in Glasgow. Here he's on his own ground, with his kilt and his Adam and his Chippendale. He'll be easier to handle in an office.'

'Five hundred is a good round sum,' I said thoughtfully.

'Too bloody round,' said Vernon (I think) but he spoke through layers of bannock.

'It's the only thing to do,' I said firmly; 'he practically laughed at two hundred. It's a question of days—hours. We've got to get his consent to-morrow and we've got to come out flat with £500—take it or leave it. Unless we do that, he can dictate terms. But if we mean what we say and look it, I think he'll take it.'

With a mighty effort Vernon swallowed his mouthful.

'Suppose he doesn't?'

'Then we're sunk.'

I spoke with fatalism but my heart was in my boots. For the first time since this mad rush was started I was faced with the possibility of complete failure. Always before, however desperate the chance, there had been an alternative. But this final offer would be my last trump, there wasn't another trick in my hand, not even half a trick. Lord Dumfries held a better card, for he only had to say 'No' and the whole adventure was at an end before it had fairly started.

Still, £500 was a great deal of money. I knew that Joe would think so.

He did think so. We telephoned him when we got to Edinburgh that evening. He nearly swooned. But he backed us to the limit.

'We shall have to save it on something else, Micky boy,' he said. 'It's too bad that he should act that way, but he's certainly got us cold. You don't think he'd fall for less? It's a big slice out of our reserve. O.K. I'll trust your judgment. Good luck, boys!'

'Good old Joe!' we both said; and we meant it.

Although it meant a trip to Glasgow next morning I had stuck to my decision to make Edinburgh my headquarters. I felt the need of allies. His letters had already made me feel I could count on Herries and as soon as we arrived I telephoned him. I liked his slow, dry voice at once. I found myself telling him all my troubles.

'Dear, dear,' his voice said soothingly, 'to think he should act like that about it after all your trouble.'

'Do you think he will consent?' I asked. An idiotic question but I wanted all the comfort I could get.

'No doubt he'll be better inclined when he's had time to think it over. You have hurried the man a little, you know.'

'I suppose so.'

'Five hundred pounds! It's a handsome offer. He'll not be likely to reject it. It's a great deal of money.'

We all seemed agreed upon that.

I had to leave for Glasgow too early in the morning for me to see Herries but I arranged to telephone him when I returned with my news, good or bad. He promised to use all his influence if I failed and altogether made me feel much better. He was a kind man.

Up till this time, I had done very little about a cast, for it wouldn't have been fair to raise hopes only to dash them. One man had been told of my plans and that was John Laurie. I had met him on *Red Ensign*, in which he played a small part; his crofter in *The Thirty-Nine Steps* nearly stole the picture; his innkeeper in another of my films was grand larceny; so that ever since the birth of the story he had been pencilled in for a part, though I hadn't yet decided which one. He came from the town of Dumfries.

Apart from him I had vague ideas but I was determined that I would use as much Scottish talent as I could find. I also intended to give a chance to anyone whom I judged to have the stuff in him or her and I was confident of my own judgment. I had already spoken to Herries, and one of the things he was doing for me was to get all the amateur drama and little theatre companies to make lists of their best players. He knew most of them himself, for he was a keen theatre-goer and a writer of plays.

In London I had been to the Royal Academy of Dramatic

Art and told the Principal that I had a wonderful chance for an unknown girl. Instead of keeping me talking while he telephoned the police he was very helpful. I saw some grand young actresses but only one of them looked capable of digging a patch of potatoes. Her name was Ruth Munro (accent firmly on the last syllable). She was a bright handful. I told her I was going to search Edinburgh—for likely talent.

'You'll be staying at the Cally?' she stated, rather than asked.

'At the. . . ?'

'Cally. Everybody stays there. It's handy for the trains and it's right on Prince's Street.'

'It seems a peculiar name for an hotel.'

'Oh, never heed it. Edinburgh is a peculiar town.'

'Good.'

'I come from Edinburgh.'

'So I imagined. Do you know anybody there I should see?'

'Ay. There's a boy. . . .'

'Really?'

'No, but he's awful good-looking and he can sail a boat and he can climb like a cat and he's brown and strong—oh, strong as anything.'

'Is he Scottish?'

'Well, his folks are. He's from Canada. He's studying medicine. He was at McGill.'

'He sounds interesting. Tell him to come and see me.'

When I drove into Edinburgh I asked my way to the Cally and eventually found myself at the Caledonian Hotel —at least that is the name outside but nobody ever calls it that. Still I thought Ruth Munro could have been more explicit; I suppose it had simply never occurred to her that it had another name. I was also worried to find 'Cally' was spelt 'Caley', but pronounced 'Cally'. This still makes me mutter to myself.

44

The Pawky Wee Body

There was a telephone message from Ruth Munro's friend
and next morning early he came to see me. He was everything she had said and rather more, for he had a Canadian
accent you could cut with a nail-file. In spite of this he was
so remarkable that I did not rule him out. I told him to
keep in touch with me.

Vernon climbed into the Auburn with me and we drove
off. It was a lovely morning but it meant about as much to
us as to victims in the tumbril. There is a wonderful road
between Edinburgh and Glasgow, wide and beautifully
engineered. It is one of the few pleasant recollections of
that trip to me. We got there ahead of time and found the
address after a little search. The office of the Pawky Wee
Body was near the top of a long street, just where it started
to rise steeply up a hill. It was a corner building, of grey
stone, and looked good for another thousand years or so.
The doors and passages were very shabby in a respectable
manner. You felt that there was nothing to prevent them
being cleaned up and chromium-plated except that all the
tenants would at once leave in a body. Lord Dumfries was
with his adviser. Presently we were asked to come up and
they received us together.

To the united horror of Vernon and myself we saw at
once that the Earl was no mean psychologist: he might be
no longer on his own ground but he had brought his props
with him. Although it was Glasgow, on a Monday, he still
wore the kilt, and, in addition, carried a bonnet and a
knobbly stick. From that moment we fought at a disadvan-
tage. The Body was an Edinburgh solicitor: any producer
would have cast him as that on sight. I liked him. His office
was an exact replica of the office of an Edinburgh solicitor.

After introductions they both looked expectant, so I
thought 'Now for it.' For the Body's benefit I summarized
what I had said yesterday to the Earl, then went on to the
more important facts behind it. Everything was at stake
and I made rather a good speech, even Vernon will admit

45

that. I emphasized the material good we should bring to the Islands and the great stir that would be made by a dramatic presentation of the most pressing problem in Scotland: the depopulation of the Outer Isles and of the Highlands. The Body showed interest and sympathy but I had my eye on the noble lord and his eye was as cold as a chilled salmon's. I told how for years I had set my heart on St. Kilda, how finally everything was ready, a ship had been bought, everything waited on the word of one man, Lord Dumfries. He had only to consent and men and women would be employed for the whole summer; thousands of pounds would pass through Glasgow and Stornoway, our proposed base; a twenty-thousand-pound enterprise depended on his nod. Finally, I had been in touch with my producers the night before; though such a thing had been quite unexpected they had agreed to my proposal, and I was authorized by them to offer £500 to Lord Dumfries in consideration of his loaning the island for the film and consenting to act as technical adviser.

Then the Earl started to speak and my heart slowly sank. As if they had never been discussed he went through all the old arguments: his birds, his holiday, his house, his privacy, the *Vedra's* siren (grunt from Vernon), the uncouth hurry of the whole affair. There would be this to arrange, that to cancel. His factor must be consulted. It was impossible to consent at once. In any case, the birds! He could not have his birds disturbed.

Polite arguments countered each other. Everybody kept their tempers admirably. Nobody got anywhere. I stuck to my guns: I had to, although I had no more ammunition. Suddenly people started glancing at watches and murmuring about luncheon appointments. Lord Dumfries, with the air of a conjuror bringing off one of his easier tricks, produced a gold cigarette case from his sporran. All seemed lost. The Body tentatively suggested that we return after lunch, by which time everyone could have thought things over; 'everyone' being, I suppose, the Earl. I made one last effort to get a plain answer for my side but he would not be rushed. I stressed once more the unique value to us of St. Kilda and of St. Kilda alone.

'Yes,' he said thoughtfully, picking up his stick and bonnet, 'I understand that of course.'

I forget where we went to lunch and I am sure Vernon does too. We faced defeat at last. We still hoped on but we felt as cheerful as condemned men on a minute-to-minute reprieve. The Earl seemed completely unimpressed by our sincerity or by the importance of our film—for after all it *was* important to any Scotsman and we were desperately sincere; so his indifference had got us down—that and his birds. Vernon said some really shocking things about the birds.

I have no affection for fulmar petrels, which breed in huge numbers on St. Kilda. For hundreds of years the islanders snared them for the feathers, their flesh and their oil, but there were always just as many. They are beautiful in flight but my chief quarrel with them is their disgusting habit of ejecting gouts of terrible-smelling oil over intruders. Men take their chance, of course, but the fulmars do it to other birds; the oil sticks their feathers together and they drown. Fulmars are unpopular neighbours. Kittiwakes, lovely birds, hate them as much as a great skua. If they had overheard some of Vernon's remarks he would have been elected an Honorary Kittiwake on the spot.

Still, things looked better after lunch. We remembered the Body's sympathy and decided he might win round the Earl. To a man of business such a chance to show a clear profit on a feckless hobby like a bird-sanctuary would be irresistible, and this would account for his suggestion of a respite. We cheered up and returned quite animated to the office. We sent up our names. The Body saw us at once. We bounded into his office with eager faces.

Five minutes later we walked out, got into the car and

drove back to Edinburgh, carrying our dead with us.

If Cumnock was our lines of Torres Vedras, that silent
drive to Edinburgh was our Retreat from Moscow. I drove
keeping my eyes on the road. I dared not look at Vernon:
the victor of the engagements at Portsmouth, Loch Linnhe,
Sunderland and St. John's Wood was in a state of collapse;
that masterful nose was out of joint; that eye-glass was at
half mast; a long sigh escaped him: I knew it was an
unspoken farewell to his first steam command.

The unprecedented spectacle of Vernon's complete despair had a galvanic effect on myself. My blood was up. Not
a word was spoken by either of us for thirty miles but my
brain was busy. As we passed the turning to the Forth
Bridge I suddenly made my decision:

'Vernon,' I said, 'we *won't* be beaten. I'll find another
island! And I'll find it by to-morrow!'

Anyone who has followed this story so far will know it
has been the history of an *idée fixe*. For seven years I had
woven my story round St. Kilda, its people and their lives.
There was hardly a scene in the completed script that did
not contain some intimate allusion or name that rang true
to anyone familiar with the islands. St. Kilda was my story
and my story was St. Kilda. The two had always been one.

I wanted St. Kilda. Well, I couldn't have it.

I had begun to analyse my story. Its appeal was a universal one. Its theme was just as vital, its story just as timely, on
any Scottish island. But it is difficult to describe what a
wrench it was to discard everything I had painfully learnt
and plan to start all over again in a different setting. I didn't
realize then how different. I still thought in terms of the
Hebrides.

'You cannot get another island,' I told myself.

'Why can't I?'

'You haven't got the time.'

'I've got twenty-four hours.'

'If you find one, by a miracle, the same as St. Kilda, one that will fit your script, with a village, half of it in ruins, with a great cliff to climb; an island not too far from a base of supplies—I say, *if* you find one, how do you know the owner will consent?'

'It's still worth trying.'

'In twenty-four hours? Remember you will also have to convince Joe that another island will be just as good. You've always stressed St. Kilda. You've oversold it, haven't you?'

'I haven't any choice. It's find another island, or give up the film, *and I won't give up the film!*'

It was then that we passed the road to Queensferry and I said aloud with such conviction:

'Vernon, I'll find another island, and I'll find it by to-morrow!'

'How?' said Vernon. He had been in cold storage for the past half-hour.

'Somehow,' I answered. 'We won't go back to-night as we planned. *You* must go and sell Joe the idea of another island. It's no good telephoning. You've got to tell him the whole story. He's got to suffer as we suffered. You've got to make him understand that it's a point of honour to get even with the noble lord.'

By this time Vernon was awake.

'**** the Dook! eh?' he suggested.

'Splendid! We'll adopt it as our motto. **** the Dook!'

From the moment Vernon coined this phrase we never looked back, till the camera turned on the first scene in Lerwick harbour. It is historic. The car which had been idling along at forty miles an hour suddenly leapt to eighty.

'As soon as we get in I'll get hold of Herries. He'll know where I can find John Mathieson.'

'Who?' We were doing eighty-five.

'The man who made a survey of St. Kilda. MacGregor speaks about him in his book. He's in the Scottish Geographical Survey. If anyone knows of another island, he will.'

'Suppose he's away?'

'Pooh!'

'You'll be too late by the time we get into Edinburgh.'

'Then I'll get him at his home. The *Scotsman* will help me. We've got to find an island to-night. It's our only chance. You must hold Joe to-morrow. . . .'

'I'll hold him.' Vernon was himself again.

'. . . but I've got to have it all settled by to-morrow night or he'll back out; and he'll be right.'

The needle steadied on ninety, as the Auburn ate up the miles to Edinburgh; and the song that the engines sang and the firm resolve in both our hearts was:

'**** the Dook!'

Chapter V

MONEY FOR JAM!

★

'The Brandon Thomas Repertory Company Present *Swords About the Cross*, a new play about Mary, Queen of Scots, by Margot Lister.'

I had seen this plastered all over Edinburgh without knowing that it affected me vitally. The first-night performance was in two hours' time. All the town would be there, including, of course, Herries. He had already left his office but I telephoned him at his home. The man was a saint. He had to get something to eat, change and be at the theatre at eight o'clock, he had never seen me in his life, yet when I told him my news he was as concerned as if he were backing the picture himself. He told me his address and urged me to come out to see him at once.

'We can talk things over and find what is to be done. John Mathieson? He will be at his home by now. You are right, he is your man. We have his address somewhere. I will get it for you. Now please do not thank me, Mr. Powell, anyone who had read your story would be glad to help. Are you sure you can find the way here? The *second* turning to the right, not the first! And the house is on the left. Ask for the Grange district. We will be looking out for you.'

Such kindness was a tonic. I left Vernon to bite his nails, leapt into the car and was there in ten minutes. Herries is tall and stooping. His eyes are pale and penetrating. His face is lined and he has as little hair as I have, with more excuse. He cannot help being kind and polite, it is in his hands and his face and his whole craggy frame. He loves the hills and the sea and good books and interesting people: and he knows a very great deal about them. The *Scotsman* is lucky in its chief reporter. ('Lucky' is an irreverent word applied to the *Scotsman*, but I don't often get the chance to patronize such an austere publication.)

In ten minutes' talk Herries was up to date. He saw the need for haste, tucked me under his arm and bore down upon John Mathieson's house on the north side of the town. Mathieson had moved recently and we wasted time looking for his new flat. It was in an endless grey road, lined with enormous houses, whose top floors must be somewhere in the stratosphere. They were built of and founded on enduring rock, as cheerful as the east face of the Matterhorn. At the door of every one was a double row of brass bell pushes which had been polished till they shone like a sergeant-major's buttons. A name-plate flanked each button. At last we found the house. I saw 'John Mathieson' on a plate. We rang the bell and started up the stairs.

Herries had phoned Mathieson to expect us and his rosy face with its crown of fine white hair peered over the balustrade when there was still another flight to climb. We met on the landing. He greeted Herries and then turned to me, thrusting out his hand with shy abruptness and with a heart-warming smile. I am not tall but I was a head taller than Mathieson. His eyes were very blue and his manners were beautiful, to everyone the same. He spoke in a soft voice which was shy and abrupt like his movements, and if either of us started to speak he listened with flattering attention. Speaking for myself, when I am with him I would rather hear John Mathieson talk of what he knows: what doesn't he know? But he won't.

It is possible that at this point the reader will put down the book with a bang and complain he is not getting his money's worth.

Money for Jam!

'Here', says my phantom reader, 'is a book that purports to be a narrative of real experiences, of things done and of encounters with real people. If this is true then the writer is a singularly fortunate man. After four chapters and a bit he has not met one unpleasant individual. Most of his characters are paragons. True, Lord Dumfries was not helpful, but he had a perfect right to refuse his help; MacGregor is a bit of a crank, but so are lots of nice people. But all the others! They listen, they telephone, they write, they rally round Powell to a perfectly sickening extent. What is the meaning of this rose-coloured world? Because it is not my own experience.'

The real explanation, I suppose, is that I had a cause in which I believed and which involved important issues, which brought me into contact, one way or another, with exceptionally interesting and intelligent men. What I had to say was to the point: in their turn, they gave of their best. Anyone whose profession brings him into technical discussion with a number of men, for instance an explorer or the captain of a merchant vessel, will understand what I mean.

That is my explanation, but it can never explain the strangers who went out of their way to help me, the busy men who wasted hours to listen to me, and all the kindness which was showered upon me all the time I was in Scotland. While as for Edinburgh (it is presumption and I shall get snubbed), every time I return, it is like coming home. I love the big, green, smoky city and its open-handed citizens.

I repeat that nothing can explain Scottish hospitality. It just is; and, in my own case, nothing I ever do will repay it.

I left myself shaking hands with John Mathieson. We went into his flat. We disposed ourselves around on chairs. Our host sat forward on his, as eagerly as if he had waited all day for this moment, instead of being completely in ignorance of the reason for our invasion. With a courteous

53

wave of his hand in my general direction, Herries gave a synopsis of my recent activities. On hearing I was a film director Mathieson looked at me with mild interest, as at a new kind of gannet, but, catching my eye, smiled in a reassuring way and resumed his attitude of absorbed attention. When Herries finished, Mathieson nodded several times in silence. He then looked abstractedly at me, smiled again, without seeing me this time, and looked out of the window.

'Another island?' I prompted.

'Ay! another island,' repeated Mathieson, looking hopefully out of the windows, as if he expected them to open suddenly on the foam of perilous seas.

'And you know them all, better than anyone.'

'He does, that's so,' observed Herries.

There was another dreamy pause, while Mathieson's soul hovered like an eagle over the Hebrides.

'I'm no' just very familiar with the Outer Isles,' said Herries. 'Skye, of course, Tyree and Iona. But Mr. Powell does not think any of those would do. Too big and not sufficiently isolated. But if you. . . . Eh? What was that?'

John Mathieson's lips had murmured something. He gave a start and repeated, in a louder voice:

'Mingulay.'

Herries looked thoughtful.

'The name is familiar. Is it near North Uist?'

'Barra. South of Barra. There's three all together, little wee islands; Mingulay, Berneray and. . . .'

He stopped, frowning, then jumped up and went out. Herries nodded triumphantly at me and I looked encouraged. Mathieson returned with maps. We spread them out. The Hebrides lie north and south in a curving line. At the top end is Lewis and the lonely isle of Rona; at the very bottom end are Mingulay, Berneray and . . .

'Pabbay!' exclaimed John Mathieson. He suddenly turned to me and became articulate.

'They are a group—very like St. Kilda—the main island is Mingulay, of course. There's a village and a church. . . . I was there once in . . . let me see. . . .'

'Is it inhabited?'

'Oh no! Its story is exactly the same as Hirta's. The last folk left it just after the war.'

'Are the cliffs high?'

'Very. I forget, but I think nearly as high as Hirta.'

'It sounds ideal.'

'Oh, it is . . . yes. . . .'

'I could get men from Barra. It's only a few miles. There are plenty of men. I had a letter from Compton Mackenzie.'

Herries nodded.

'Ay, he should know.'

'Who owns Mingulay?'

'Ah, now, that's just where you may have some small difficulty. . . .'

Herries and I exchanged glances.

'. . . it seems to me that I read the other day . . . and I believe it was in your paper, Herries . . . that Mingulay was for sale.'

To me that was good news.

'But that's grand. If they'll sell, they'll rent—to me anyway. Think of the advertisement to the place. It would be worth their while to hold up any deal for this summer.'

'We can find out all about it in the files,' cried Herries, fired with my enthusiasm. 'Let me see, who is on duty to-night? Stafford! I'll give you a note to him.'

'Splendid.'

Herries rose to his feet, his face beaming.

'I'm really sorry, Mr. Powell, but we must be off.'

'Of course. Look here, Mr. Mathieson, you've given me new hope but I've got to have a second string. This place may be tied up, or already sold. I've only got till to-morrow. Can you think of another island?'

Mathieson shook his head.

'You must have the same characteristics as Hirta?'

'It's essential.'

'Then there's no other that I know of and I know them all.'

'He does, that's so,' said Herries, moving towards the door.

We all went out. I was pleased but I wasn't satisfied. Twenty-four hours was too steep. Two chances would halve the betting. As we picked up our hats:

'Of course,' murmured Mathieson dreamily, 'there's Foula!'

Prose has its limitations. For there is no doubt that deprecating suggestion marked the moment between success and failure, not only of the expedition, but of the completed film. But I merely stopped and said:

'Foula? Where is it?'

Mathieson already seemed to blush and regret his suggestion. He really is too modest. He said hurriedly:

'Oh, it's much farther north, in the Shetlands, nothing like the Hebrides at all.'

By this time I was beginning to know Mathieson and I realized that he wouldn't have thought of Foula without good reason; so, although Herries was shifting restively, I lingered and said:

'What made you think of it?'

'Well, its position for one thing. If you want a lonely island, there are none lonelier. Then there's always been a kind of dispute, between Foula and Hirta, which has the highest sea cliff. One of them is certainly the highest in Great Britain. The official survey gives Conachair on Hirta as fourteen feet higher than the Kame on Foula. But there's little in it.'

He did not add that he had made both surveys, one of them in his own time and at his own expense.

'Is it like St. Kilda?'

Money for Jam!

'Like Hirta. There is only one island, you know. Conditions are very much the same.'

'Is it inhabited?'

'Oh, yes, certainly, about a hundred people.'

'Who owns it?'

'Well now, there again Mr. Herries can help you. There was something about the owner of Foula last year, if he can find it.'

'If it's in the files, we'll find it.' (The *Scotsman* speaking.)

'Can you show me Foula on the map?'

We turned and hurried back to the sitting-room. I had a prickly feeling up and down my spine. Mathieson dragged out the ordnance map of the Orkneys and Shetlands.

'There is Foula!'

I looked. The Orkneys bunched together close to the north-east point of Scotland. Then came eighty miles of sea with Fair Isle a half-way house. For a hundred more miles the Shetlands straggled northward, from Sumburgh Head, where the tides always run one way, to Muckle Flugga, the northernmost lighthouse in the British Isles. Out to the west lay Foula. It roughly resembled Africa in shape and was about three miles long by two broad. It stood alone, like a valiant champion, for the whole coast of Shetland, against the ceaseless attack of the grey Atlantic rollers, nonstop from New York; and, like a champion, the great cliff of the Kame seems to ask no help and need none, even in the full force of a south-west gale.

I know Foula so well now that as I look again at the map which I shared with Mathieson, the restless tides of those Northern Seas start to surge and flow through the smooth surface of the paper. I can see the white water where the Hoevdi grund is breaking and the streams of bubbles where the tide rip runs round Strem Ness. I can hear the breakers on the long shelves of Helliberg and watch the waves of cloud pour day after day over the summit of Hamnafeld. I lay no claim to second sight but something of this was

57

there for me in that first sight of the map of Shetland, with Foula out to the west. Mingulay, which had so excited me a moment before, receded to second place, while Foula loomed bigger and bigger.

Herries was quite agitated, for he would certainly be late for the theatre. I tore myself away from the map, thanked Mathieson with all my heart, arranged to meet him next morning, rushed down the stairs after Herries, dashed with him across Edinburgh, talked all the way, dropped him and returned to the Caley to tell Vernon my news.

Now that we had two alternatives up our sleeve we decided it was time for Joe to take it on the chin about St. Kilda. The blow would be softened by not having to sign a five-hundred-pound cheque but we expected a cry of anguish; also we feared a drop in enthusiasm. We had this advantage. We had been through the depression and Foula was round the corner. As we had dinner we planned our sales talk. It was to go something like this:

VERNON: 'Hullo, Joe?'

JOE: 'Hullo, Commodore! Well, is it in the bag?'

VERNON: 'Any minute! Micky's at the offices of the *Scotsman* now.'

JOE: 'What doing?'

VERNON: 'Locating the owner.'

JOE: 'But Lord Dumfries. . . .'

VERNON: 'Oh, of course [light laugh] we've been so busy I forgot you don't know. St. Kilda's out.'

JOE: 'What!'

VERNON: 'Hold on! We've found another island.'

JOE: 'But . . . !'

VERNON: 'In the Shetlands; better climate, better location.'

JOE: 'Great Grief! The Shetlands! Why, they're way up in the Arctic Circle or something. . . .'

VERNON: 'Not quite.'

JOE: 'But it's the story! Why, Micky said. . . .'

Money for Jam!

VERNON: 'He's changed his mind; and another thing, Foula is inhabited.'

JOE: (weakly) 'Foula?'

VERNON: 'The new island. We shan't have to bring people in. No food and shelter to provide. That will save another thousand pounds. If we get Foula. . . .'

JOE: 'Then you haven't got it?'

VERNON: 'Practically. Micky is chasing it now; and we've got another if it fails.'

JOE: 'I give up. Where are you? The Thousand Islands?'

VERNON: 'Joe, we've got a million of 'em!'

I outlined this with some enthusiasm. Vernon looked doubtful but guaranteed to keep Joe calm until next morning, by which time he would be back in Elstree. We agreed that the end of twenty-four hours was our deadline. If I failed to get Foula or Mingulay by then, the option on the *Vedra* would expire, Joe would back out and the whole structure would collapse. If I succeeded, the advance guard could be on the island in ten days, and we could be shooting by 20th June.

Herries had told me to go to the offices of the *Scotsman* at about nine. We wished each other luck and I went off. The Castle was floodlit. It was a foggy night and wreaths of cloud circled the battlements, which looked like the citadel of a dream. Luck was with me all through our adventure, but one of the luckiest things of all was to see Edinburgh Castle that night, when it was still new to me, glowing with light, the battlements throwing solid shadows over the steep grass slopes, the fog lifting and parting uneasily round the grey walls; and all this, hundreds of feet up in the air above me, with a few quiet footfalls in the gardens, the traffic in Prince's Street muted by the fog and the distant clanking of a train in Waverley Station.

Edinburgh is a city of bridges, not over water but over busy ravines of men. The most impressive of these glens divides the Castle and University from Prince's Street and is spanned by two wide bridges. The offices of the *Scotsman* stand at the south end of North Bridge, overlooking the town. I approached it from the gardens below and, after climbing steadily, came out into a street called Fleshmarket Close. I was very pleased with this name which seemed to me Scottish and uncompromising, though on reflection I suppose it was not very different from a street in my home town of Canterbury, called Butchery Lane. MacGregor, being a vegetarian, would not approve of either. This reflection brought me up short. What about MacGregor? His chief value to the expedition was his first-hand knowledge of the evacuation of St. Kilda. The answer looked pretty obvious. I was rather worried, still I decided to suspend judgment until I found another island. If it resembled St. Kilda no doubt his knowledge would be almost as useful.

By this time I had arrived at the foot of an enclosed stone stairway, connecting the Close with North Bridge, eighty feet above. Although a public passage it was part of the *Scotsman* building and several mysterious swing doors opened off the various landings. If a mental picture is to be formed of this part of Edinburgh words like 'bridge', 'building' and 'stairway' must not be judged in the light of ordinary experience. In Edinburgh they build things to last and their idea of a wall to keep out draughts is two feet thick of granite. The Druids may have felt pleased with themselves when they hauled the last block on Stonehenge, but if they had seen the offices of the *Scotsman* they would have felt like jerry-builders. North Bridge, seen from below, is a work of giants; it is almost impertinence to call that colossal dingy structure by the same name as a couple of planks over a brook.

I arrived, rather winded, at the street level. A stone terrace led to the main entrance of the newspaper. I passed through revolving doors, noting with respect on my way another door which bore a plate, 'Headquarters of the

Money for Jam!

Northern Command'. There was nobody in the long entrance hall but presently a man came through and directed me to the reporters' room. I went down a huge staircase, with a stained-glass window, which told me bluntly: 'Nemo me impune lacessit.'

The reporters' room was more cheerful. Stafford was expecting me and had already found the item about Mingulay. I have it no longer but it briefly announced that a firm of agents off Prince's Street had been instructed to sell it, together with its dependent islands. The owner was not named but I knew I could obtain all I wanted from the agents. So far, so good. Nothing more could be done about that till the morning. The next thing was Foula.

There we were stumped. Reporters came in and out. Some of them knew of Foula but nobody remembered the item, nor who owned the island. I was introduced to half a dozen men. It was nearly ten o'clock, so we dived through underground passages, passed a watch-dog in a glass-fronted kennel, and emerged into one of the many alleys which are a feature of Edinburgh, as steep, picturesque and narrow as any in Marseilles. We returned ten minutes later ready for anything. I can recommend the beer in Edinburgh; and the company.

Somebody new arrived and said the owner of Foula lived near Edinburgh. My spirits soared. He wasn't sure where. Somewhere in East Lothian. Dalkeith or some place like that, it began with Pen, he thought. ('Penicuik,' shrieked somebody. 'No, no,' said the oracle, 'don't confuse a man.') Ah, he had it. He remembered the name because a team from there had done so well in the Drama Festival; it was particularly surprising since such a small village, practically four crossroads and little else. . . .

'What is its name?' we all yelled.

He looked surprised.

'Have I not told you?' he said, fumbling for matches. 'Pencaitland.'

'But that's a bare twenty miles away; ye go by Mussel-
burgh and Portobello, Mr. Powell.'

I received this aside with a nod of thanks, though the
names meant nothing to me. What did excite me was the
news. The owner of Foula could so easily have been living
at the other end of Scotland, or on the island itself. To hear
that he was within easy reach was too good.

'If he lives at Pencaitland, then I know the owner,'
announced Munro, a slim, dark young man, with clear
eyes and a friendly smile.

'Who?'

He named a big landowner of those parts. The others
seemed to think he was probably right. (But he was wrong.)

Stafford had pounced on a large book.

'There's no mention of Pencaitland or Foula in the index,'
he reported, 'nor yet of the owner. The only way is to go
through the files till we find something.'

I shall never forget those reporters. They had the paper
to get out but they snatched all the time they could to help
me hunt. I had told them of my time limit and they were
all as keen as I was. The slim young reporter was full of
enthusiasm. He knew the Shetlands and had Manson's guide
at home. He promised to bring it next day for me to see.
He had Highland blood in him and evidently spent all his
spare time on the hills. Herries appeared, to write his review
of the play. He heard my news, sympathized, wished me
luck and went home. Vernon looked in before his train left.
I was able to cheer him up and give him details to tell Joe.
Midnight passed. The paper was put to bed and some of the
staff went, too. Still we searched, turning feverishly the
sober, close-printed pages of the *Scotsman*, running our eyes
down column after column, reaching the end of a file,
heaving it aside and selecting another. The big L-shaped
room, with the arched windows and the bare lights suspended over each wooden desk, grew quieter, while down
below us the granite shook to the thunder of the presses.

Money for Jam!

Only three of us were left now. My eyes were aching. My companions were tiring but their enthusiasm did not lag. I was prepared to go on all night, for my whole future turned upon my success, neither more nor less. Then, at half-past one, we found it.

Somebody said quite quietly:

'Here it is.'

We all crowded round and read over his shoulder.

It was a half-column story, on an inner page. It was a news item and an obituary notice. It regretted to announce the death of Professor Holbourn, M.A., F.R.G.S., of Penkaet Castle, Pencaitland in East Lothian and of Foula, in the Shetland Islands. It gave a brief history of his career. He had been a lecturer of international reputation. He had been a great traveller and had been shipwrecked three times: he was one of the *Lusitania* survivors, had been picked up after hours in the water. He had bought Foula thirty years ago, after seeing it on a visit. He divided his time when not on his travels between the island and Pencaitland. He had stood for the Chair of the Academy of Fine Arts in Edinburgh but had not been elected. One gathered that there had been rather a battle about this. He was survived by his widow and by three sons, Hylas, Alasdair and Philistos.

The impression was created of a remarkable personality, restless, intolerant, learned and imaginative, with little sense of humour. Everything I have since learnt confirms this impression. I wish I had been able to meet Professor Holbourn and I feel that the world is poorer by his absence; but it was fortunate for my plans that I arrived too late to do so. I do not think he would have looked with favour on a film company as temporary tenants of Foula.

I read and re-read the half column. The item was eight months old. The man who could name his sons with such autocratic definiteness would have been an adversary to reckon with, and it was possible, in fact probable, that the sons of such a father would be as individual as their names. It was unlikely that they would all be at Penkaet Castle. I wondered with whom I would have to deal.

I thanked everybody all round, walked back to the Caley through quiet streets and went to bed.

Next morning I was at the estate agents' at half-past nine, enquiring about Mingulay. A charming partner saw me and was very sympathetic. Mingulay had just been sold to a lady in Essex. They had not met her personally but would write at once to her agents, to enquire whether she would consider a sub-let for this summer. I explained the need for haste, authorized them to send a telegram, reply paid, and was off to see Mathieson by ten. A hunch is unmistakable. I was not in the least cast down by the lady in Essex (I never found out her name) for, although I was determined to clear my titles on both islands, I was as certain of Foula as I had been of St. Kilda on the previous morning.

The Geographical Survey is located somewhat mysteriously in a huge building, of a rather frivolous design for Edinburgh; inside there are pillars and archways and colonnades in bewildering profusion. The main entrance leads to a cinema and is plastered with stills and posters; I passed it several times. Finally I ventured in and found, across the hall, a broad stairway. I came into a room running the whole width of the building, filled with books, maps, charts, secretaries and a friendly official who took me down another corridor to Mathieson's room.

He was pleased to see me and as excited as I was by my discoveries. He had some more maps to show me, particularly the six-inch ordnance map of Foula, which gave the island in detail. I was struck by the multitude of unusual names, totally different from the Hebridean, and then learnt, for the first time, how the Shetlands were Norse-speaking until 150 years ago, and how a Foula man was the last to speak the old tongue. The Shetlands and Orkneys were never Gaelic-speaking but of course it is sung and spoken in the Hebrides, and I had introduced a lot of it in my script. I saw I was in for a lot of changes. Then Mathieson showed me another map, an old one, that thrilled me to the marrow, for it *was* my story. It was engraved in black and white, about 30″ x 20″. Foula, on a scale of one inch to a mile, was in the left-hand corner. Round the island, roughly following the contour, the map maker had drawn a series of wavy lines which finally flung away from the shape of the island to reach down across the map in giant embracing loops. But all that they embraced was blank, just the empty sea; it filled the whole of the other surface of the map, except where, high in the right-hand corner, a fragment of the coast of Shetland seemed to extend a helping hand to its lonely neighbour. Everywhere else was the sea.

He had some books for me too. Government reports and Hibbert's *Journal* and Tudor. I skimmed through them in half an hour, gathering up facts and legends to be used on Joe and Vernon and in my conversation with whoever barred my way at Penkaet Castle.

An elderly man came in to see Mathieson. He was just such another, and when I was introduced he looked at me wonderingly in just the same kind way. They talked together while I bent over the books and made notes. Finally I thanked Mathieson and was off again, to Herries this time.

I had already found out that Penkaet Castle was not on the telephone so I sent a telegram saying I would be there at three to see Holbourn (unspecified) on a matter of business. It seemed only polite to do so, particularly as I left them no chance of refusal. I guessed that I should arrive on the heels of my message.

Herries and I talked things over. Until I stormed Penkaet, nothing further could be done. Nineteen of my twenty-four hours had gone but they had not been wasted. I left Herries, made a quick lunch and took the road for Mussel-burgh and Portobello.

I passed through Musselburgh, near Prestonpans, turned south and wandered through flattish country which became more wooded as I approached Pencaitland. The roads were white and dusty and the landscape changed to a different scale, more like England. I came to four crossroads and asked my way to Penkaet Castle. It was a shock to learn that the man had never heard of it. I insisted and he looked worried. Finally I mentioned Holbourn's name and his face cleared.

'Oh, ay,' he said, pointing up the narrow lane in which he was standing, 'follow the road over yon field. You will find the house among the trees.'

'Penkaet Castle?' I insisted, for I was puzzled.

He shook his head obstinately.

I drove up the lane as there seemed no other choice. The mystery of the name would solve itself. The road turned into a track over a field of beets, then it turned sharp left and bore along towards some factory chimneys I could see in the distance. The country had quite changed now into rolling fields and miles of woodland, till I could have fancied myself in Hampshire. The trees were mostly oaks. I met another man who turned me round and sent me back again to the beets. There I found another road, so rough and narrow that I had never even considered it as a possi-bility. With a shudder I turned the Auburn up it. I thought my springs would snap, as we lurched from one fearful pot-hole to another. Fortunately it was dry and did not last long. A cottage appeared on the left and some farm build-ings, all rather unkempt. The road widened and suddenly shot down a very steep pitch into the trees round an old shed. I clapped on the brakes and it was just as well, for the hill became as steep as a house and turned sharp to the right. I found myself driving through the gates of one of the loveliest houses I have ever seen.

It was long and all of grey stone. It was not only the loveliest but the oldest-looking house I had ever seen. Age showed in the stones and the weathering of the masonry. Age was in the way it slept there in this fold of the hill, settled down, embedded, as if it had always been there. The windows which faced north, where I stood, were small and narrow and sunk in the walls. The door was in a turret, which ran the height of the house, three storeys. At the other end of the house was an archway, as well proportioned as the rest. A glimpse of a sunny courtyard could be seen beyond. I stopped the car on the drive, which circled round a big flower bed, full of simple colours. I seem to remember snapdragons. For at least five minutes I stayed in my seat. Nobody had heard my arrival. Two great yew trees guarded me like fat sentinels.

As I sat marvelling at this wonderful house hidden in the woods I was brought back with a jerk to the present. A uniformed nurse came through the archway. She was as stiffly starched as if she had just stepped out of a hospital ward. She took no notice of me, I don't believe she even saw me, but vanished into the house through a side door which I now saw for the first time. The introduction of that unexpected figure into the old-world setting gave me a queer feeling and I did not altogether like it.

I got out of the car, approached the door and pulled the bell. After the jangle died away nobody came for a long time. Then I heard a shuffling and the door was unbolted and opened. The play was evidently to continue along the lines of the opening, for I saw in the doorway exactly what any student of drama would expect: an old woman, who regarded me in shrivelled silence.

'Mr. Holbourn?' I said.

Without a word, she nodded and made a rough circular

sweep of her arm which I took to be a cordial invitation to enter. I stepped inside. I was within the wall, and a circular stone staircase of the real old type, each step slotted into the central stone pillar and a corresponding slot in the wall, rose directly up from my feet. There was just room for me and my guide. She closed and bolted the door. I followed her round and round until I stumbled out, through a stone slit in the wall, into a long room, with a blazing fire at the far end and a table, at which was sitting an idiot boy.

He goggled at me with very goggly eyes. He had a hare lip. He was clean and well dressed. I looked behind me and found the servant had silently disappeared in the approved manner. Good heavens! I thought, can this be Mr. Holbourn?

The boy went on staring at me. He had been reading a book and presently made a noise like an empty soda-water syphon, and half rose from his chair. I smiled pleasantly and put the table between us. It didn't seem quite the right time to say, 'Are you Hylas, Alasdair or Philistos?' He might reply: 'Both,' or still more likely, fly into a passion at being reminded of the trick his parents had played on him.

Apart from its occupant the room was delightful. It faced south and the sun streamed in through large recessed windows. It was furnished with taste, the panelling was good, the ceiling was low and there were books and flowers. The view was wonderful, clear for at least fifty miles, for the woods which surrounded the house dropped away on the south side in waves of green oak leaves.

Much of this I saw later for I had only half an eye to spare, my host naturally taking up most of my attention. I had already picked my weapon if he started a stealthy approach. However he appeared to have lost interest; of course it might be a blind, but I was in command of my nerves now and only jumped about a foot as another door opened on my right and a man came quickly in.

He was short and square-shouldered. His hair was a wild,

mouse-coloured thatch which fell forward in a thick fringe
over his forehead. His eyebrows were bushy and rather
beetling and he stared out from beneath them like an un-
combed Shetland pony. His clothes were rough and stained
by work and weather. At first sight he might have been
any age: he was actually twenty-six.

His voice, when he spoke, was slow and cultured and
had a pleasant rhythm of its own:

'I am Alasdair Holbourn,' he said.

'How d'you do. I am Michael Powell; did you get my
telegram?'

'No.'

'No?'

'No.'

'I was lucky to find you in.'

'You would be lucky to find me out, this time of the
year.'

'I wanted to make a business proposition to you.'

'Come inside.'

Nobody mentioned the idiot boy, who had placidly
resumed his reading. Holbourn led me out of the cheerful
room into the adjoining one, which was evidently a drawing-room and seldom used. The windows were sealed and
it was almost as cold as a celler. Holbourn did not appear
to notice it. We sat down and he looked at me with no
expression whatever.

My attack was a model of directness.

'Mr. Holbourn,' I said, 'I am a film director and I want
to make a film this summer on your island of Foula. For
permission to do that I am ready to pay £200.'

I was impressed by the way he took it. He looked at me
from under his shaggy eyebrows with some attention.
Most people would have made all sorts of remarks, exclamations or questions. He did not. He said finally:

'How much did you say?'

'Two hundred pounds.'

'I shall have to ask my mother . . . and my brothers.'

'Are they here?'

'My mother is. My brothers are both at Oxford.'

'I am sorry to hurry you, but I must have an answer at once.'

'That's impossible.'

'You could telephone your brothers.'

'I will speak to them this evening, after seven.'

'Not before?'

'We have no telephone here. I shall speak from the office at the colliery, up the road. We have an arrangement with them. I shall put in a personal call for 7.30. Then I shall be sure of getting my brothers.'

'And your mother?'

'She is in Edinburgh. She will be back to-night.'

'Can you at least tell me this, Mr. Holbourn. Do you think they will consent?'

'I don't see why not.'

'You, yourself?'

'I think it could be arranged.'

I could have kissed him for the unemotional way he said those reasonable words, but I restrained the impulse.

'You will probably wonder', I said, 'why I offer money for the privilege, instead of first trying to get it for nothing.'

'You want a quick answer,' he said shrewdly.

'Yes. I knew you would take me seriously from the start. Two hundred pounds is a good lump of money.'

'It is,' he agreed.

I was glad to find at last somebody who thought so.

'How did you know we were the owners of Foula?'

'I read the article in the *Scotsman* about your father.'

'Are you familiar with Foula, Mr. Powell?'

'No.'

'Then why do you want to make a film there?'

I explained my story and as much of my recent doings as I thought politic. I had already far too high an opinion of

Holbourn's shrewdness to let him think he had the market to himself. He brought out an album of photographs of the island and dozens of others, large and small. They took my breath away. The place had everything: streams, inland lakes, moorland, every kind of croft and cliff such as I had never seen or imagined; walls of sheer sandstone, worn and polished till they were almost white; thousand-foot cliffs that dropped like plummets to the sea; hills that swept down in long lines to a broken, savage coast. My exclamations of delight made Holbourn unbend and he talked with real love of the island. That led him to speak of his father and, by a natural sequence, of Penkaet Castle. I told him what a jewel it was.

'Yes,' he said, 'my father was twenty years looking for it. It was his ideal of a house. He loved it from the moment he saw it. So did we all. He used to say on all his travels that he was looking for the most beautiful house and the loveliest island in the world, so that he could buy them and leave them to his children.'

'His dream came true.'

'Ay.'

He led me over the house. It must have been in a sad state when they bought it. They had been working on it for years; all the panelling was their work. Fireplaces had been built, wells sunk. It was plain what fine plans the old man had made for the house, some of them finished, some still only half done, others too ambitious, abandoned for ever when he died. The man had been a poet and a dreamer; and a man of his hands, too.

Alasdair talking of his father's dreams was very different from my first impression of him. By common consent of the rest of the family he was acting as factor for the estate. At the same time he was carrying on his work as an Ergo-therapy Occupationalist. He took pity on my blank face and went into long explanations about treatments of patients suffering from nervous diseases, usually arising out of physical disability. I listened, I hope, intelligently, but my chief sensation was relief; the idiot boy and the nurse were at last explained.

They both appeared at tea, a cheerful meal, with thick bread and butter and strawberry jam. The nurse was a pleasant person and the idiot boy proved to be not at all an idiot, it was only his appearance that was against him. He produced several nifties on the subject of films and altogether seemed to be quite the Average Patron that some critics talk about.

I left immediately afterwards. Alasdair went with me to make his call at the colliery and to show me the way out, which was very different from the way I came in. I told him that nobody had heard of Penkaet Castle. He grinned.

'That's just their obstinacy,' he explained. 'The house dates back to 1490 and used to be called Penkaet 'Wood Head'. It changed hands several times: one of the owners was the Dick-Lauder family. Sir John, when he was made a 'Law Lord', said he couldn't be known as 'Lord Woodhead', so he changed his name and the house's to Fountainhall. That remained its name for many years, but when we took it, there was always confusion with the other Fountainhall, near Stowe. So we found out the old name and changed it back; but the folk round here will have none of it, so we still have trouble.'

I had obtained a promise from Alasdair that, if his family consented, he would come with us on the expedition as technical adviser. I had decided he would be invaluable for his local knowledge and I also thought that, with such an interesting job in view, he would be a good salesman for me.

He dropped off at the colliery and gave me my directions, and in a minute I was sliding down the road to Dalkeith, on my way back to Edinburgh. I glanced at the clock. It was exactly twenty-four hours since our Retreat from Glasgow.

Money for Jam!

I had reason to be pleased. My hunch had been a good one. John Mathieson had been right. As far as I could see from the photographs, some of which I had brought away with me, Foula was better than St. Kilda. The island itself was not so barren, in fact parts were beautiful. Life was not concentrated on one little village street, as in Hirta, but spread all over the island among a score of crofts, each one a different and interesting location. Then I groaned as I thought of my script, so carefully worked out; practically every line of action would have to be changed and much of the dialogue.

There was another person who would have no cause to rejoice and that was MacGregor. Try as I might I could not fit him into the expedition. His knowledge of the Hebrides, of Gaelic, of St. Kilda was useless to me now. Holbourn would have to take his place. I was sorry for he had been the first of my allies.

I dashed into the office of the chief reporter in a most indecorous manner. I showed him the photographs. We rejoiced together. I told my other friends of my good fortune. Munro gave me the Shetland guide which he had promised. I met Forsyth Hardy, the film critic; he had not been at the office the night before. This was our first meeting, though we knew each other by reputation. Then I was off again to my friendly estate agent. He had a reply about Mingulay, but a negative one. The new owner's agents were going to approach her and would let us know in due course, etc. We knew that meant they refused to be hurried. My agent was very distressed but nothing could depress me, I felt so certain I had got Foula.

Back to the hotel where I telephoned Joe; Vernon had convinced him and I pledged my immortal soul—if any— that Foula was in the bag. At eight o'clock the telephone bell rang. It was Alasdair.

'Hylas is not keen on the idea. I did not think he would be. By the way, your telegram has just been delivered.'

Talk about suspense! I managed to say:

'Well?'

'Oh, he accepts, on condition that I go with you. Do you know what my young brother said?'

As if I cared! But I answered:

'What?'

A grim chuckle sounded in my ear:

' "Money for jam!" '

Chapter VI

WE TAKE THE AIR

★

The sixtieth parallel of latitude runs through Oslo and Petrograd. It touches Cape Farewell in Greenland, and it misses South Ness on Foula by a few miles. This is quite far north but is seven degrees outside the Arctic Circle, of which Joe spoke with such horror.

St. Kilda is farther south, latitude fifty-eight, and those two degrees make a lot of difference.

Before leaving for Elstree, I held a lunch-party: Herries, Mathieson and Alasdair. Alasdair at once embroiled himself with John Mathieson on the vexed subject of Britain's highest cliff. I should imagine that all Holbourns take themselves seriously, but Alasdair could give points to Hamlet. Besides, a Holbourn holds as an article of faith that the Kame is higher than Conachair on St. Kilda, and that Mathieson, who held the contrary, should have his theodolite thrust down his lying throat. Mathieson gazed in wonder at the gloomy ferocity of his accuser, much as a kind woolly sheep-dog would stare at a bristling Aberdeen.

It was Wednesday, 20th May. I pledged myself to be back in Edinburgh, with the members of my advance guard, in exactly two weeks' time, on 3rd June. Herries, on his part, promised to have all the available actors in Edinburgh waiting to see me.

We all slaved to such good effect that on Wednesday, 3rd June, as I had promised, I was shaking hands once again with Alasdair in the lounge of the Caley. He was in rough tweeds and looked as dour as if we were starting for the Pole.

'I never expected for one minute to see you.'

'A promise is a promise,' I answered airily.

'With film-folk?'

I saw that Alasdair was going to try and gain a moral ascendancy over us and would be successful, unless checked, for at present we depended upon him utterly for all our information.

George had been bouncing rather restively during this duel. He felt he was missing something important. George always felt he was missing something important. It gave him a rather restless look.

'This is George Black, our production manager. You will have a lot in common.'

John ambled up, with the look of one who sees visions.

'This is John Seabourne. He will stay behind on the island with Syd Streeter, until the unit comes out.'

John shook hands absently with Alasdair.

'How do you do? Micky, I've just been on Prince's Street. It's all round you, everybody's talking it, just the same stuff that you pay good money to hear Will Fyffe speak. And it's all free!'

'Where's Syd, John?'

'He can't find his box of tools on the train. He almost cried last night because they wouldn't let him have it in his berth with him. "I told them it shouldn't go in the van," he was saying to the stationmaster, very pink and self-controlled (Syd—not the stationmaster) and the. . . .'

'Here comes Streeter, now,' said George.

George had only joined us two days before and was inclined to be managerial, since he knew none of us well. We had no objection to George so long as he managed and made no fuss about it. We had not figured on a P.M. It had been Gerry Blattner's idea—he said he must be represented by someone, he said we must have a manager, he said—'Well, as to that, Gerry,' John had said, 'we're pretty good at managing ourselves. . . .' Anyway, here he was, looking rather worried about his exact position. Syd came up, pink and self-controlled, his spectacles gleaming, his beloved box of tools in one hand (it weighs 70 lb.), his personal effects (weighing 20 lb.) in the other. He was much the most respectable member of the party and nobody seeing him would have guessed that he was embarking on a series of labours, which would make Hercules look like a sissy.

'Syd Streeter is our chief of construction.'

'What does that mean?' asked Alasdair.

'Oh, he'll be in charge of all manual labour, build the camp, construct light railways for track shots and—I'll tell you what, Holbourn—he'll put a false top on the Kame for you, so that you can confound Mathieson and win the palm for Foula.'

Alasdair smiled in a manner with which we were all to become very familiar and which earned for him the title of 'the Smallie': 'And where will Mr. Streeter obtain his "manual labour"?'

Even George realized that something unpleasant was coming. It was Alasdair's weakness that he had no talent for under-statement. He wanted to make our flesh creep. At the beginning, he succeeded, for we were Babes in Shetland. After a week, even a newborn babe would laugh merrily up at Alasdair's most troll-like mutterings. But at the Caley, on 3rd June, we knew not our Smallie. We all looked scared and said:

'Labour? Why, the islanders, of course.'

Alasdair sniggered.

'You are welcome to try. Father did.'

'You mean they won't work?'

'I mean what I say. You can try.'

'Come clean, Mr. Holbourn. Can we get labour on the island or can't we?'

'It's the middle of the fishing season.'

'The men will be away?'

'Many of them.'

'But some are crofters. They must look after their farms.'

'The women do that.'

'And who looks after the sheep?'

'Och, the girls and the old men.'

'But there must be some able-bodied men on the island. Who runs the mail-boat?'

Alasdair looked slightly confused.

'Oh, ay, there's the mail-boat crew. But', recovering, 'try and get Walter Ratter to do anything he doesn't want to do.'

We looked doubtfully at one another. George shook his head with foreboding. Syd looked trustfully at me. John said confidently:

'I'll take care of all that. The whole island will be feeding out of my hand in two weeks, or my name's not Seabourne.'

George had engaged a sitting-room for me. I retreated there after breakfast; the lobby was already filling with ambitious Scots. Herries and Campbell Robson arrived just before ten. Robson had put in a lot of work on the list of suggested players and was himself suggested by Herries for the part of James Gray or the Catechist. His own description of himself is 'Character actor; thin face; 5 ft. 6 in.'. My own note is scribbled against it and describes him as 'a good type, small, excitable, fox-terrier'. He had just had a big success as producer of a play on Dickens, in which he took the name part.

The morning passed in interviews. One by one, thirty people came in, all shapes, sizes and sexes. I greeted them, asked for their names and addresses, made notes, but all this was only to cover a keen inspection, which few of them passed. You can tell a good actress or actor when they walk into the room: it is more than poise, more than personality; it is, I think, a faculty for doing a thing right. From a good deal of experience, I consider this is the outstanding characteristic of a good actor; it is a habit of mind, of training, which has taught them adaptability: to coordinate their nerves and mind to instant obedience. Also, their bodies. For example, I had a scene in a film, where a car had to be driven up a drive, swerve suddenly, back and stop. If the car failed to stop exactly in the right place the shot was useless, for a low camera covered the whole action and finally centred in close-up on a significant piece of detail on the car's running-board. To save time, the producer engaged a crack driver to double for the actor who was in the car. I explained just what I wanted and why I wanted it. It had to be done at a good speed. The driver nodded, went confidently through the scene and finished a car-length off the spot. He tried again. He kept on trying. Finally the actor said in my ear:

'Let me have a shot.'

'Have you ever driven a Bentley?'

'No, but it's just a car.'

'All right, but don't kill anyone.'

He got in, drove down the road and back and said he was ready. The crack driver sucked his teeth loudly. We started shooting and I signalled the actor. He came roaring up, swerved, stopped and shot back. The running-board came to a bang-stop exactly in the centre of the screen.

'Can you do it again?'

'A few inches farther away,' suggested my camera-operator feelingly.

He did it again.

'How was that, Monty?'

'Too good!'

The crack driver was paid and went home, and we went on making pictures.

With this at my back, I was able to make up my mind

quite quickly in those interviews at the Caley. Some of the girls were pretty, some plain, nearly all had sweet expressions, but there wasn't an ounce of poise or self-assurance among them. This statement of what I consider important for a young woman's screen career will be received by many people with impatient snorts, but I can assure them that personality, sweetness, even genius, are no good in an interview unless the candidate has made up her own mind about it. One of two things is necessary for an untrained girl, looking for a job. Unusual good looks, or a thorough knowledge of her own good points. If she has the first, she usually has the second. If she has the second, she can make people believe she has the first. That is all I have to say about a burning question; it has certainly been said before but I may as well say it again.

No. 12 on the list made by Robson was 'Hamish Sutherland. Six foot tall; athletic, good Scotch type; hardy; fine talent; powerful reserves.' He was suggested for the part of Andrew. He came in, smiled at Robson, glowered at me, sat down and held his hat between his knees, leaning forward and daring me to not cast him for a part. I see on my notes: 'Big—twenty-five—cross-looking—John Shand'. His largeness, earnestness and determination tickled me profoundly. I said tentatively:

'Well, Mr. Sutherland, can you act?'

'I can!'

The answer came pat on the end of my question. It was said with convincing energy and admitted of no argument at all. Hamish Sutherland was impressive.

I said cautiously:

'You are in business in Edinburgh?'

'I am. An insurance inspector.'

'Do you think, if it were necessary, you could get away for the whole summer?'

'I could!' With exactly the same tone and conviction as before.

'I am on my way to Foula now. I shall be back by Monday. [Vanity of man!] Will you let me think things over till then. I may have a proposal to make you.'

A gleam of triumph came in his eye.

'Ay. I will!'

He got up, seized my hand, seemed about to say something, then nodded curtly to the room generally and strode out.

Harking back to what I said just now: Hamish Sutherland knew what he had got.

The door opened quickly and a dark, thick-set man came neatly into the room. He was dressed in a business suit and wore gold-rimmed eye-glasses. His thick, black curly hair was neatly brushed and he would have been an ornament to any board-meeting. Yet before George Summers had sat down, the part of the Trawler Skipper, a nebulous possibility till that moment, had suddenly taken on shape and enlarged, and the end of the film had been changed to suit it.

These are the fascinating possibilities of leaving a character like a pencil-sketch, until you find the man to fill it in.

I made him the same proposal I had made Hamish. I offered the part of the Laird to Campbell Robson. There were a few more people to see and I saw them, but there were no more discoveries.

My chief disappointment was the girls. I had nobody at all in mind, except Ruth Munro, and she was too round-faced and young for the girl I had imagined. Her voice and her experience were good, but I had hoped to find a real Scottish peasant lassie. With more time I believe I could have succeeded. If many Scots girls have the same spirit as

Miss Pagan, then I am certain. She was a frail-looking old lady, with a fine, intelligent face, who came to see me. She wrote later to Herries, supplying information I had asked for: 'Perhaps I ought to add that I have had experience of camp life and in varying weathers. Even slept on straw and bathed in a chilly stream, though I trust conditions will not be quite so strenuous as that. It was ten years ago—and I'm older now!'

Talk about Flora MacDonald!

John Seabourne had meanwhile vanished on a mysterious errand which was explained when he suddenly appeared at my elbow, accompanied by a huge, soft-spoken, neatly dressed man, with striking eyes, who was proudly introduced to me as none other than Busty Hawkins, hero of 'The Rocket Has Gone Up, Sir!' I had known the fabulous Busty Hawkins so many years, through so many of John's inspired reminiscences, that I could only gape as anyone would gape on suddenly being presented to Long John Silver, Terence Mulvaney, or Porthos, in the flesh. I shall always have a grudge against John that he rushed him in and whisked him out that morning. Heroes of antiquity should not be treated that way. John told me that Busty Hawkins had spent his last years of service at Edinburgh Castle, where he was loved and feared. He had then retired and taken a civilian post. He had met John by special appointment. I said I bear a grudge, and yet I am also glad. The songs the sirens sang and the name Ulysses bore when he hid amongst the women may not be beyond all conjecture, but they are even better as the stuff of dreams.

Somebody—it may have been me—gave Alasdair a good opening, as we crossed the Forth Bridge. Somebody—I am sure it was *not* me—said thoughtfully:

'What time do we get to Aberdeen?'

'About eight,' said George.

'Four hours. When do you think we shall be on Foula?'

'It depends,' said George wisely.

We Take the Air

I saw Alasdair's face change, his lip curl, a troll-like look come into his eye. George had his back to him.

'What arrangements have you made, George?' I asked innocently.

George looked fretful.

'There's a boat to-morrow night for Lerwick. We can catch that but we have to wait all day.'

'What about to-night?'

'Too late.'

'Can we fly?'

'That's what I can't make out. Some people think there's a plane from Aberdeen, some say Inverness.'

'Surely there's a schedule?'

'But there isn't. I can't understand it. Nobody knows anything.'

'Heh! Heh! Heh!' said the Smallie.

We all looked at him.

'What's that mean?'

'What are you laughing at?'

'All of you. Complaining about aeroplanes that don't exist. Your troubles are only starting.'

'Tell us the worst.'

'When we get to Lerwick, we aren't at Foula.'

'You're kidding.'

'All right, laugh, but we'll have to find a boat to take us over.'

'So we can get a boat?'

'Weather permitting.'

'O.K. Jonah, we can always throw you overboard.'

'You'll still have to get back again.'

George looked worried.

'Are we likely to get bad weather?'

It was enough. Alasdair was off, with chapter and verse of the storms he had been in, the privations he had suffered, the risks he and his brother ran every day of their rugged island lives. George lapped it up.

We Take the Air

I owe Aberdeen an apology. It is a fine city but each time I was there I had a lot of other things on my mind. The hotel district, where the big shops are, is on a hill as steep as any in Edinburgh. I remember a sensation, on Union Terrace, of being high up in wonderful air and looking down over public gardens to the docks far below. The air is galvanic in Aberdeen; it ought to be bottled for export to the enervated south.

George found a friend in the young hotel manager and was delighted to discover that there *was* an air service to Shetland—we could leave at ten in the morning and be at Lerwick for lunch. But again the same air of mystery prevailed when we tried to get details. Nobody seemed to know or care that the service was unknown in Edinburgh. There it was. Surely that was good enough? It reminded me of the Italian air service when I was in Albania in 1929. The planes were war relics; they maintained a service from Tirana, to the main towns; but on all time-tables only the time of starting was ever given, never the time of arrival. After a brief study of this significant fact I went by car.

The morning was fine and a car took us out to the flying field. The driver did not seem very sure of his way. Finally we drew up at a bungalow and got out. A small enclosed plane was waiting and quite a crowd of people who stared at us hungrily. We met the president of the company, though what he was doing there we could not imagine. There was a wind blowing and the sparse grass of the rough field waved tragically. I have not done much flying. I do not care for it except to save time, and my only experience had been with the termini of the big air-lines. I looked in vain for smooth asphalt, white lines, little flags and cool mechanics, all so reassuring to the public. The only official-looking figure was the pilot, a tall young man in a uniform so gorgeous and unexpected that he was at once dubbed 'Maurice Chevalier'. Our baggage was stowed in the tail, we shook hands fervently with everyone, and took the seats carefully assigned to us by the pilot, with an eye to balancing his machine. I saw through the window the president's companion shake his head ominously and point, but a minute later they were specks below us and we were following north the banks of a busy river. The map told us it was the Don. We soon left it and were winging over the limitless brown moors of Scotland; they seemed to stretch as far as we could see, with now and again a lonely croft with its cultivated fields around, long straight dusty roads, every ten miles a school or church and then nothing but the moors, every shade from light brown to purple, with sweeping hills in the distance, stone dykes and, plain to see as we flew directly above, mysterious rings of stone and peaty pools of water. We swung right to avoid the high hills of Banff, passed over Lossiemouth and were suddenly above the North Sea, which creeps far inland by the Moray Firth and then, by the Caledonian Canal, winds through Loch Ness and Loch Linnhe to the Atlantic. For forty miles we droned above those shallow waters and our shadow passed across the sails of fishing-boats from Buckie or Banff. We could see clearly dark shapes of shallow reefs, invisible from the water level, except when they break in an easterly gale, while around them the sea-bed spread in carpets of fine sand. We met some air-pockets and bumped badly; John was discovered being quietly sick into a paper bag but declined sympathy. I watched him with some anxiety. John's health had been a debatable point with all of us. One of the fittest men in the army, as soon as he left it in 1920 he developed duodenal ulcers and has had intermittent trouble with them ever since. Doctors failed to explain or cure them. John accepted them fatalistically, sometimes down but never beaten. He fought like a hero and the last years had shown slow improvement but to take him on to a lonely island took some courage. I was the one afraid, not John. He said:

'I've tried everything with the bastards except thumbing

my nose at them. Let me come, Micky. I believe it will do me good. Kill or cure! If I don't go, I think I shall die anyway at the next haemorrhage; then I shall haunt you.'

His wife nodded and said:

'Yes, let him go.'

He saw my worried face and smiled. He said:

'Take that look off your face; I know you. How can I die with twenty weeks' work guaranteed in my contract?'

John is of the same gallant clan with the Mizners. When Wilson Mizner was working in Hollywood, just before his own death, he heard that his brother in Florida was dangerously ill, not expected to live. He cabled: 'Stop dying. Am writing comedy for Joe E. Brown. Wilson.'

The plane was circling round and I looked out. There were fields surrounded by queer-looking fences, thin slabs of stone placed end to end, and one of the fields by the road had a new shed in it, nothing else. I cast a hasty look round. Beyond was the coast and a few miles off some islands which must be the Orkneys. To the east a distant green point of land was visible. To the west, a castle guarded a fine bay where a little, grey old town shepherded a river to the sea. We were at Thurso and the distant point was John o' Groats.

'Maurice Chevalier' made a rather bumpy landing. Some surprised people greeted us. There was quite a little mob who looked like passengers. We stretched our legs while a conference took place. Suddenly George gave an indignant exclamation. We looked and saw our baggage being dumped out on the grass. We dashed up with that peculiar indignation an Englishman always feels about his baggage. Syd, who had already had trouble with his box of tools, was particularly touchy. I forgot to tell that when our baggage was weighed at Aberdeen the pilot flatly refused to take Syd's box. Syd, yes. Box, no. Syd threatens not to go. Pilot shrugs shoulders. Syd pleads, pilot deaf. We all plead, explain box is Syd's father, mother, fiancée, aunt.

Pilot moved but says plane won't; already overloaded. George tells Syd bid farewell to his tools, they must be sent by steamship to Lerwick. Affecting parting. Syd morose for rest of trip, expects the worst, lying stevedores, inefficient purser, barratry, shipwreck, never see his tools, product of ten years' selection, again.

Syd was therefore to the fore, as we rushed to defend our rights. 'Chevalier' explained that the other passengers were for Orkney. The local agent had expected an empty plane. They had all booked passages. The only thing to do was for us to stop at Thurso and have lunch. Meanwhile he would flip them over to Kirkwall and be back in an hour to take us on our lawful occasions. We did not like it—it would make us very late at Lerwick, to get a boat for Foula—but we lumped it.

Alasdair had been so thrilled by the air journey, which was his first, and by the realization that with luck we might be in Foula that night, a journey which usually took him four days, that he had no comment to make on the delay.

Thurso lies along the west bank of its river, so that we crossed an old bridge as we entered the town. It has one main street which forks in two as the quay is approached. We strolled around. It was high tide and some boats were loading lobster pots. It seemed to be an ordinary fishing village but a sudden turn revealed a bathing-beach where some children were playing. It was sunk below the level of the houses, well sheltered, and you could easily be for days in the town without knowing it was there. But the most exciting thing in those parts is Thurso Castle, which is very tall and stands on the east bank of the river facing the town, with its battlements in the water of the bay.

During lunch, 'Chevalier' showed up and started to eat. He told us that another pilot would take us on to Shetland and was waiting for us. We arrived at the field to find our baggage already in. A small brown man in a battered hat and overcoat conferred with the despatcher over maps, then climbed into the pilot's seat, and we soared into the air. We had been eyeing him rather askance, for he was as different from 'Chevalier' as a brown moth from a peacock butterfly, but he evidently knew how to use his wings and we were soon at ease. John was soon sick but announced he was beginning to like it.

Our flight was to be non-stop, for the Orkney passengers were taken care of and we had no more room anyway. Alasdair pointed below to the perfect harbour of Scapa Flow; he was as excited as we were to get such a gull's-eye view, to see clearly the limits of the little inland sea, for that is what it is, to follow the lines of the shallow bottom and point with a thrill to the great rusty hull of one of the German warships, sunk so gallantly eighteen years before and now only just raised back to the air and skies of Orkney. We passed over Kirkwall Cathedral, a landmark recommended by *The North Sea Pilot*. The scattered islands became smaller and smaller, and at last we left North Ronaldshay behind and were over the open sea. The pilot set his course north-east and we roared steadily along at 2,000 feet. There was a thin haze over the water but it was a fair day with a breeze from the east, and we could see for miles. None of us had realized how far the Shetlands were from Orkney and eighty miles of water looked neverending. For the first time, I appreciated Lindbergh. He had no idea of whether he would get there; neither had we: I glanced at the pilot but he was scratching his nose with a calm more reassuring than many brass buttons. He was also friendly and let us look at his charts and instruments.

'There's Fair Isle,' he shouted suddenly (a shout was necessary to be heard above the engines). We all saw it, a dim blue shape dead ahead. It took form quickly and we passed low enough above it to see the two lighthouses, Skadan and Skroo, names as good as Gog and Magog; they stand like two friendly white giants, at the north and south of the island, guarding its reputation, which is none too good with passing vessels.

Fair Isle was as unknown and as poor as Foula until a canny Edinburgh factor wrote to the Duke of Windsor, then Prince of Wales, and asked him to help the island by wearing a Fair Isle pullover. The Prince did; and a trade was created overnight which has kept the island prosperous ever since, though all is not Fair Isle that now bears the name. But the bright colours in the Shetland patterns were unique to Fair Isle and their origin goes back in history, for they were taught to the women of that stormy island by the Spaniards, cast ashore in the wreck of their galleons from the Spanish Armada. Lonely islands keep their secrets and their traditions untouched, a treasure-house for an historian or philologist, which is why the bright colours were not used on Shetland until the Prince performed this one of many kind acts for his people. I think there ought to be a statue to him on Fair Isle, with his golf clubs and his cap and pullover and the earnest look we all know so well. Here is a chance for an ambitious young sculptor.

Alasdair had crossed to the port side of the plane, earning a frown from the pilot, for we had been nicely balanced; unconscious of any blunder he had been staring out of the window for some time. I watched him and wondered at his solemn look of concentration. Suddenly he stiffened and an almost religious look came over his face. He stabbed at the window and in the tone of Othere saying 'Behold this walrus-tooth!' he said:

'There is Foula.'

There was a simultaneous move towards the port side which almost caused the machine to do a barrel-roll and summoned an audible protest from the pilot. We all stared. There was nothing to be seen though we looked till our eyes ached. We told Alasdair he was mad. He smiled in a superior manner, for after all it was fitting that Holbourn (of Foula) should be the first to see it; then, one by one, we all saw, far to the west, a blue haze, a solid shape, an island, as dim and distant as anything could well be, but a reality, the solid land itself after weeks of an empty name, our future home for five months, the centre of all our work, our hopes, our fears and for me the culmination of seven years' dreaming, the very sight of it a direct throw-back to that first misty photograph of St. Kilda. It was fifty miles away. Soon it vanished from our sight.

After that, everything was an anticlimax, even the slow approach of the black coast of Shetland, with Sumburgh Head at the end of its long isthmus, looking like the head and neck of a plesiosaurus. From above we could plainly see the long, narrow path, worn by the lightkeepers, winding across the grass of the head, following the long knife-edge of rock, no wider than itself and finally scrambling on to Mainland, as the principal island of Shetland is called by the islanders, not caring a fig for the rest of the world, as in Dymchurch they say that the world is divided into Europe, Asia, Africa, America, Australia and Romney Marsh. There is a great deal to be said for such a point of view, it is only an extension of our own, for are not all our continents islands, does not the great sea surround them all and is not the whole multi-coloured world a drop in the ocean to Somebody? The Shetland people are wise to realize that their world is small and is their own and the daily knowledge of that realization is what makes the strength of a small people.

The North Sea Pilot says of Sumburgh Röst: 'This is a dangerous race, in which the sea rises to a great height, and breaks with violence, at times even in calm weather . . . so that small vessels often become completely unmanageable and have sometimes foundered. It should be given a wide berth.' We passed right over the race, which was breaking mildly in the easterly breeze, and there seemed something almost indecent in leaping gaily over what had been a terror to good sailors for 2,000 years. Alasdair evidently felt this deeply for he stared down at it with excitement, pointing out Horse Island and Fitful Head and starting to tell me an interminable saga of a trip round there with his brothers of which I heard cantos during our entire stay on the island, but of which I never heard the end, either because it took too long or because I never gave him a chance to finish it.

By now we were circling over a grassy plateau, broken everywhere by vicious-looking outcrops of rock. There seemed no room at all to land; there were no signs, no flags. At last we made out a battered car standing by a clear piece of grass, about as big as a medium-sized billiard table.

'There we are,' said the pilot and dived straight at it. It was ridiculous to think we could land anywhere without a smash, so I accepted it as inevitable. At the last moment the pilot bore away again, circled round over the rocks, brushed over a cornfield and made a perfect landing on the smooth spot, which, I admit, turned out to be larger than the largest billiard table. The chief fright to a layman in these trips, as I said before, is the absence of all marks and dotted lines; they act, at any rate to me, like a light guard-rail on a bridge which I should otherwise cross on all fours.

We congratulated our taciturn pilot on his perfect landing; we hardly taxied twenty yards.

'Thanks!' he said. 'Yes, it is a bit trickier than I thought. It's my first trip over here.' Then, with a look at our faces: 'I thought I'd better not tell you until we'd made our landing.'

We agreed with him.

Our pilot was returning at once; there was no hangar for the plane at Sumburgh, there was nothing at all except the battered car and the flat open space. But that last was unique in Shetland. Nowhere else, at least in the southern half of the Mainland, is there another spot possible for a plane to land. We soon found this out, for an hour's drive to Lerwick awaited us. The road was narrow and had a fair surface, but the drive in a closed car was interminable, unless you knew the country; it all looked alike to a stranger, except where the sea sparkled on our right hand.

Lerwick lies in the middle of Bressay Sound and can be approached from either end. As you open up the town from the southern channel it is a city of ships with the clock tower of the Town Hall rising high above them. But it is a sea-town only. Approached from the land it is drab, and it is not until you see the crowded harbour below, the millions of wheeling gulls, the green slopes of distant Bressay and the narrow streets, paved with smooth flags, that you feel its fascination.

The herring season was in full swing, which meant that three hundred drifters were packed into the harbour and a thousand girls were in town, gutting, salting, packing the herring, living in huts by the North Harbour and parading the town of an evening with hands in their pockets, long lines of them, Scottish and Irish, tough as men, with broad lively faces, and broad, muscular arms, and broad, powerful hips. The buying and selling was over and soon the drifters would be off on the evening tide; at present their crews picketed the town, bought tobacco, patronized the cinema or dance hall, while their skippers walked up and down the harbour, talking and looking at the weather, and occasionally vanishing into each other's cabins. Shetland is officially dry, which of course means that, with a little local knowledge, you can drink twenty-four hours out of twenty-four.

By the time we drew up at the Queen's Hotel I had decided to make some sequences in Lerwick. I had already in my mind some scenes on a trawler at sea, to provide contrast to my island sequences. I would still keep the trawler but the bulk of the action could be enlarged and staged against the busy background of the Port of Lerwick. I went down to the harbour, while George and Alasdair telephoned. I planned a sequence of Andrew looking for work and meeting with the Trawler Skipper; then I saw how it could be worked up to show his hatred of all trawlers.

This is an important point, the difference between a trawler and a drifter, and I had better clear it up. The drifters are primarily after the herring, following them and casting over the side their deep fine nets, buoyed with big air-filled floats called 'bows', half a dozen nets to a man and sometimes ten in a crew; they drop a light anchor and then drift with the tides and the winds, snatch an hour or two's sleep and at dawn pull in their nets and count what the night has brought them; sometimes only a few cran, sometimes fifty or sixty, sometimes an hundred. A 'cran' is four baskets and is about three hundred fish. Though each man has his own nets to look after, the shooting and raising is all team work: one man will lash on the 'bows' as the nets go over the side; another will give the loaded nets a skilful heave that will send most of the fish flying into the hold, while a winch for'ard helps out the heavy work. Then, light or loaded, they head for home and the first boats in to the waiting fish-salesmen get the best price, if herring are plentiful.

Trawling is quite another matter. I hesitate to describe it because whatever I write will be derided by Vernon; ever since the North Sea trip, when he made his film *Men Against the Sea*, he has been quite unbearably knowledgeable about trawlers. As may be remembered I was understudied by Buddy on this pleasure cruise, which has always made me humble in my ignorance. So, without prejudice, here are the facts.

There is only one net, heavy, strong and narrow, whose mouth is kept apart by two great iron-bound pieces of wood, called otter-boards; the water resistance splays them outward like a paravane while a heavy chain about 100 feet long connects them together. These otter-boards are the villains of the piece. Their chain drags over the sea-bed, ruining the new spawn, and tearing up the bed. The trawlers steam to and fro over their fishing ground until their catches cease to yield big fish. Then they haul the nets in and make for fresh grounds, until at last their hold is full or their food gives out, when they head for their home port.

Now in theory, especially political theory, the deep-sea fishermen of the Outer Isles have all the fish they want inside a three-mile limit round their shores, so a benevolent Government rules that no trawler shall shoot a trawl inside that limit. They even provide a patrol boat to enforce that law. In practice, there are objections. Some of the best fishing grounds, banks sacred to the island fishermen since fishing began, are far outside the limit. In the old days the men of Foula and St. Kilda used to go out in their big six-oared boats into the Atlantic for three days at a time, to come back loaded to the water with fish. Sometimes only a piece of wreckage returned. Nowadays most islands own a power-driven boat, those with good harbours have a fleet. They still regard the banks that their fathers fished as their personal property. Then the trawlers come and in a few years the shoals are swept bare and the trawlers steam farther out, in ever-widening search of fish, till the cost of coal eats up all profit. Many of them laugh at the three-mile limit and dodge the patrol boat, and if an island boat puts out to yell protests, a dunt on the head with a lump of coal is all the satisfaction likely to be given. Conditions like these make for bitterness and despair; it is little wonder that the young folk give up what they see is a losing battle and go to work on company-owned drifters or even on a hated trawler; while their fathers, dumb and dogged, see their lives change and their homes vanish, with croft after croft falling into ruin, until at last the day comes when they have to face evacuation and charity.

Yet many acts of kindness are done by trawlers to the islands. They are only doing their work, earning their bread and earning it hard. Trawl is shot every three hours,

day and night, in every kind of weather, handling the heavy
net in bitter cold, cleaning fish, loading the hold, a never-
ceasing toil during the whole voyage of two or three weeks
at sea, a few days at home, then off to sea again. St. Kilda
would have been evacuated years before if the trawlers who
sheltered in Village Bay during bad weather had not given
the islanders fish, tobacco, newspapers and help of every
kind.

It is the method and the system that are wrong. Deep-sea
fishing by steam trawl is destructive to the banks, but there
is also no doubt that it is profitable to the owners, though
it is a question how long it can remain so. These owners
are certainly not going to go back to the old ways of lines
and nets and small boats; it is the difference between the old
pioneer buffalo-hunter and the organized drives made for
the Eastern market; the new hunters killed thousands of
buffalo and made thousands of dollars, but where are the
buffalo which once covered the plains? That is Progress.

At present nobody has produced a better way of profitable deep-sea fishing than by steam trawlers; nor has any
serious attempt been made to enforce restrictions on them.
The Conquest of Nature by Civilization is a fine theme and
is always printed in big capitals, but what good is civilization if it drives a strong, hardy, independent people back
from the outposts to live in towns?

I seem to have been led by a description of trawling into
a discussion of the theme of my story, but the two are
closely interlocked. There are other contributory causes.
Failure of the peat, bad harvests and mortality. Restlessness
of youth. In the old days too, the young men left the islands,
shipped on merchant vessels, joined the Navy or went to
the colonies. But they always looked towards home; when
they had their pile, or their strike, or their pension, back
they came and settled down. There is hardly an older man
of Foula who has not been round the world, some of them
many times. But the young people now hear other sirens

sing; what is more, they make honest women of them. Easy living is as potent a drug in the Islands as in London. The boys and their girls like newspapers, cinemas, new gramophone records, dance halls, and they don't get those at home. They naturally do not look ahead to middle-age, when they will want land and a croft of their own and peace. So they marry and are unwilling to bring their wives back to their old homes; and only their fathers or an on-looker, who has seen the west wind sweeping down the Daal, the blue-green surges eight hundred feet below, the cloud of kittiwakes over Mill Loch, the seals basking by the Gaada stack, the shadowy boats fishing for piltock on summer nights, the spray of a south-easterly gale drifting over the island, only an older man could tell them what they are sacrificing.

When I was finally driven from the island with only a few scenes left to do, I made them on the coast round Lerwick. I needed two boat crews and, as it was late in the year, I had quite a number of the best fishermen to choose from. They lined up on the quay one morning for me to pick the types I wanted. I went down the line once and then again. There was not one single face in all those fisher-men (two, at least, the best boatmen in Shetland) which would pass for the face of a man of Foula. There were two qualities that were missing, peace and an inner strength. There were honest faces, strong faces, weather-beaten faces, but I had studied and lived with and photographed the men of Foula too closely to be deceived; and this was in Lerwick, a rugged, remote fishing-town which is only a name to the average traveller.

Alasdair came quickly past me as I stood on the quay.

'I phoned Moore at Scalloway,' he panted, 'but they say he'll be here yet.'

'In Lerwick?'

'Ay. I know where. We're in luck.'

'Weather permitting.'

He grinned.

'There's two bodies asking for you at the hotel.'

'Me?'

'Inkster and Johnson. One's from the *News*, the other from *The Times*. They'll be wanting a story.'

I thought fast as I walked up the sloping alley to the hotel. Joe's last words to me had been: 'Remember—no publicity!' In case anyone should think Joe had been standing in the sun, I must explain that he had a theory that a film of this kind would pack a bigger punch if totally unheralded.

'We can't avoid them knowing that we are making the film,' he said, 'but if we don't talk about it they will forget it. Why should we go to a lot of trouble and expense building people up to say "So, what?" All we can give them is promises of something different. Nothing else. So let's all of a sudden slide it under their noses.'

'Like selling dirty postcards?'

'Yes,' said Joe doubtfully.

I said, 'It's good psychology,' which is a good safe remark when talking to a film executive.

'Isn't it?' said Joe, pleased.

So what was I going to say to Mr. Inkster and Mr. Johnson?

I temporized.

Mr. Inkster was a dark, shrewd-looking man, with eyes that missed nothing. It was a paragraph in the *Scotsman* which had put them on the watch for us, that, and of course the new aeroplane service.

'Was it a good passage?'

'Excellent.'

'May we have your impressions of the flight?'

'Well—if you like—but why?'

Mr. Johnson chimed in; he was a short, compact, little man, with a cheerful face.

'It's such a new thing to us here. We're all still quite excited to think we've got two regular services all at once.'

'Where does the other start from?' asked George.

'From Inverness.'

A light dawned on me. We were all listening by now.

'And they're both new?'

'Oh, dear, yes. On 1st June. We had the inaugural flight the other day by the first company. They have been preparing it for a long while.'

'And the other company?'

They exchanged covert smiles.

'Well, you see, *they* had *their* inaugural flight a day later, using the same landing ground; of course it's the only one possible; still—it was a bit of a surprise to all of us. Nobody knew of their existence till then.'

'And they used the same landing grounds?'

'Ay.'

'And came from Aberdeen, which is a much handier base than Inverness.'

'Ay.'

'And suddenly descended from the blue?'

'Ay. Of course, we don't know the rights of it all but it's very healthy to have competition, eh, Johnson?'

The mystery was explained; the subdued excitement at Aberdeen, the vague suggestion of official send-off, the confusion at Thurso, the pilot who had never landed before at Sumburgh, the hastily summoned car—all was clear. It was also clear why we had not been told about it.

'Then are we the first regular passengers?'

'Ay. Did you not know?'

We looked at each other in awe. John stood up and saluted. We were pioneers!

We Take the Air

But both reporters came round to the subject of a film on Foula. I told them that this was a trip of inspection; if the island was suitable for my film, I would consider it, but it was impossible to say more. I thought I did very well for Joe, but I knew they didn't believe me and they knew that I knew. They smelt a story and they were both smart reporters.

'Mr. Alasdair Holbourn is with you, is he not?' said Johnson shrewdly.

It was useless to deny it because at that moment he walked in.

'I was just telling our friends here that we cannot decide on Foula until we have seen it,' I said.

Alasdair knew what I meant, for his family had fallen in gladly with the suggestion of no limelight, but it went against the grain to admit that Foula could be anything less than perfect. However, he produced a noncommittal grunt and told George that he had found Moore and a motor-launch would be waiting to take us from Scalloway at six.

'We'd better have tea and be off,' he added, 'it's five now.'

'Is Scalloway far?'

'Six miles—twenty minutes in the car.'

'So we may say it's a reconnaissance, Mr. Powell?' said Mr. Inkster softly.

'If you can spell it.'

'And possibly we shall hear your decision when you return?' This was Mr. Johnson.

'Er . . . yes.' That was Powell.

'When are you returning?'

'On Saturday. I have to be back in London.'

'You won't wait until Monday for the mail-boat to Walls?'

'No,' said Alasdair, 'these gentlemen are in a hurry and can afford to hire the mail-boat specially.'

Everyone looked respectful and we went in to a huge tea in the dining-room, whose windows look over the crowded harbour.

Chapter VII

'GALE WARNING'

★

I have many times been near a violent end but never nearer than in our drive from Lerwick to Scalloway. The car was a good one, the driver was tall, taciturn, with high cheek-bones, the road was dusty and narrow, with several hairpin bends which were like a direct challenge to Fate; we met few people on the road but when we did, we accelerated, we were on the outside edge of the road most of the way, and all I can say of Shetland sheep is that they think fast and keep one jump ahead of their thoughts.

At the end of eight minutes we leapt over the last hill and saw Scalloway Sound below us. I called to our demon driver to stop and next second regretted it as I nearly shot through the glass partition. John, who was in my way, regretted it even more. As the dust subsided from our four locked wheels we descended. With leisurely and detached calm our driver lit a cigarette.

The Sound and the harbour were like glass. There did not seem one movement in the little white town, from the great black curing sheds to the four-square, roofless shell of the Castle. The two tortuous channels wound through a dozen tiny islands to the sea, three miles away, where a light swell moved on the horizon. The westerly sun turned the water into a mirror; town, islands and Castle were all in duplicate. An outward-bound drifter in mid channel set the round, green reflection of Greenholm shuddering. The nearest channel of the harbour reached almost to our feet where two old hulks lay together, leaning heavily on their sides, their wood burnt by the sun and wind into patches, white as silver. The land all round was a monotone except where the fields of two crofts on West Burra showed a bright yellow, speckled with scarlet poppies. Alasdair pointed west over Greenholm. We all looked and saw again the blue mass of Foula, only twenty-five miles away. There was an evening haze and it was hardly more distinct than from the aeroplane.

We climbed in again, our driver thoughtfully extinguished his cigarette, slowly got into his seat and we were off like a scalded cat. Hunched over his wheel he tore down the side of the hill, made a murderous rush at the narrow bridge over the burn where two boys were paddling, and ascended the opposite hill in standing leaps. An old woman, in a black dress and shawl and white sunbonnet, with a 'kesshie' of peats on her bent back, was toiling up the other side. I quite expected to see her give a loud yell on seeing our approach, hurl herself and her peats into the ditch and cross herself; but she just stepped aside as we thundered past and before the cloud of dust hid her I saw her resume her painful way, without a second glance. There are so few cars on Shetland that I suppose their stormy passage is accepted as an act of God.

We went straight to Moore's boat-shed which is at the far end of the town. While Alasdair and George vanished I took stills. A rickety old black pier, covered with gulls, delighted me for its contrast; every one of its wooden supports was at a different angle. From this side, with the sun flat on the walls, half in the water and half out, Scalloway looked bleached by the sun, against the dark background of the hills.

Alasdair returned with the news that the boat was waiting at the quay, so we drove around to the other end, passing close under the walls of the Castle. I said:

'They look as good as new. The Castle only wants a roof and windows to be as good as ever.'

Alasdair said:

'That's eggs.'

'Where? Anyway, you mean "those are eggs", don't you?'

'No, I meant the Castle; it's built of them.'

We looked at each other in dismay.

'George, sit on his head if he becomes violent.'

Alasdair smiled pityingly and condescended to explain.

'When bad Earl Patrick built the castle, about four hundred years agone, his architect told him that if he used white of egg to bind the mortar, the castle would last for ever and a day. So he exacted a tribute from all his people of two eggs per head, under pain of death by torture.'

'Gulls' eggs?'

'They had to be hens'; and there weren't more than a few dozen hens in the whole of Shetland.'

'But they got them.'

'Oh, ay, they got them. You see, they knew he meant what he said.'

'His architect must have been pleased.'

'No doubt. He did a good job. When it was all finished the Earl was so pleased he hanged him.'

'What would he do if he was displeased?'

'Oh, hang him, just the same.'

'They knight them nowadays.'

'Ye see, he didn't want another castle like it; also this architect had built him a secret room.'

'Where he could smoke with the boys?'

'It's funny you should say that; the legend says that was how he met his end. The castle was stormed but they couldn't find the Earl, he was in his hiding-place, they searched three days. Then he couldn't resist a pipe and they say he coughed and gave himself away.'

'He wasn't smoking KENSITAS!'

Sure enough the launch was at the quay. It was about twenty feet long, decked over, with a little wheel-house. The old skipper's face could be seen by the wheel, while his crew of two were on the quay. We dumped our things aboard including a packing-case of food. George arranged with our driver to come to Walls to meet us on Saturday. Alasdair conferred with Moore. I needed a yacht for the prologue, and if the Holbourn's boat was suitable I proposed to use it. It would have to have an auxiliary engine which Moore would install. The yacht was lying at Walls.

By half-past six we were thumping down the Sound, on the last lap of our long journey. We cruised about a bit then set our nose to the open sea.

At once we felt the swell and a chill wind blew spray in our faces. The boat was not fast and the tide was against us. Four knots was our top speed. Foula had vanished in the fog that often closed down in the evening. We prepared ourselves for a dreary trip.

Syd, whose box of tools had been on his mind all day, now cheered up and became the life of the party. On arriving at Lerwick he had gone straight to the office of the steamship line, although his treasure-chest could not yet have left Aberdeen. I suppose they had reassured him, for he had returned somewhat eased in mind. He now knelt well in the bows of the plunging boat, snuffing the salt air and staring towards Foula with an air as trusting as the Infant Samuel's.

John began to look sick, but declared he could hold out.

'Alasdair,' I said, 'where shall we all sleep to-night?'

'There's no telling,' he answered helpfully.

'Is there room for us all in the Haa?' (Haa—Hall).

'There is not; and there will be the catechist.'

'What sort of a man is he?' asked John.

'A wee bletherer.'

'I thought you said he was leaving?' I remarked.

'He is. But he's not left yet.'

'Gale Warning'

'Perhaps he left on Monday.'

'Not he.'

The hours went by. We were all cold, tired and hungry. The boat ploughed endlessly along. The fog had vanished and the black bulk of Foula broadened till it filled half our horizon. The last three miles were very long and we were crossing the uneasy tides around the Hoevdi Grund. Except for the swirl of the water and the bump of the motor the night was very still. Although it was still light enough to read, distant things were blurred and lost detail. It was midnight and we had been nearly six hours at sea. We made out the lighted windows of crofts as we approached Ham Voe. The five peaks of the island lay black against a sky which was almost violet. I made Alasdair name them over and over until I knew them as well as he did: The Noup, Hamnafeld, The Sneug, The Kame, Soberlie, five magic names, the master words of a pentagram which is the key to the island, for me and every one of us.

Suddenly the island drew very near. We could see that a few boats were out under the cliffs, lying in the shadow, their rods propped in the air, silently watching our approach. On the port bow the moon laid a path to us across the sea and on the starboard the sun, close above the horizon, was still shining, so that the gold and silver ripples met in the wake of our boat. I never again saw Foula with the sun and the moon shining on the sea, but I shall never forget it.

A lantern appeared from the square black mass, with one lighted window, which was the two buildings, the Haa and the Shop. It stayed for a moment on the little hill and its bearer was evidently looking out to sea at our boat. The lantern twisted, vanished and reappeared in an undecided manner. Then it moved jerkily down to the quay and waved encouragingly. Then it was still. Its owner had placed it on the sea wall and we were close enough now to see him dart back to the house.

'Is the man daft?' demanded Alasdair. The will-o'-the-wisp was evidently the catechist.

Nobody felt like answering him and at that very moment, by the irony of fate, within five minutes of our goal, John could hold out no longer and was very sick. We did our best to comfort him but he announced, between gasps, that he much preferred to get it over before he landed as now he would be able to eat a good supper.

The tide was high, as we doubled the end of the jetty and clawed at one of the iron rings in the cement; there were only half a dozen steps above water. The catechist was already staggering down the long concrete ramp which led to the road above, an enormous package in his arms. He was thrusting it on board our boat before we were fairly off it.

'How are you, Mr. Holbourn?' he panted. 'It's Mr. Alasdair, isn't it?'

Alasdair gruffly assented.

'Skipper, please can you tell me if you are staying long?' the little figure went on almost in the same breath.

'We'll be off as soon as paid,' replied our skipper, combining, in one short sentence, information, common sense and business ability.

'Oh wait, please wait, I have been packing all day, you must take the things I have ready!'

He was off like a hare up to the house without waiting for the skipper's declaration that he didn't intend to stay a minute longer on Foula than he had to, he and his crew had all got beds to go to if other people had not, and having beaten all the way to the island against the tide he did not propose to wait until it turned so that he would have to beat all the way back again, all this delivered in a sort of rumbling shorthand which was perfectly intelligible although not a word could properly be distinguished.

We all climbed on to the quay, with our baggage and our packing-case, chilled by the endless journey and this extraordinary welcome. The island loomed above us and around us. Everything was wet and salty from the sea mist. Nobody could be seen clearly. The catechist was only an agile little beastie in badly cut plus-fours. Alasdair was grumbling, George was disputing some demand of the skipper's. We three shivered and changed our bags from hand to hand. Our island felt and looked like the very last place on earth. One of the fishing boats shot in from the darkness and a voice greeted Alasdair in low tones.

The catechist was staggering down again, this time with an enormous easy-chair on his shoulders, to be lowered on to the boat with a volley of instructions and admonitions. He was off again, but by this time George had reached an agreement and paid off our boat. We all followed the catechist up the ramp, Alasdair rather hanging back, but we would have none of it. We were Fed Up. We told him to lead the way. The path to the Haa turned off from the road and we passed across a strip of long grass. The Haa, so pretentiously named, was only a four-roomed house. In front were the walls of an unfinished porch, on a grand scale, evidently intended to give the plain front of the cottage a baronial look. I recognized the same hand that had planned the ambitious schemes of Penkaet; like many things at Penkaet the walls were unfinished, there was no roof, weeds grew where the floor should be and we entered the house through a door of rough boards. An open door on our left showed a grate with a peat fire blazing and we went right in. The room was long and the windows had been enlarged. There was an amazing wood ceiling, in panelled squares, and a filthy carpet on the floor. There was a good big table and chairs, two wonderful Dutch cabinets, with heavily carved doors, and a cheap oak bookcase. It was a jumble of good, bad and dirt, but it was comfortable and it was warm and to the end of our stay, however much it was abused, the Haa remained as I first saw it—a haven from a cold and dark world without.

People always ask me if Foula was very cold. It was and
it wasn't; in direct sunlight it was often hot enough to strip
to the waist but at other times it was cold enough to wear a
sweater, sometimes three. In June and July people were
tempted by the heat of midday to go in swimming; they
were out in a minute, blue with cold. The sea became
warmest in October when Bill Paton and Frankie, our
bathing beauties, went swimming in the Voe while I was
struggling to get a scene with Belle and the ponies up by
Brae. I first knew that Frankie had appeared in swimming
costume by turning round from Belle to find my whole
crew, especially the cameramen, facing the other way.
Frankie attributes this to S.A. but she should remember
that this was in the fifth month of our isolation from the
world, the flesh and the devil. Most women will agree that
too much fuss has always been made of Thaïs: no competition and all the time in the world—who couldn't get her
man?

As we clustered round the fire the catechist bumped
down the passage with another case in his arms and pattered
past the window. Alasdair was looking about him with
disgust. He went out and could be heard thumping about
upstairs, then there was an exclamation and a scramble
down the stairs and a splendid black Cocker spaniel burst
into the room, kissed us all round and rushed down to the
quay after his master. Alasdair came grumbling downstairs.

'The house is filthy and there's hardly a stick of furniture
left.'

'Most of it went off on Monday, I expect.'

'Except what's in the packing-cases,' added John.

There was a laugh at Alasdair's expense. The combination in the catechist of embarrassment at our arrival with
anxiety lest his goods should miss the boat, all in the confusing darkness, was rather funny. We had not been long
enough on Foula to appreciate what a unique occasion it
was to have two boats going out in one week. Later on,

particularly during the Great Cigarette Famine, we understood.

'Let's get supper,' said John practically. We found a stump of candle—the sitting-room was lit by a hanging oil-lamp—and explored the kitchen. It was as well lit and ventilated as any medieval dungeon. The walls were rough stone and had been white-washed about the time of Earl Patrick. There was a small, flat stove, greasy and dirty. There were two rickety tables, dirty and greasy. There were greasy saucepans and frying-pans everywhere; and dirty crockery on the tables; and a fine big dresser dragged out from the wall so that a cupboard could be opened behind it and—on the nearest table were spread some sheets of paper. I glanced at them gingerly. They were sheets torn out of *Good Housekeeping*!

We started to clean up. Then a bumping was heard again in the passage. It was the catechist but with the same package, not a new one. He was in great distress, the skipper had kept his word and gone without more ado. He put the case down in the passage, where it was an infernal nuisance, and came into the kitchen full of apologies for the mess; he spoke as if it had accumulated since lunch time.

George and Syd went off up the brae with Alasdair to find somewhere to sleep. Although it was so late there were quite a few people moving about and lights were burning. In Foula there is very little conventional sense of time; it's not much good having a set time-table when you have only one hour of real darkness in summer and about one hour of good daylight in winter; if a man feels like milking the cow at 2 a.m. he does, and neither his wife nor the cow is surprised. During our stay, we rather threw a spanner into this carefree life, for we were great on time-tables, although some of my crew, especially Skeets and Bill Martin and Niall, would have preferred the Foula tradition. Still our band of Foula 'Regulars' adopted our schedule quite placidly, although one of them, who was prominent in the first weeks of our stay, finally got tired of it all and went to bed for the rest of our time on the island; that is, during the day; I believe he was sometimes seen strolling quietly and thankfully about at midnight.

John was doing wonderful things with fried bread and bacon by the time Alasdair returned. He had found them a bed in the best room at Leirabach, and they had turned in right away, refusing supper, but saying they would make up at breakfast. I am telling them now that it may have seemed too much bother to return to the Haa, but they can have had no idea of what they were missing.

Michael approved highly of this extra supper and was allowed to lick the plates. He was a beautiful spaniel, though how the catechist kept him in condition was a problem. He always had to be on a lead like the other island dogs, and his master used to feed him on bully beef and sardines and other things which would have crisped 'Bob Martin's' hair with horror.

John and I found a few blankets and took the two beds in the big room where Belle and Frankie slept later on. We piled our clothes on top of us and slept uneasily. Alasdair and the catechist had meanwhile begun a sort of conversation.

We heard sleepily the twittering and grunting going on beneath us (the floor of the best bedroom in the Haa was a good sound-conductor as Belle and Frankie were to find out), but at last the adversaries went to bed, the catechist in the far room which was occupied by Mrs. Rutherford (at a later date, of course), Alasdair in the little room next door, where he slept the entire summer, except when ousted by little Margaret.

I tried to be excited by the thought that this was my first night on Foula, but before I had become even mildly interested I was asleep.

By half-past eight Alasdair was leading us over the foot-bridge across the burn. We were going on a tour of inspection of Foula. We did not yet realize what we were in for. On the face of it, it does not look a big job to walk round an island three miles long by two broad, even if you are out of training. If we had been wise we should have recognized on Alasdair's face the grim smile of the Smallie; but it was a grand morning and we frolicked up the hill.

Syd and George were loud in praise of their quarters at Leirabach and of their hosts, Dodie Isbister and his sister, Robina (Dodie is short for George). We climbed the path to Leirabach, which stands on a grassy bank above the burn, with a view of the sea and of Mill Loch, with its hundreds of wheeling birds; so close is the croft to Hamnafeld that the shadow of the great hill falls across it early in the evening, clear and sharp as its own outline. We saw their bright little room, facing east, decided it was too good for them and struck off across the heather to the War Memorial, a tower of rough stone blocks which stands in a commanding position on Baa Head. The men built it themselves to the design of Professor Holbourn; the inscription is inset on the west side so that the reader faces the open sea and the coast of Shetland, distant reminder of the world. We read:

> TO THE GLORY OF GOD AND IN
> MEMORY OF THE MEN OF FOULA
> WHO GAVE THEIR LIVES IN THE
> GREAT WAR 1914-1919

Five names followed.

The effect of a War Memorial is always impressive, but reduced here to such simple terms, it was profoundly so. On this remote island, the folly of war became plainer: five able-bodied men taken from a community that could not spare one of them. If their boat had overturned or rope given way, a rough headstone in the kirk-yard would have been their memorial. But they had died for their country, far from their own island, and their fellows had laboured many days to raise these stones to their memory and to the Glory of God.

We regained the road and made for Hametoun, where it ceased to be a practical highway, forked in two, squeezed through two narrow gates and broke up into a hundred tracks. Where the road forked it was roughly circular in shape, and covered with large, smooth stones. This became in due time the Roundabout, terminus for the car and rallying point for the kirk or the Sneck. We bore left to Punds, where we interviewed Walter Ratter, captain of the mail-boat.

Walter can build anything, do anything and, at times, say anything. He is an ex-Navy man, a gunner. His chest is huge, his moustache an epic growth, his movements are deliberate, he speaks at the rate of one word a minute, but every word counts. Alasdair talked a good deal. Walter talked not at all. He consented to be photographed by his croft. He regarded us with reserve.

We took a delighted look at Hametoun, about twenty crofts scattered round this sheltered hollow in the south of the island. It is a saucer, set to catch the water which drains from the Noup and Hamnafeld into the Daal. This valley runs from west to east, cutting across the island, and one day the sea will break through by the Sneck and there will be two islands at Foula. Most of the crops are in Hametoun and the fields were all laid out in oats and barley and potatoes. We made straight down the path and crossed the burn by a plank bridge. A green mound on our right was marked on my ordnance map as Whirly Knowe. I lingered fascinated by the name and by the mound itself, but Alasdair hurried us on. A well by South Biggins was my next discovery. It was by the path, lined with great round stones; steps took me down to the water until my head was out of sight. But Alasdair was determined we should see the old church. It was no longer used for worship though its walled yard was still the place of burial; the grass had grown long over the graves and the path had vanished, the wall had gaps in it and there were slates off the roof.

'It looks uncared for,' apologized Alasdair, 'but we will have that right in a week.'

'Don't do anything of the sort,' I said, 'it's just how I want it for the opening of the film. Afterwards we can repair it and cut the grass. Meanwhile you must tell whoever looks after it . . .'

'Robert Isbister.'

'. . . tell him that it mustn't be touched. Can we look inside?'

'They'll have the key at South Biggins.'

But they hadn't and Robert was at the Shop. So we went on to the stone wall at the edge of the pasture and looked over.

It is no good saying that it took my breath away because that happened a hundred times on my first visit to Foula. I can only describe what I saw. There was a cabbage patch ran right up to the wall and there was a small gate in it. Suppose you could lean on your own garden wall and look down three hundred feet of tumbled cliff to the shelves of Helliberg, white with the foam of a long Atlantic roller, then brown as the wave pours back into the sea, white again, then brown again, white . . . brown, till your eye was hypnotized; suppose you could watch this, it might be bad for your cabbages, but it would be good for your soul. We followed a sheep path down the face of the cliff, known as Back of the Noup (which it was). Four months later when we were all careering down there full-tilt, in half a gale from the south-east, cameras and boxes on our shoulders and Belle carrying her own props, it was difficult to remember how steep and dangerous it seemed the first time. I know I stepped with care and looked a lot at the hungry sea below. Alasdair had no nerves at all, so enjoyed himself, showing off with the gusto of a small boy.

We scrambled back up the cliff and made off along the base of the Noup towards the Daal. Alasdair chose a path that was all rough stones. We began to realize that he had the cheerful intention of walking us off our feet. We had by then covered about five miles of very hard going and had most of our day in front of us. The Smallie was already getting in sly remarks like: 'Call that steep? Wait till you see the Ufshins. Tired? It's only ten o'clock.' I was in good training myself for I do a lot of walking, so I made a private resolve that climb he never so goatishly I would be with him, step for step, until the end.

We passed Stöel, a little croft under the Noup, which had wooden wind-baffles, like a milking-stool, on top of its chimneys, to ward off the wind which swoops straight down the mountain at that point and sends the peat flying. Nanny and Jenny were pottering about outside and, although not knowing us from Adam (except that we wore clothes), they gave us a beaming smile and both said in chorus: 'It's a bonny day, Mr. Holbourn.' They were sisters and were at once christened the Apple Dumplings, because apple dumplings are wrinkled and brown and rosy and good, or are if home-made. They later acted with great poise in the Lullaby scene at Sloag.

We started the trudge up the Daal, the only walk on Foula which is really dull, like a great slab of bread and butter which has to be done with before cake, the only walk which was really hated by everyone, from first to last, literally, for our first base camp was at the end of the Daal, at the Sneck, the last shot on Foula was made there and it was in that tent that we were playing 'Spelling B' in the drenching rain when the flaps were burst open and Len . . . but I am ahead of my story.

We were now painfully approaching the Sneck of the

Smallie: 'What's a Smallie?' I had asked when shown the picture of the great cleft at Penkaet.

Alasdair said with relish:

'Oh, it will be a wee troll that lives down at the bottom of the cleft—a kind of bogey, squatting down there and weaving spells and chuckling to think of all the evil in the world.' (It will be seen how Alasdair got his by-name!)

'Does it ever come out?'

'Whiles. But it loves to sit in the Sneck and drag things down to keep it company.'

These descriptions were meat and drink to Alasdair. It was evident he had been brought up on tales of the Sneck, until he had come to look upon it as worthy of Sinbad the Sailor. His father had drawn a picture of it, rather stylized but effective, with Arabian Nights' clouds of smoke swirling up out of the abyss and a caption in archaic lettering, something about 'the Sneck of the Smallie on the island of Thule, where the turning fog-wreaths creep up from the Devil's breath' or something of the sort, lovely stuff to impress a small boy.

What usually happens in such a case is that the impression on the child's mind is so strong, that when he thinks about it, he sees the place as he saw it then, not as it is now. I imagine that something of the sort happened to Alasdair, for he cannot really be as excited about the Sneck as he pretends to be. Yet it is remarkable enough and, to a child, would be really terrifying and a fit home for trolls.

We came on it suddenly; a tumbled hollow in the ground where the cliff is falling in and then, leading from it, a chasm with smooth perpendicular rock sides, about ten feet in width, at least 300 feet in length and from 100 to 180 feet deep. The whole island above Mucklaberg is sliding towards the sea, with huge fissures opening on the hillside, but this is the largest of them all. It runs through to the face of the cliff and, from the sea, the great slot, level as a rule, dividing the 200-foot cliff from top to bottom, is most

remarkable. Near the sea end a number of chock-stones
have jammed together in the opening of the slot, making
a very handy bridge and a nursery for puffins, whom I
could hear grumbling all round me in their holes as I
scrambled down. They have most peculiar voices for their
size and appearance and when safely in their holes sound
more like an irritable bulldog than a bird.

Puffins are often called sea-parrots and *look* like sea-
parrots, which explains it. They are about a foot long,
with huge red and blue beaks; they swim and dive well
but their flying is desperate and their landings are really
awful—they would never get a first-class pilot's certificate.
They are very inquisitive. We soon noticed that if we
stopped on the edge of the cliff we became a point of great
interest. Squadron after squadron of puffins, all in line,
would sweep up, hover four feet away, eyes left, stare into
our faces, eyes front, sweep on and round out to sea half a
mile away, right round and back again, still in perfect line,
hover, eyes left . . . and so on as long as you stood there,
thousands of squadrons, millions of Tiller Puffins (John's
name for them). The parents—there are many bachelors
—hunted sand eels, silver fish, like tiny whitebait; they
brought them back, a row of a dozen at a time, held neatly
in their beak (John says always head to tail like a sardine is
packed; but he is inclined to see double). With their fish
they had to make a landing on their special stone. There
were always half a dozen puffins on it already who made
not the slightest attempt to make room, so that the unlucky
fisherman often made a bumpy landing, bounced once or
twice and then had to drop off into the air and round again,
perhaps ten times before he made it. With it all, their faces
were so serious, they were born comedians.

The Sneck is worth the price of admission when you see
it from the greatest depth inside. Then the smooth sides
can be seen, with the hanging ferns and highlights where
springs are dripping on to the green jumble of rocks and

skeletons that lies at the bottom, far from the daylight. Voices boom up, like the Smallie himself, setting the puffins whirling, while the narrow slit frames to the north-west a sight of the blunt cliff of Wester Hoevdi with, far below, the cliff path of Mucklaberg, sheep everywhere on the rock face and every kind of bird sitting, walking, flying, diving, swimming, running, jumping in a grand Olympic meeting at which every competitor is a champion. Except, of course, the puffins.

We left the Sneck and flung ourselves on the Ufshins. This was our first encounter with a real Foula scramble. It is only six hundred feet from the Sneck to the Hooses of the Burrie but it is smooth grass, so steep we could hardly stand and every step meant the effort of lifting our whole bodies. Alasdair bounded up like an antelope—or a Foula sheep—while we followed, more or less. Alasdair reached the top and turned, grinning; I was next but I thought my heart would stop. He pretended not to be at all winded but I saw that he had to take long breaths not to show it. The others were right behind me, but John frankly gave up half-way and made the rest in ten-foot stages. Of course he should have taken it easy for the first week or so but it was no good trying to tell him that.

The Hooses of the Burrie was a fold in the side of the Ufshins, a natural shelter for the sheep, with a view right down the Daal. Any place of shelter can be a 'hoose' (house). The Burrie is the rank grass which grows there. It was an eyrie, a rampart, impregnable until an enemy came over the top of the Ufshins and took it from above and in the rear. This was our next stage, not so steep. When we reached the top we looked down on Wester Hoevdi, which ran out in a rounded platform. Our ridge led along towards the Kame and the Sneug, the peaks of the island. I decided to carry the war into Alasdair's territory: I suggested that we two run down and look at Hoevdi, then work along up the cliff edge to the Kame, where the others could join us. He agreed and we fell down the steep slope in giant leaps, over Hoevdi Burn, and in a minute were looking down into the bay of Nebbifeld. It was my first encounter with the great cliffs of the island. Alasdair stood on the edge. I lay on my face and felt giddy. It was two years since I had been up a mountain and I had to recover my head for heights. The cliff on that side is 800 feet and straight as a wall; then in one superb sweep the wall circles round and upwards to the point of Nebbifeld, exactly 1,000 feet and sheer all the way. There is no beach at the foot of this enormous wall until Nebbifeld is reached; the cliff goes straight down into the water and ten feet out there is no bottom at 100 fathoms (600 feet). The wind dashes against Hoevdi, slides around the curve of the cliffs and is thrown off Nebbifeld, as if it were the crest of a switchback, out to sea again and so for thousands of years until the face of the cliff is a mass of swirling lines, of every colour and width, but all swinging round till the eye which follows them finds itself out over the sea again and the cliffs are left smooth as if sandpapered, with not a ledge or blade of grass to be seen.

We were looking for a spectacular place for Andrew to stand on a 'dare', so Alasdair obliged by posing in some horrible spots. We saw the others, little dots above us, working their way along. We followed up to the top of Nebbifeld and there before us was the Kame!

Imagine a cliff whose summit runs up into the sky and juts out like a diving-board, so that it overhangs the sea. Beneath it a sheer cliff drops 800 feet to a grassy ledge as big as a small meadow; then on again another 400 feet to the sea. The Kame is over 1,200 feet high, nearly a *quarter of a mile* sheer drop. When I looked over for the first time and saw the birds dropping down, down, until they were invisible, and the sun shining on the white surges of the waves round the stacks, with every gust of wind trying to tear me off the rock to which I was clinging, while the roar below and round me and the cries of birds added to the general effect, I was scared stiff. Once or twice I have thought I was nervous, but now I know that the real feeling is an ache in every muscle and nerve of your body, till the more sensitive portions feel as if they had frost-bite.

We all had a look, then had lunch and thought it over.

I had quite given up the idea of the race being up a stack and had decided on one of the big cliffs. It seemed hardly likely that the actors would agree to the Kame. On the whole I thought the south side of Wester Hoevdi looked the most promising. I had seen it from above and it was all broken up in ridges and rock-falls; also the burn went over the cliff just there and I reasoned that if the water could get down, then climbers could get up. There was still Soberlie to see; its plateau lay below us, but Alasdair assured me it was overhanging all the way.

We slithered down the grass slope of the Kame, as steep as a roof, and followed the cliff edge to Soberlie. At least Alasdair and I did; the others had had enough and some-body had to go back with John, who was beaming but all in. They set off across the moors to Overfandal, where they could drop down into the road again by South Harrier. I plugged along step for step with the Smallie for the honour of Films. The cliff here is about 700 feet high, regular as a wall and weathered into folds like an elephant's hide. I fixed on the place for the 'Gone Over' stone and found some fine spots for cliff climbing. All of a sudden we were on the top of Soberlie, with a grass slope down, like the Kame but steeper. Half-way down, a rock platform jutted out into space. As I stood on it, the black curve of Soberlie was above my head while below was empty air, to the rocks below. There were ledges all around with guillemots nesting. A little higher was a cave in the cliff. This was Maggie Henry's Hoose.

Long ago, in the old days, when every croft on Foula

was standing in full bloom, a little boat with a sail and one figure in it came drifting into the old boat harbour at Grisigarth Mill. The whisper went through Hametoun that the lonely passenger was Maggie Henry, come back to the island where she was born, but her own kin would have nought to do with her, and barred their doors, for she was stricken with leprosy. She wandered up the long, winding road, past Mornington, past Mogle, past Gossameadow and Burns, and everywhere folk ran from her and barred their doors. She left the road and toiled up the steep side of Soberlie and her black, fluttering figure disappeared towards the great cliffs. Then the watchers looked at one another. But although Maggie Henry had come back to her home to die, it was not yet. She found on Soberlie Hill a house with no door to bar against her and there she lived. While it was summer the birds kept her company, but when the winter storms came they flew away and she lived alone. People brought food and laid it for her on the pulpit-rock and, with winter, a man returned from the fishing who had once loved her. He found Maggie Henry's Hoose and went to see her every day; so once a day, storm or sunshine, she heard a human voice. For two years she lived on in the cave. Then one day, when her old lover came, she told him she was dying; and the next day she was gone, and only the waves know her last resting place.

At night, fishermen from the North End, casting their lines off the Freyer Rocks, have seen a mysterious red glow, high on the sheer face of Soberlie, under the overhang of the cliff, where a climber from the top cannot go. It is strongest on moonless nights. They call it the Carbuncle, and nobody knows the meaning of it. It is a queer, haunted place, the Hill of Soberlie.

On we went again, down almost to sea-level, half walking, half sliding. I was determined to set the pace, as we jumped the wall above the Logat Stack and saw the seals lying out on the reef like great slugs. As we shouted they all slid into the water, then twenty-three blunt muzzles appeared and looked up enquiringly, while the bay filled with their mournful singing. Alasdair threw a stone and at once there was nothing but twenty-three widening rings on the water.

On, once more, past Ristie, the neatest croft on Foula and the loneliest, at the extreme north of the island, with clean, white-washed walls and a garden gay with flowers, as well as potatoes (Jimmie was out in his boat and Tina was at Ham), then down on by the flat Parliament Stone to the long, curving beach which is all of rounded stones, every size from a few ounces to half a ton, but all rolled and polished by the busy tides, till we stopped by Springs, not long deserted by Andrew Gray (he lives now at North Harrier). The turf roof was already falling in; the fire had been in the middle of the floor, with a hole in the roof to let the smoke out, and all the beams and upper walls were crusted inches deep in hard soot. A hundred relics of a dozen generations lay about, abandoned or forgotten; a rusting gun, an old spinning wheel, a broken quern, a mildewed Bible, open at the first chapter of St. Paul.

On again, along the low cliffs of the east coast, pink granite at Ruscar Head, sandstone at the Stack of the Gaads, black basalt at Taing Head. Even Alasdair was silent now while, if he had only known, I was moving quite mechanically. If he had stopped I should never have started again: I was only trying not to think about my feet although they were all right, no blisters. We headed over a peaty moor, cut to pieces by water channels, so that my right foot never knew where my left foot was going, then suddenly the Haa was in sight. We plunged down into Sloag burn, up the other side on to the shaly path above the Blow-hole and the Haa was only a few hundred yards away; Syd appeared waving a teapot, my load of care dropped from my back, my legs were moving like pistons, we came striding in at full speed, to find a huge meal spread and two places waiting; this was the final test of the Battle with the Smallie: Alasdair looked expectantly at me but I went on standing by the fire, talking and describing the North End, until with a sigh, he sat down. Then, and not until then, I sat down; last and at last!

I noticed admiringly during the meal that John already had the catechist leaping smartly to the word of command, fetching kettles of water and generally being a little treasure about the house; and by the respectful and admiring looks which he gave John I could see he had already heard portions of the great Seabourne Saga, an epic narrative which, if pieced together, would rival Gargantua and Munchausen, and of which the reader has already heard a fragment in the Story of Busty Hawkins and the Rocket is Gone Up, Sir!

One of the things I had noticed with concern on Foula was that there were no Shetland ponies on the island. A film of Shetland life without ponies would be like coffee without cream, an egg without salt or whisky without soda. Alasdair explained that the family used to own a few themselves but they ate a lot of grass and were not much use, so they had sold them. Could they be bought on Mainland? Ay, they could, all I could want, for five pound apiece.

We were all discussing this, when suddenly Alasdair sniffed the air sharply and said:

'I was expecting it!'

We all knew that our Smallie would not have been expecting anything pleasant, so took no notice. But George said sharply:

'Expecting what, Mr. Holbourn?'

'A change of wind.'

We all listened. It did seem to be stronger, but like most townsmen, or English countrymen for that matter, we were vague about the points of the compass.

'Where to and what of it?' I said.

'Gale Warning'

Alasdair looked whole volumes of Sailing Directions at me:

'It's gone into the west,' he said, 'from north to west; and you won't be here long, before you'll know what that means.'

Anybody speaking with knowledge is impressive and Alasdair evidently knew what he was talking about. I said:

'What *does* it mean?'

'Come outside.'

We all went out. It was already much warmer and a drizzle was falling. Alasdair sniffed the air:

'Due west!' he said with satisfaction. After all, everyone likes to be proved right. 'It's rising every minute. We'll have a gale before the morning.'

'Do you really think so?' said George. It certainly did not look like it. I looked around to the west and exclaimed:

'Look at Hamnafeld!'

The others were not sure where to look but followed my look. Hamnafeld dominates the Voe, as Table Mountain lords it over Capetown. It rises straight from the ground as abruptly as a slag-heap, and it is about the same shape, if you can imagine a slag-heap a thousand feet high and a mile long. The peak is directly opposite the Voe; from it, the shoulder runs down to Hametoun, on the left, as straight and sharp as a rule; and the side of the hill all the way is at 60°. When the sun is on it, in the morning, it is like a friendly garden wall; but in the evening, when the hill is in shadow, it is a black rampart.

All day Hamnafeld had been sharp and clear with the north wind blowing along its back, but the change of wind had changed the shape of the mountain. Great billowy clouds from the wet Atlantic were pouring over the sharp ridge, like rollers over a breakwater. They thinned out and floated off over Shetland but always more came rolling up, faster and thicker and blacker, till we felt that the Smallie was over the other side, mixing bad weather for the whole sixtieth parallel. The west wind and Hamnafeld—how often we had to watch those rolling clouds and whistle for fine weather.

At the moment we were rather excited and impressed. We had no thought of the morrow. The mail-boat had been ordered for eight o'clock so we were going by it, as confidently as we always took a bus in the morning. But the catechist was bending over his radio as we came in and the words we heard were:

'GALE WARNING!'

For the first time in our lives we listened with a quickened personal interest. Sure enough; it was for the Faeröes, Orkneys and Shetlands. It was Alasdair's moment of triumph, his vindication, and he rose to it nobly:

'Good night, everybody,' he said. 'Pleasant dreams and, whatever you may have planned, don't bother to wake *me* in the morning!'

Chapter VIII

A BONNY PLACE IS FOULA

★

John and I died that night at half-past nine and came to life again at seven next morning, to find a full-sized gale roaring over the Haa. At first we failed to realize how impossible it was to leave the island, for the Voe was to windward of the island, and there was only a light swell running. But Alasdair made us look farther out, beyond the shelter of the land and then we saw the whole horizon was moving uneasily, while over the Hoevdi Grund great round boils heaved up abruptly into the air.

'The Hoevdi will be breaking as soon as the tide turns,' said Alasdair, with relish. His island was certainly putting on a good show for him. 'It will have looked just the way it is now, the day the *Oceanic* was wrecked.'

This was Alasdair's titbit; he had been saving it up for a suitable moment. That moment had arrived. We all said:

'The *Oceanic*?'

'What?'

'When?'

Alasdair swelled with pride.

' 'Twas in the war. She was an armed auxiliary merchant cruiser. She was on patrol-duty—but she made a mistake when she came up here; she didn't know *our* seas.'

'What happened?'

'She was in the channel between the two rocks though nobody knows what she was doing so close in to Foula. Maybe she was going to send off a boat. The tidal stream had set towards the south-east, it runs five knots over the shoals. She turned broadside on and it carried her on to the Hoevdi before she could get clear.'

'Is it so shallow there?'

'Shallow? There's not two fathom of water!'

'Did anyone see it happen?'

'The whole island heard it. They said it was a crash like the cliff had fallen.'

'She was a big ship?' I asked, trying to remember.

'A fair size,' offhandedly. 'About 17,000 tons.'

'But that was terrible!'

Alasdair looked gratified.

Yet he is a kind-hearted man. It was just that the magnitude of the disaster reflected to the glory of Foula. All the Holbourns boast that the seas round Foula are the most dangerous in the world; they all say so, so it must be true; the *Oceanic* to them is the concrete proof of it. A Holbourn tourist poster would read:

COME TO STORMY FOULA
Where the sun never shines for long.
TRY   a diet of dried piltock;
a jump off the Kame;
a walk in one of our gales.
WE DARE YOU!
SEE   the Sneck of the Smallie;
the Suicide's Grave;
Foula and Die!
Special Wrecks arranged.   No extras.
No life-belts.
Save Money this Year by Taking a One-
Way Passage to Foula.

Walter came down to the Voe, took a look out to sea, shook his head and stumped off home. Dodie wiped his moustache thoughtfully and went back to his workshop, with Andrew by his side. Peter Manson went to the Shop to buy some flour, before he started back to Blowburn. The door was locked but a shout or two brought Jimmy Isbister hurrying down from Ham. Peter Gear had not bothered to bring down the mail-sack; they all knew the weather was hopeless, though etiquette compelled them to wait for Walter's decision. John and I went into the Shop, curious to see what it provided. There were three customers standing about without speaking. Jimmy o' the Shop was behind the counter, his knuckles resting on it, his fair hair disarranged. Peter had his flour under one arm and his ditty-box under the other. (All the mail-boat crew had their box, with food and other things, for they never knew how long they might be cut off in Walls by a storm.) Peter stood with his legs well apart, purposefully chewing tobacco. He was dressed in light blue overalls, thrust into short sea-boots, a short, tight dark blue jersey and a tight-fitting, weather-stained cap. His face was lean and muscular; and he radiated the same physical impression from his whole body. I always imagined that if he thumped his chest it would sound like well-seasoned teak. We blinked a bit in the gloom, getting our bearings. Jimmy looked tactfully away as if he hated selling anything. The other men looked straight in front of them, without moving. Everyone went on saying nothing. I felt that this suspended animation was not quite normal, like the feeling, on entering a deserted waxworks, that the figures have just hastily resumed their proper positions.

The Shop was the whole ground floor of the house; a third was general goods, a third was sacks and tools and a third was standing room. A short ladder led to a granary, with a hoist to the shop below, and there was another little room, matchboarded off from it. I was confused by our silent audience and murmured something about looking around, but John never lost his poise and after considerable chat, in Scotch, bought a white china egg-cup, of which there were about forty in a row above the door. I saw some bottles and enquired if they were lemonade but they were acetic acid, five quart bottles of it! When we knew Jimmy better, John tried to solve the mystery of the row of egg-cups and the acetic acid. There never was a good explanation of the first, but somebody on Foula had been told by somebody else that acetic acid was good for rheumatism; they asked Jimmy to get some and he had to order six quarts. So if anybody knows of a good use for large quantities of A.A. a postcard to J. Isbister, Ham, Isle of Foula will be appreciated. I compromised with some ginger-wine, which I thought might help John and Syd through the long summer evenings. When we got outside I said to John:

'Why the egg-cup?'

'We had to buy something; an egg-cup is cheap; an egg-cup is an ornamental object.'

'The shopkeeper seems to think so. What on earth can he want with forty-two . . . ?'

'Forty-one.'

'Forty-two!'

'Forty-one!'

'Forty-one egg-cups on Foula?'

There was no answer. John has an answer for most of life's problems but forty-one egg-cups on Foula beat him.

I was quite pleased that we were marooned. We had plenty of stores and there were still a hundred things to decide. Even if there had been no gale, I should have stayed. I gathered everyone together for a council of war.

First there was the question of our base camp. Alasdair had three suggestions: at Brae, on the opposite bank of the Voe; at Mornington, a large and well-built croft on the brow of the hill towards Hametoun; or at an old ruined croft by Mill Loch. I had already decided that the Haa, with the jetty and the Shop in easy reach, was ideal, but we went on a tour of inspection.

Brae was awkward for transport and open to every wind

that blows. The croft by Mill Loch was so old and picturesque that it hurt, but not so much as it would to live
in it. The biggest joke was Mornington: it was a fine croft
right enough but completely roofless. Alasdair spoke as if
this were a minor matter but Syd spoke his mind and, by
the time he had finished, Mornington was out. But, for our
other purpose, it was quite good. There were three interior
sets in the picture: the church, the Manson croft and the
cabin of the trawler. I was not going to strike a false note
by making them in the studio. The two island sets I had
planned to do in a roofless croft, the other in the chart-
room of the *Vedra*. Mornington looked good to us. The
big room could be dressed to look like the church and the
smaller one the croft. The idea was to get general illumina-
tion from the open roof, which we would control with
blinds, like a photographer's studio; and to use mirrors and
reflectors (tinfoil on three-ply, gold, silver and dull silver)
to light the actors and make high lights on the walls.

We went back to the Haa and I tackled Alasdair. There
were obvious objections to all these places, there were none
to the Haa. On the contrary. The camp would consist of
five huts, four beds to a hut. The kail-yard at the back of
the Haa was ideal. There was nothing in it and a wall all
round it. The big dining-hut, twenty-five feet long, would
just go in the space between the Shop and the Haa; and
they would protect it from the gales. ('Heh! Heh! Heh!
you haven't seen *our* gales!' said the Smallie.) With a
clean-out, a sink, electric light and a new window, the
kitchen would do; it was big and we had to have a big
kitchen. (We did, but not for the reasons I meant.) The
girls and Mrs. Rutherford could sleep upstairs, and the
girls could have the sitting-room as their own property (I
can hear ghostly female laughter at this point). Alasdair
could still have the little room where he slept last night.
(Sarcastic thanks from the Smallie.) The whole unit—crew,
actors, domestic staff and technical adviser—would be al-

most under one roof. The Shop was next door. The *Vedra* would be always in plain sight for signals (this was a grand piece of unconscious humour). The Camera Hut could be placed near by. The Sound Department could be put in the big porch, which Syd would roof over (Syd nodded and Alasdair visibly brightened). It might cause the Holbourns inconvenience if they wanted to come this summer to their island, but it would leave them with an improved property at the end of our stay.

Syd and George at once plunged into estimates and measurements, for George was to take back with him the orders for timber and materials. I got to work on my script, with Alasdair by my side. John put the catechist to peeling potatoes for lunch and wandered off on his own devices.

With all I had seen and heard, I changed action and names, planning the sequences to give a complete picture of the island. With Hamish Sutherland in mind, I built up the part of the Catechist, making him a serious young man with a call, a man of the island, so that he would share with James and Peter the authority of the community. I was inspired to this, partly by Alasdair telling me of the previous catechist, now dead, who had been an islander and much loved, and partly because I thought I had in young Sutherland 'a find'.

The Lerwick sequences worked out beautifully and I could see that the noise and bustle would be a welcome relief from the austere silences of Foula. Alasdair was a mine of information on everything I wanted to know.

The wind had brought up a thick mist and the rain was soft but steady. George and Syd came in, soaked and with huge appetites. Between mouthfuls Syd described the church; they had got the key from Robbie. He was professionally enthusiastic about the work on the seats and the pulpit. It was all plain, unpainted wood and was as solid and good as when it was put in fifty years ago. The building itself was more like two hundred.

'You must see it, Mr. Powell,' he insisted, 'it will give you a hundred ideas. If only we could shoot it as it stands! Of course I can manage the pews, but the best thing of all is the way the windows are recessed, almost two feet deep. They give such character to the place. You wouldn't see that in a studio set, in a hundred years.'

'What about the outside? Will the roof stand a belfry?'

'Easily. I thought in the middle; then the rope from the bell can run down the roof and through an iron loop on a bracket out from the wall, like this.' He scribbled on a piece of paper. 'I've seen them done that way.'

'O.K.'

'What's this about a bell and a belfry?' said Alasdair suspiciously.

'The bell is in the script, part of the sound dissolve that brings the island back to life. The belfry is to carry the bell, of course, but chiefly to make the church look more like a church to a film audience.'

Alasdair said nothing but he said it in a withering manner.

After lunch John set the catechist to washing up, saw him well started with plenty of soda and suggested a stroll to me and Alasdair. The latter looked worried.

'I'll need to be working out something to say to-morrow.'

'Why to-morrow?'

'It's the Sabbath.'

'And the next day is Monday.'

'It's no joke. Someone must take the service.'

'You?'

'Why not?'

'Isn't it the catechist's job?'

'He's already preached his farewell sermon.'

'Oh.'

However, Alasdair agreed to leave theology till the evening and accompany us. We crossed the field behind the Haa to a long croft on a hillock, called Veedal. It was half in ruins; a little man, thin as a rail, with a fair moustache and puckered eyes, was tending to his cows, one of whom was blind in one eye. This was Andrew Manson (and his 'coos') and at this time he would have nothing to do with us. He was the only one left of a large family and, living alone and brooding on his misfortunes, he had sunk into melancholia, as many lonely crofters and shepherds do. But we saw his croft and I liked it better than Mornington; it had more character, it was older and in one corner was a complete quern (hand-mill of two round stones, with a hole in the centre for the grain, a wooden handle in the top stone to turn it and a ridge to catch the coarse flour as it squeezes out of the edge). Veedal was much handier for us, too.

As we struck across the moor Alasdair told us that Andrew was only one of several, equally sunk in apathy, with no relatives, no money and no prospects. Then and there John and I decided we had a mission: to see that every croft on Foula benefited equally from our presence; so that those who could not work should act, or hire their crofts for a location. We also vowed, by the time we finished, to have every victim of Giant Despair out of his dungeon and dancing on the green. I date from that time the start of our personal interest in Foula; for to many of us, by the end, Foula had been not only an adventure but a spiritual experience. Foula did as much for us as we ever did for Foula.

As we took the road to the North End we looked back and found the dog, Michael, had followed us. We were annoyed because he had a bad reputation for chasing sheep. We yelled 'Go home' and made all the usual gestures but he stuck, so we gave in. We soon regretted it.

The road pushes through two sheep gates, under the shadow of Hamnafeld, then winds past Burns, the largest croft on the island—it has two storeys—where Peter Gray and Old John Gray, his father, live. A wicket-gate leads down to a bridge across the burn, which runs deep and clear, while behind the house is a long, dark peat cutting, cut along its whole length by such regular, narrow slices of the 'tusker' that from the end it looks like a board fence. Beyond lay the whole watershed of the island: Netherfandal, Overfandal and the great undulating ridge from Hamnafeld up to the Sneug and down again to the Kame.

Then the road stopped and a narrow pathway took its place, cut out of the peat, so that it shook at every footstep. Presently this branched, one fork to Harrier and the Wilse, the other to Blowburn, high up on the side of Soberlie. But although these seemed to be the last crofts, they were not the true North End, which lay over the hill on our right, as I knew already. Mucklegrind is there, where David lives, the brother of Jimmy o' Ristie. I thought that now I had seen them all, but looking back I saw a little croft before Burns, hidden from the road and cuddling under Overfandal. It was Gossameadow.

South Harrier was gay with white-wash and its gates had *patent latches* on them, which shows the sort of man Scotty Umphray is. It gets the sun most of the day and the burn comes down from Flick and Overfandal, meeting the other from Blowburn, so the fields are well watered. North Harrier was more dour. Andrew Gray came out to meet us. He was a fine, tall man, one of the best boatbuilders on the island, but, since he left Springs, he too had relapsed into melancholy. He was convinced that nothing awaited him but death. His sister kept the house. He took us to his kail-yard, which had been an old Norse burying ground. There were dozens of great flat stones, some of them still standing, relics of kistvaens. He told us a Norwegian professor had spent two weeks digging there and had earned the great respect of the entire community by describing different places on the island, so soon as he heard their names. He had told them that the settlement around the Voe was called Ham, because it means 'harbour'; and that Foula was pronounced 'Foola' because it comes from Fugly: 'bird island'; and that people had once kept pigs at Grisigarth and horses at Hestinsgarth and lambs at Lammigarth, until they thought he had second sight. . . .

There was a sudden scream from Andrew's sister. He turned and the next second was outside the yard throwing stones and cursing. Alasdair turned pale:

'That damned dog!' he exclaimed.

We all rushed out but were too late. The Grays were coming to meet us, the woman with a tiny lamb dying in her arms. Andrew's face was black with anger. Anywhere it would be bad enough, but on Foula, where wool is the only thing to be sold, and many a family's only possession, it was far worse. We could do nothing except beat the dog and apologize. But his rage was all against the catechist; apparently this was not the first time his dog had run loose. The black criminal was very pleased with himself, of course —like most spaniels, his skin was as thick as his coat.

The rain came on heavier, with a shift of wind to the south. We were glad to get home and change into dry things. After a heart-to-heart talk with the catechist, Alasdair squared his elbows, spread out a big Bible and concordance and started to compose a sermon. George and Syd wrangled amiably over lists of timber. I pored over my script. John cooked kippers over the fire. Outside the rain blew past the windows and the gale roared overhead. The smell of kipper and the voice of the radio announcer reading the news filled the low room. Suddenly John dropped a kipper on the fire. The announcer was saying:

'. . . in the Shetlands. Three film-technicians from Elstree are marooned by the storm on the lonely island of Foula, twenty miles off the coast.'

Alasdair's face rose appalled from his sermon.

'They left on Thursday in a small motor-boat to survey the island for a film, intending to return almost at once, but a gale sprang up and they were forced to remain on the island.'

Mr. Inkster and Mr. Johnson, I thought grimly.

'It is not known if they have any provisions with them. There is no means of communicating with Foula and the gale is still raging. . . . Ahem. . . . Stay-in Strikes in Paris . . .' but he was switched off by common consent.

John thoughtfully dusted off the fallen kipper.

'If we're as near starvation as they say,' he said, 'we may need it.'

'Remember—no Publicity,' I thought to myself; and already we were in the News on Saturday night, which meant headlines in the Sunday papers as well as items on Monday. Poor Joe! That would be the end of his campaign to hide his spotlight under a bushel. Besides, from now on, Foula was News! If they acted like that over three of us and a cap-full of wind, what would they say to a whole unit in a real gale?

I had to wait five months to find out.

On Sunday 'the gale was still raging', but it was fine, dry weather. The church service was at 5 p.m. George and Syd promised Alasdair they would attend, so John and I, deciding they could represent the maroonees adequately, stuffed oranges in our pockets and set off up the Sneug. We went by the Daal as before but branched off before we came to the Sneck and climbed up at our leisure from the south. We saw several figures about in the distance and supposed they were taking the Sabbath air but I suspect now that we were being spied on, after the illuminating broadcast of the night before, which had revealed us to be no ordinary 'towerists'. We noticed one figure in particular, light and swift, with a fluttering black shawl, which circled around us, about a mile away, with the agility of a Shetland sheep.

We made first for the Kame, as the wind was dropping. It was a different day entirely and we were able to sit on the edge and throw orange peel to the seals. John posed obligingly for a horrifying still to show to his wife. Then we followed the ridge up to the Sneug. It was only two hundred feet higher, but we first had to dip down into a saddle-back of marshy land which was exclusive Bonxie Territory. Anyone ignorant of Bonxies, their habits and appearance, is in the same position as we were. My first introduction to them was a loud yell from John who hurled himself flat on his face. Before I could adjust myself to this I saw, out of the corner of my eye, a huge shape rushing at me through the air; the next second I received a stunning blow on the head from the body of a large bird, which soared up again into the air, turned and dived at me once more, before I had clearly seen what it was. This time I copied John and it roared over my prostrate body like a Handley-Page. We got to our feet and ran like hares, pursued to the limits of their nesting grounds by these wild fowl.

We paused for breath and looked back. Dozens of the huge birds were circling round and round, giving angry barks.

'Nice birds!'

'Like getting mixed up with Hendon Air Pageant,' agreed John.

'What are they!'

'Humming-birds, do you think?'

'Too far north.'

'It's been puzzling me for days', said John slowly, 'to see the inhabitants of this benighted island walking about certain parts of it with their walking sticks held in the air like umbrellas. At first I thought they were genuinely under the impression that they were carrying an umbrella and I was on the verge of pointing it out to them. Then I decided they were nuts. Now I see the point.'

'You'd be dumb if you didn't.'

'You mean dead.'

As we panted up the last slabs of the Sneug I saw a black shawl flutter to our right. It was our Mysterious Watcher again; this time quite near. I mentioned it to John.

'She'll probably rush in and bring us both down with a flying tackle,' he suggested. 'Anything goes on this island!'

'There's never a law of God or man runs north of 53,' I suggested.

'You took the words out of my mouth.'

'There should be a cairn on top, according to the report in the Government Survey. Do you see it?'

'No.'

'And a holy well, whose water has miraculous healing power and used to be bottled for export.'

'What would it look like?'

'Just a well.'

'There's the cairn,' said John suddenly; and it was. In a moment we were standing on the highest point of Foula.

It is worth the climb. Everywhere else the land is in the line of sight. But on the cairn of the Sneug the sea is all around, wherever the eye turns. The island, distinct and complete, alone in the waste of sea, lies below on every side. It was a clear day and the whole coast of Shetland filled the eastern horizon. We made out Ve Skerries and Papa Stour, the curving cliff of Sandness, the dent in the hills where Scalloway stood, and the distant hump of Fitful Head. John said:

'I believe I can see Fair Isle.'

We both stared hard and there rose out of the sea a rounded, blue shape, as dim and distant as the Sneug itself had looked when we first saw Foula from the aeroplane, over Fair Isle. We felt unreasonably pleased with ourselves and, as a matter of fact, we *were* lucky, for I only saw Fair Isle three times.

Suddenly we saw that the Mysterious Watcher had approached within biting distance. As Jemima is a remarkable person, I had better describe her in detail.

She was not a pretty woman but her face was striking. Her body was thin, her hands were worn, her feet were in old shoes but her figure had natural grace. It was impossible for her to move, or to stand or to sit in an ugly way. Even her plain black shawl, worn by all the women, was caught by her in an individual way round her shoulders, crossed over her breasts and tucked into her waist, so that the rather clumsy outline was transformed into something graceful. She was very light on her feet. Her face was brown and lined. Her mouth had a humorous twist to it and her eyes were her best feature.

She saw us looking and smiled and looked out of the corner of her eye. I said:

'Good afternoon.'

She said eagerly:

'Good day to ye both, it's a bonny day to be out on the banks, ye'll not often see so far or so clear as to-day, so early in the year.'

I said: 'Oh?'

She said: 'I saw ye both from down by Hoevdi. I saw ye were crossing over to the Sneug and I knew fine the Bonxies would be after you and I called to you and waved my shawl but ye never heeded it and I was afraid they might do you a harm.'

John said: 'They. . . .'

She said: 'Before this day I have seen a man with his head bruised and bleeding and his eye blackened from going too near the Bonxies and the Allens.'

I said——

She said: 'And he lost his cap too.'

I said firmly: 'What are Bonxies and Allens?'

She said: 'Skuas, their proper name is, there's a many, too many on Foula. "Bonxie" is only our name for the Great Skua and the Allens are the smaller ones you'll see down by the Haa, they're smaller but they're fiercer; do ye no' hear the Bonxies now calling down there: "Skua! Skua!"?'

We listened and she was right.

I said: 'They are big birds.'

'Big as an eagle,' she agreed, 'four feet and even five across the wings and they weigh a lump. There was a time there were only two pair in the world and they on Foula but now there's too many.'

'Why don't you like them?'

'They're robbers and they kill smaller birds. They live by robbing and they drive the other birds away. They're a fine large bird but they're nothing but thieves. Do ye like birds?'

'Yes.'

'Maybe you collect their eggs?'

'No, but Mr. Seabourne has two sons who do.'

She was fumbling in a fold of her shawl and then held out a fine guillemot's egg, larger than a hen's and much more pointed, of a rather rare pattern of pure white and chocolate, with beautiful bunchy pigment markings at the rounded end. She held it out towards John and something in the manner with which it was presented told me that it was a calculated ambassadorial gift, and that if John accepted it, he would be 'taking seizin'. He stretched out his hand. Jemima smiled and placed it carefully in his palm. We were formally 'seized of Foula'.

Alasdair would disapprove of this phrase, for Foula is held, not by feudal, but by udal tenure; the land is held not by permission of any human authority but by the sun and by God; it must be gained in battle and held by force of arms and no money has anything to do with it. Alasdair insisted that this holds good to-day though, when I enquired if his father became the owner by personal combat with the previous laird, he admitted there had been an arrangement, by which the udal tenure remained, though money changed hands. We turned this information against the Smallie later on, by pointing out that he was one against many and that if we had trouble with him we would fortify the *Vedra* and Ham Voe, set him adrift in his dinghy and become udal owners of Foula, *vi et armis*.

Jemima told a long story about just finding the egg on the grass by Nebbifeld and slipping it into her shawl and then thinking we might like it. She pointed out different places that we had not yet visited and described things we had not yet seen.

'A bonny place is Foula in the soft summer weather,' she said. 'The work is hard and there's little enough to carry us through the winter but all around there's beauty and there's things to see if you have the mind to see them. They say this will be a lightsome summer. Ay . . . a bonny place is Foula.'

Now I am as sure as I can be of anything, and I challenge Jemima to deny it, that she had set out that morning, with the guillemot's egg in her shawl, with the firm intention of tracking us down, catching us in a favourable spot and selling us Foula. The radio report had told the island who we were and Jemima's quick wit had seen that if we could be convinced that Foula was an ideal location, it would indeed be a lightsome summer for the whole island. She was quite right; for her friendliness and personality dispelled any doubts that may have lingered about our possible reception from the islanders. The present of the egg, though naïvely staged, was a master-stroke. Jemima was undoubtedly Real Estate Agent, Welcome Committee and Syndicat d'Initiative of Foula all rolled into one.

She showed us the Healing Well, which is difficult to find, for its little cup is not marked in any way but by a small pile of stones, like a hundred others. It was empty, but Jemima assured us it sometimes held water through the driest summer. We said good-bye and struck off along the ridge to the top of Hamnafeld. I looked back once and saw her graceful black figure standing looking out towards Shetland. She was too polite to look directly after us, though no doubt we were in a corner of her eye.

All the way we kept to the ridge, so that the east side of the island lay below us. We could not have had a better view from an aeroplane and the stills I took look very like air views. We discovered that the source of Overfandal Burn was a beautiful round lake, hidden on a shelf under Hamnafeld, about 500 feet up. It was covered thick with Bonxies bathing and making as much noise as the bathers in Highgate Ponds, so we avenged our recent rout by rolling stones down into their swimming pool. Then we watched them settle again; they came down on the water with a rush like a flying-boat, and individual pilots were better than others. There was one big fellow with a very broad white bar across his brown wings, who sent a fountain into the air every time. There were plenty of Allens about too—birds half the size of the Great Skua, but streamlined, swifter and fiercer, and more grey in colour. One of the Bonxies blundered into their territory and four of them set on him and drove him out, wheeling under and over and at him in mid-air like fighting scouts round a clumsy bomber. The Bonxie did not try to fight back but just ran for home and I saw brown feathers float down the wind. Alasdair told us later that Overfandal Loch was known as the Bonxies' Bath; also that the full name of the Allens was Allen Richardson Skuas.

We went down the sloping ridge of Hamnafeld until we were above Mill Loch. The kittiwakes covered the shallow end with a white blanket of moving bodies. They were bathing, aquaplaning, landing and taking off without ceasing and the air was full of 'Kittiwaakes!' At the other end there were quite a few Bonxies and, if one of them approached the kittiwakes, there would be a storm of wings into the air and a general chorus of protests. The 'kitties' love to wash the salt off their wings in fresh water and all the lochs of the island used to be covered with them. But the Bonxies, which nest on the high hills, have gradually muscled in on the kittiwakes' territory. Robina, Dodie's sister, told me that a few years ago Mill Loch had thousands of kitties all the summer.

A Bonny Place is Foula

'The water would be hid and the air full of the pretty wee birds and none of us here at Leirabach could hear the other speak, from the noise of their crying. But we loved them. They always meant the summer to us, and the long days and the flowers, and I always wept to see them go; and now the cruel Bonxies are driving them out, they are bolder every year. They would be over Rosie's Loch, too, but the Allens will not let them. The Allens are the only things they fear.'

Ishmael though he is, the Bonxie is a splendid bird and a fine flyer, unafraid of the fiercest storm and capable of ranging for food as far as the eagle.

We launched ourselves over the edge of Hamnafeld and went down like rolling stones. The kittiwakes must have thought us a new and fearful kind of Bonxie; they took one look and were all off to Kittiwakes' Haa, before we could say 'Skua!' I stubbed my toe on an eider duck which was comfortably inserted into a hole in the heather. She took no notice and continued to exhibit perfect poise when John and I stared in her face, photographed her and discussed her private life, with as much freedom as a gossip-column treats a débutante. She even let me lift her up, in a warm unprotesting lump, while John counted her eight greenish-white eggs. I replaced her carefully and she cuddled down without even a disdainful look at me.

The heather turned into stones and lastly into bright green grass, which proved to be a disastrous bog, where a spring ran out from the hill. I went in up to my knee without any effort at all. The whole of the length of the hill was a line of springs, a never-failing supply of crystal drinking water. Hamnafeld must be a great hollow tank for the whole watershed, honeycombed with fissures and underground lakes. This would lend a good deal of credibility to the story of the Lum of Liorafield, of which more later. We had looked for it on the summit but had the usual failure—luckily for us, if the legend is a true one.

A Bonny Place is Foula

As we arrived at Leirabach, George and Syd were on the point of church, leaving behind them the remains of a high tea, upon which we swooped, for Robina's scones are something to sing about. Alasdair called for his converts, looking very preoccupied, his Bible and notes under his arm and an old B.A. gown over it. He looked expectantly at John and me but we were welcoming the arrival of jam and a fresh relay of scones and home-made bread and were unlikely converts. Dodie had already left with the big Bible and the key of the chapel, so the new catechist gave a sigh and left us wallowing in sin and a fourth cup of tea.

The wind had dropped by now, and although a heavy swell was still running on the coast of Shetland it would be almost gone by next day. I sketched out my plans to John. It would be two weeks to our starting-date. I had a week's shooting in Lerwick and Scalloway, with the trawler and the fishing-fleet. Three weeks to build and organize the camp, line up labour to do it, overcome prejudice, and establish a fair wage-scale was not much, even with Syd in charge. But John said they could do it and they did, Vernon and he and Syd and Buddy. I shall never know how, for I only heard vague reports and they will not talk, strong, silent pioneers all.

There was a bad skerry at the end of the jetty, making it useless for any but the smallest of sea-going craft. The *Vedra* would never be able to come nearer than a hundred yards and that only in mill-pond weather. How we were to land most of our stores was a problem, let alone the huts, which were very heavy, even in sections. I also planned a small car, or a tractor, and there would be a power engine for charging batteries, and tons of heavy material. The mail-boat would be a tremendous aid, for it only drew two or three feet; it was an open boat, with a small cabin over the engine and a mast immediately aft, shallow and broad in the beam like all Shetland boats, which ride the waves like a gull and are extraordinarily graceful and seaworthy, a striking contrast to the deep, heavy hulls of the south. The mail-boat was about twenty-five feet over all and her beam about eight. She could take a surprising number of people and their goods, and I always felt safe in her, though whether this was the boat or the presence of her crew, I am not sure. Anyway, we planned a good deal on her assistance and we were not wrong.

Much refreshed by seven huge cups of tea, John hurled himself into the preparation of a gala dinner, to celebrate the marooning of Crusoe Seabourne next day, for Syd and Alasdair were going with us to the mainland, one to enquire about timber and carpenters, the other to put the yacht in commission and line up several things for me. The *plat du jour*, John announced, was to be a huge omelette for six people, made with eight hens' eggs, two Bonxies' and what was alleged to be an Allen's. The catechist had not attended church, preferring to leave the field to Alasdair, and was packing the last of his goods when we arrived at the Haa. John was grieved to see the state the kitchen had got into during his absence all day and put him on to clearing up, while he delivered a lecture on domestic hygiene. Between them they had an impressive meal ready by seven o'clock, to welcome the churchgoers. Alasdair looked as if he had a weight off his mind but George and Syd were subdued. They reported that their preacher had soared into realms of theology as abstract as the Fourth Dimension and as intimidating as the Binomial Theorem. But it had gone down well to a crowded house.

The omelette was an inch thick, as golden as a buttercup, as rich as Rockefeller. John took five curtain-calls. After dinner we held a last council of war, then turned in early.

The islanders were down on the quay next morning and for the first time we saw most of our future friends and neighbours. I was struck by the predominance, among the girls, of a Northern type of face, almost tending towards the Eskimo, which I saw later was very common in Shetland; a flattish, pleasant face with humorous mouth and rather small, almond-shaped eyes, which screwed up when their owner laughed, which was often. The men were every kind of type but all had the quality of personality which I have described. We were not the only passengers on the boat. Nurse Dodson, a lively little woman, with curly black hair, was going out for her holiday. Scotty Umphray, of South Harrier, was leaving for three months on a drifter, which was waiting for him on Shetland. He was a strong, sandy, splendid type of seaman, with a keen mind and a neat way with his hands. He was dressed, of course, in his 'Sunday blacks' (which are actually 'Navy blues'), and he carried his kitbag under his arm.

Jessie and Bessie from North Biggins were there, Mrs. Henry's two strapping daughters, with soft, sweet voices; the Henry twins from Gossameadow were there, both knitting and giggling furiously. The mail-boat crew looked serious and important, saw to their cargo and discussed the weather. Jimmy o' the Shop impressed on Dodie some specially important purchase. Finally we were off and everyone waved and cried good-bye and God-speed. John, left all alone, joined in as if he meant it.

If all this excitement seems excessive, for a boat that is only going twenty miles over the sea to return the same day, let anyone imagine herself in the place of one of those women. Their men are in that boat and until they see it again they will be ignorant whether they are alive or dead. The mail-boat has sometimes been *ten weeks overdue*. Storms come up suddenly. The boat might have left Walls, been caught in a squall and sent to the bottom. Nobody on Foula would know until the gale went down. Their men might be ten weeks dead and they could never know it; ten weeks of peering every morning out to sea; ten weeks of doubt and fear; so it is little wonder they crowd to the jetty to cry 'God-speed!'

The catechist poured a last cascade of bundles into the boat and we all had to wedge ourselves in as best we could. In spite of that it was a wonderful crossing and I never again enjoyed it half as much. There was still a good swell running but with our load we were well ballasted and Walter managed the boat in a way that was a treat to watch.

The harbour of Walls is entered by two passages round the rocky island of Vaila. It is not until a boat has gone a mile down Easter or Wester Sound, that the village is opened up at the end of a fine bay of clear water, where the regatta is held, with the steamer pier on the left. This was intended to be our mainland headquarters, but for various reasons, it was soon changed to Scalloway. The mail-boat ran right up to a little pier in the shallow water by the village. There was quite a crowd of people waiting. Some pedlars, with a battered saloon car, were transferring their goods to packs, more suitable for Foula. There were one or two islanders; and an elderly gentleman, with a charming, gentle face, who came up and spoke to us and then immersed himself in conversation with Scotty. Dodie told me his name was Greenaway; he was the husband of the late schoolmistress of Foula. They had been twenty years on the island and loved it as much as they themselves were loved. He lived in Edinburgh now but came to stay on Foula every year at South Harrier. I liked the look of him immensely and began to plan a school sequence, in which he could play the dominie.

George went to telephone for a car, while Syd came with the rest of us to inspect the Holbourn yacht. It was larger than I had expected and was in fair condition. The deck was canvassed over but we planned to plank it, if we had the time. The painting and rigging were already being overhauled. I told Alasdair it would do, and we took measurements for the auxiliary motor, to be fitted at Scalloway. The sails were all good; they needed washing, but altogether she was a sound little boat, very seaworthy and quite pretty when under sail. Her fittings were especially good.

This took a big weight off my mind, for it meant we could have a yacht standing by all the summer for suitable weather, rather than attempt to make the whole opening sequence of the film within a limited time—practically an impossibility, for there are only about ten days in the whole year when a small boat can make the circuit of the island, as there is nearly always a deep Atlantic swell on the west. The yacht could lie in the Voe, moored from side to side with a chain hawser, and be at our beck and call. Like most of our plans, however, this also turned out to be full of unconscious humour.

We took Scotty and Nurse with us in the car, for the only bus had already gone to Lerwick. The catechist bade us good-bye. He had some friends in Walls and was going to stay a few days and get his scattered possessions together. We had got used to the queer little man and he had been very helpful about the house, as John pointed out, so we wished him better luck in his next job.

Although Walls is only a few miles up the coast from Scalloway it is much farther from Lerwick, fully an hour's run through rolling heather hills and salt-water lakes, sometimes over a causeway with the sea on each side of it, until, at a bridge in the hills, we met the familiar road from Scalloway and in ten minutes were in Lerwick. We dropped Nurse, who was profuse in her thanks and made for the Queen's, where Scotty left us to go down to the harbour and find out where his boat lay. Mr. Inkster and Mr. Johnson were waiting for us, with such beaming smiles over their front-page story that I could not resist their entreaties to be able to say that I had decided on Foula for the film. They showed us cables from all the news agencies, asking for our story. We were blameless anyway, so I gave them what they wanted and told them we were flying south next morning. They dashed off to their offices, we snatched some lunch, then George and I went with Alasdair to see Shetland ponies, while Syd departed on a timber-hunt.

The pony-breeder, whose name was Smith, had his fields near Scalloway, at Berry, where dozens of the little ponies ran wild, wickedly tossing their shaggy manes and tails, their feet twinkling over the rough ground. They would not allow anyone to come near, the only way was to stand still and have them driven up for inspection. We chose about a dozen; one beauty was marked like a pinto, with a cream-coloured mane, and there were two mothers with foals. The smallest of the ponies was a friendly little thing, with curly hair and a twinkle in her eye; we named her Shirley Temple.

Syd did not have much luck with timber or carpenter; we realized that we should have to depend on ourselves alone; apart from scarcity, everything in Shetland is very dear. All luxuries and most of the necessities have to be imported. The only steamship line is the 'North of Scotland'. Where there is no competition, freights are always high. So serious is the difference in price that we considered sending the *Vedra* back to Aberdeen each time she coaled; it would be cheaper than coaling in Shetland, in spite of the fuel burnt on the voyage; but we eventually made a special arrangement.

Syd was bitter with steamships and the world in general. He was aching to fly at something with a hammer and chisel and, first, he had no wood and, second, he had no tools. Straight as an arrow's flight had been Streeter's to the offices of the company, his voucher held before him like a reprieve for a condemned prisoner. But his box of tools had not arrived. Nobody had ever heard of them. Nobody had ever heard of him! He returned a shadow of his former self. The next boat was not until Wednesday. The mail-boat would have to sail without him. He would have to wait in Lerwick! No man of Foula ever lamented his fate more bitterly. We comforted him and arranged by telephone for the mail-boat to return on Wednesday—weather permitting.

The morning dawned foggy and rainy, but the airway company could take it. The car arrived at nine. Nurse was going to a village near Sumburgh, so we took her with us. There were only George and I now, our forces were scattered all over the map. 'Maurice Chevalier' was our pilot; we came down in a field at Kirkwall but nobody was waiting and we roared up again, flying blind until we sighted Thurso below us. The fog was so bad that it looked as if we would have to stay there, or else go on by train. We went to the hotel, had lunch and inspected the dreary little station; eighteen hours was the fastest train to Edinburgh. But the pilot decided to go on, the weather cleared over Wick and we made Aberdeen in grey but clear weather. All the way down we had been objects of glamour and reporters awaited us at Dyce Aerodrome, also the president of the airways, not displeased with all the publicity; but he did not offer to transport us and our heirs free for ever. We left that night, George through to London, myself to Edinburgh once more, where I met all my friends again, chose maps of Foula and Shetland for the beginning of the film, bumped into Hamish Sutherland in Prince's Street and offered him a contract for the duration of the picture, arranged dates and terms with Robson and Summers, telephoned Vernon at Sunderland to find him horribly busy but anxious to hear about the island, lunched at the Caley with the whole Edinburgh unit—Herries, Forsyth Hardy, Sutherland, Robson and Summers—had an encounter with Leslie Henson in the writing-room upstairs ('Of course, madam, of course,' said a fruity, abrupt voice, 'I quite agree that if it is your chair you are entirely in the right, madam, entirely—entirely,' as she steamed majestically away—'Hullo, Mr. Henson, what are you doing here?' 'Opening a new show, my dear boy, come and see it.' 'Sorry, but I'm off to-night') and I was, on the night train, which was beginning to look like home to me.

Everything was now in hand. Sectional huts, beds, timber, camera equipment, stoves, stores and props were already pouring in on Vernon at Sunderland, to leave as soon as the *Vedra* could sail. Vernon took one look at the huge sections of the huts and sent them on to Aberdeen, to be left at Walls until he had time and room for them. Alasdair was to leave his yacht with Moore at Scalloway and join Vernon at Sunderland, to act as local pilot for Shetland. Buddy, who was now officially enrolled on the production, would converge from the south, with two camera assistants, and an electrician to install the power-plant.

I found Joe resigned to all the publicity and, since he was only human, anxious for more. The excitement was all over then, of course, except in the Scottish papers. Joe showed me the clippings. One headline read: 'Four Men Marooned On An Island'; another 'Three Elstree Men Marooned'; the *Era* said, plainly and simply, 'Michael Powell has been marooned on the Shetland Isle of Foula'. It did not state whether the paper was for the idea or against it.

I hurled myself into casting the picture and turning out a final script. John Laurie was dancing with impatience but I had an idea of playing Malcolm Keen as Peter, with his own son, Geoffrey, to play Robbie. They were not very alike in face, but their voices were extraordinarily similar and they were unmistakably father and son, which would strengthen the reality of the picture enormously. They were both anxious to do it but Geoffrey was opening in a play in September and Malcolm was doubtful about his other engagements. He asked me to dinner to talk it over, and a very excellent dinner it was: I ate alone and Malcolm arrived, full of apologies, in time for coffee; also in time to open a wonderful bottle of port which I seem to remember finishing about midnight. In spite of this he decided they could not risk it and at the same time I received an ultimatum from John, refusing to play James.

That settled it, for I was determined to have John in the picture, so John became Peter Manson; and a wonderful performance he gave: he *was* the man.

Picot Schooling (who is an agent, not a kind of tea) was assigned by Chris Mann to dig up talent and in her first spadeful were Eric Berry and Belle Chrystall. When I saw Belle I could have kicked myself for having wasted so much time. I knew what a grand actress she was and in looks she was ideal: a fine young face, with deep eyes, and a broad forehead, the hair sweeping naturally off it, a sensitive mouth, a head set cleanly on good shoulders and a strong supple figure. Everyone knows how splendid she was in *Hindle Wakes* and I had also made a test of her for a part at Warner's; she only failed to get it because of the very qualities of strength and confidence which made her ideal for Ruth. My mind was made up at once. Not so Joe's. Belle went out to see him, in some sort of ravishing creation, and he shied away like a startled horse, screaming that she was too sophisticated. I soothed him by promising to make tests of her and any other girls he could dig up. This seemed the best scheme to get my own way, as I had no doubt at all about the outcome of the tests.

Eric Berry was unusual. He was tall and dark and his eyes were intolerant. He was not quite tough enough for an islander but he was an actor, that was evident. It was important that Robbie should have charm and intelligence and Berry had both. I could not quite make up my mind about him. I decided it was because I had not yet found Andrew.

I had been worrying for a long time about a man, in

Turn of the Tide, who had shown great promise, in a secondary part. He came from Dublin and his name was Niall MacGinnis. He had done good work in several pictures since then. I went to see Bill O'Bryen, who has an office exactly like the film-agent's office of fiction—the only one I have ever encountered—as difficult to enter as Paradise, panelled in rare woods, carpeted with mink, or something like it, and lined with photographs of Elizabeth Allan, his wife, whom he calls Liz.

He had big plans for MacGinnis, but when he heard a description of the part he sent him along to see me. I was going to dinner with Frankie and we both waited at my flat to meet him. He came in at last, looking earnestly about him, his face half scowl, half shy smile. He looked rather as if he had parked his caravan outside and, as soon as he had seen me, he would be off on the long trail into the sunset, with a hey nonny, nonny and a wind on the heath. An actor like this was unusual. He talked in a liquid Irish voice and was rather given to long, dark stares and Celtic silences. He carefully concealed the fact that he had a sense of humour but he could not hide the poetry in his voice and in his movements. In looks and personality he was a complete contrast to Berry. I decided on them both, at the same instant.

I still had nobody to play pawky, far-seeing James Gray, father of Andrew, and although I saw many people I got no further. George Summers, who was to play the Trawler Skipper, could have done it, but he could only get away from his work for a short time.

Vernon was ready to leave and reported to the studio for orders. Gerry Blattner was in charge of all the organization and Gerry had a map, with a lot of little flags on it. He deployed this before Captain Sewell.

'Here, Vernon,' he said impressively, 'is a map of the area which you and the *Vedra* will cover. This flag is the *Vedra*. Now as soon as you arrive at Lerwick or Scalloway

or Foula, you must telegraph me and then I will move my
flag and then we shall know exactly where you are and
what you are doing.'

'What good will that do you?' asked Vernon reasonably,
but it was evidently the wrong answer. Gerry frowned as
seriously as it is possible for him to frown, which is not
very alarming. He answered:

'This office is the nerve-centre of the production.'

'Oh, I see,' said Vernon, surprised and tactlessly letting
his surprise be rather obvious.

'Unless we know Where You Are,' said Gerry, very
crossly indeed, 'how can we Communicate With You and
Decide What You Are To Do?'

This was unanswerable so Vernon saluted, advanced
three paces, saluted again, shook hands and departed for
Foula with a very undermanned ship, a pessimistic pilot,
two mutinous cameramen, one tolerant electrician, and, of
course, Buddy.

Two nights and a day brought them to Foula in the
dawn, a morning of scorching sun and blue haze over a
still sea. There was not a ripple on the coast of the island,
and the mountains, rising out of thick fog, seemed to float
high in the air like a mirage. Vernon says that Ballantyne
himself could not have pictured anything more like his
Coral Island and he himself would not have been at all
surprised to see a fleet of catamarans come speeding to meet
him, instead of the mail-boat, which brought him in a
grand sweep to the jetty, where a bronzed and bearded
gentleman, whom he identified incredulously as John Seabourne, grasped him by the hand and shook it heartily as
they both exclaimed in unison: 'Dr. Livingstone, I pre-
sume?'

Gerry was not able to record this swift arrival on his map
until the next day, as the radio had yet to be installed on the
Vedra. John and Syd had lined up sixteen men to unload
and build the camp. They reported that after two days'

work with crowbar and hammer, Walter had finally penetrated the two-foot wall of the kitchen and a window was
almost in place. The barn was ready for stores. The Haa
had been cleaned from top to toe by a Women's Battalion,
headed by Maggie Gray o' Dykes ('Up the Grays!'). John
and Syd had just finished the enormous ham imported by
the advance guard and would appreciate a change of diet.

In return Vernon informed them that he had been obliged to log Able Seaman Skeets Kelly and Ordinary Seaman John Behr for mutiny and incitement to mutiny, in
that they did refuse to take a trick at the wheel, saying they
were cameramen and supercargoes, not crew, and did scoff,
sneer and hurl gibes at Horton, who, in defiance of the
Union of Electricians and the Board of Trade, consented
so to do.

In reply to this, Skeets and John Behr told a tale of hard-
ship and privations which their appearance belied and went
on cutting bread and butter—for this conversation took
place over breakfast in the Haa.

All day they unloaded with such speed that Vernon was
able to leave for Walls before sunset, with Alasdair comfortably ensconced in the cross-trees, where Vernon reported
he had spent the greater part of the voyage, criticizing
audibly and subversively the seamanship of all on board.
They made Walls before dark, which was fortunate, for it
is a tricky entrance. In the morning Vernon sent a wire to
Gerry (who pounced upon map and flags) and loaded his
deck with huts, whose huge, flat, projecting sections made
the *Vedra* look like a drunken aeroplane-carrier and caused
all vessels sighting them to give them a wide berth.

By arrangement, the huts were cast overboard opposite
the bay of Ham Little, about 200 yards from the Voe. Here
they could be towed in and dragged up on to the cliffs,
whence they were carried, eight men to a section, round to
the Haa and assembled under the eye of Syd and Walter
Ratter, who was proving a figurative as well as actual

tower of strength. The rest of the huts had been delivered, mysteriously, at Scalloway, so Vernon was off again, collected them, left Alasdair to see to his yacht, and reappeared in record time. The weather continued set-fair and the whole of the *Vedra's* first job was done by that evening. It was a smart piece of work.

Vernon's experience of the two harbours decided him at once that Scalloway was the better one for entering in all weathers and seasons. It was a larger place, too, and although farther from Foula by sea, it was very much nearer to Lerwick than Walls. So Scalloway was decided on as our base.

Smith, the owner of the Shetland ponies, was very anxious that Vernon should take them off his hands, presumably to save him feeding them. For the next two weeks, whenever the *Vedra* was sighted in the Sound, Smith would come charging down to the quay, with Shirley Temple and the Pinto under each arm and a mob of others running behind, and would try to park them in the saloon cabin. Vernon would have none of him and some spirited engagements were fought, I am told, all hands lining the bulwarks to repel boarders.

After the final trip to the island, Vernon took Wullie Gear on board, as pilot in place of Alasdair, and set the *Vedra's* dirty nose for Aberdeen.

At Elstree the last week had arrived, with Joe and myself still locked in combat *re* Chrystall. Kitty Kirwan arrived at the studio and was at once engaged for old Jean, the grandmother. Only Ruth and James Gray were not settled. Finally I had a glorious day of tests in the open air, in a field of blowing grass on the Studio Lot. Everybody was in costume. For the men it was a final test for make-up, accent and clothes. The girls, Belle Chrystall among them, were all candidates for Ruth.

There were eight of them, some very pretty, some pretty and some what are happily described by their agents as

'interesting types'. Belle took one look at her rivals and
nearly ran away, for she is the most modest person alive
and, like most good actresses, hates tests worse than poison-
ivy. But her panic did not stop her from walking away
with the honours of the day; and Joe, who was watching,
handsomely admitted it, even before we saw them on the
screen. The men all showed up well, especially Berry in his
rough, blue jersey. We decided John's hair was too white
and made another test to fix it definitely. The production
crew were all set. Belle started a mad dash to get clothes,
but still there was no James Gray!

I was at my wit's end. I thought he would have to join
us later. Then I got a hurry-call from Picot, rushed to her
office, and there, in the largest chair, beaming all over,
in grey tweeds, grey-hair and glorious suède shoes, sat
Finlay Currie.

'Finlay!' I cried, 'is this true? Would you play this part?
It doesn't carry anything like your money, you know.'

He waved his hand in a lordly manner.

'I hate the stuff, chief,' he said. 'It's the wonderful summer and the wonderful part in a fine film that I'm after. If
I can bring Maud, I'm your man.'

'Maud?'

'My wife. Don't worry. I know there's no room on the
island. She will stay in Lerwick for the present and she will
love it as much as I did, for you know, Michael, I have been
to Foula.'

'You haven't!'

'Aha, that shook you! Thirty years ago in a wee boat. So
you see it's fated. Well?'

'It's a deal; and Finlay, I'm tickled to death to have you.
I never dreamed you would be able to get away.'

'Did you think I would miss a trip like this? Besides this
is the third picture where we've nearly worked together.
We have got to break the spell. When do we leave?'

'The day after to-morrow.'

A Bonny Place is Foula

'Maud and I will be ready,' he said with the calm assurance that only sits on an old trouper of many theatrical seasons and countries. So there was my final difficulty solved.

Belle was having trouble with her clothes, her flat, her maid, her plans, her belongings, her packing, her—I seized her by the hand and tore into West End shops. At first I thought I should find what I wanted at the cheap little places, but we finally got the rough tweed skirts, and shirts, and little Sunday frock at Swan and Edgar's, where they must have thought us mad, for we were in and out like a whirlwind, making snap decisions and talking unintelligible jargon about colour filters and panchromatic film and No. 28 make-up; Jaeger's proved to be a mine of wool jumpers and, as the clock struck one on Saturday, Belle was outfitted. We were to leave next day. She and Frankie were following us on Monday.

I have left Frankie to the last because she was a special piece of casting and my own personal problem. I had to have another girl for the opening sequence of the film on the yacht. She was also essential as a companion for Belle. I had to have someone who was very beautiful, because her part in the film was pure decoration and only justified by that, and also very level-headed and personally attractive. She would have to share rooms with Belle and live with her for five months. That was asking a good deal of two girls who, unless carefully chosen, might hate one another on sight. I was sure of Belle, that was the deciding factor that had made me insist on her; I had to be equally sure of her companion. It does not require a great imagination to picture the havoc that could have been caused by the wrong girl. I saw many beautiful young women who would have been as good company as rattlesnakes among twenty young men; and others who would have had their throats quietly cut by Belle after one week. I thought it over and asked Frankie if she would take the part. With great courage, she accepted.

157

A Bonny Place is Foula

On Sunday evening, the 21st of June, I stepped leisurely out of a taxi on to the pavement outside Euston. Forty seconds later I hurled myself back into it, with my bags on top of me, and drove hell for leather to King's Cross. The making of the film had begun.

PART II

'Iꜰ——': Rudyard Kipling

Chapter IX

THE EDGE OF THE WORLD

★

Every successive edition of my script (there were four) bore a cautious legend: 'This script, although complete in itself, must not be regarded as final.' This was true of the last version as well as the first. It is every producer's pipe-dream that one day he will find a director who will shoot a film word-for-word with the script that has been handed to him. It remains a dream, even in the studio; on an expedition, where an outstanding sequence often results from a freak of nature, or a quick decision by the director, it is a nightmare. However, the main continuity of the film was settled.

Whatever the changes, not one of the bones in my original skeleton was missing in the final construction. When editors, cutters, producers, sound-recorders, composers and critics had done their worst and best, the grim outline of the island itself still dominated the picture. That is how I wanted it.

THE EDGE OF THE WORLD

The Final Story

A hundred miles north-east of the Orkneys lies Ultima Thule—the Last Landfall—the Edge of the World—named and charted by the Roman galleys of Agricola. On modern charts its name is Hirta. Its towering cliffs rise out of the Atlantic, sheer walls a quarter of a mile high. It looks as impregnable as Gibraltar, as remote as the Lost World. But on the east the precipices fall rapidly to a low jagged coast-line, pierced with hundreds of rocky inlets but with no safe harbour. The largest of these inlets is Ham Voe and a little jetty marks a landing-place for boats.

In the long valleys blooms the late spring of the North. Wild iris grows along the burn and a hundred other flowers struggle against the wind. On the scanty pastures tiny lambs gambol round their brown, shaggy mothers.

A cruising yacht discovers the island and drops anchor off the Voe. As the sail rattles down, the Captain's hail echoes over silent crofts. The churchyard is deep with weeds which hide all but a few gravestones. No feet come running in answer to the hail. No voice replies. The island is deserted.

Andrew Gray, the pilot of the yacht, is a man of Hirta. He takes *The North Sea Pilot* from the Captain's hands:

'Your book was right when it was published,' he says, 'but you were wrong just now when you said that little changes on these islands. There is not a living soul now on Hirta.'

'That was the old name for the island?'

'Ay. It means death!'

High above them an eagle sights a quarry. Its great neck stretches, its iron beak snaps and it launches down the wind. The lamb runs panic-stricken, bleating for its mother, who stamps and glares up at the circling death. The report of the Captain's rifle brings an unexpected rescue.

The Captain and his wife explore the island, bringing Andrew with them, a reluctant guide. Voices haunt him. Phantom footsteps follow him. Memories crowd around him of companions and old things gone. He sees his home in ruins. On the Kame stands a crude memorial stone, at the very edge of the precipice. It bears in rough lettering the name of a man: 'Peter Manson' and at the foot two brief words: 'Gone Over.'

'They never liked to talk of death,' says Andrew; ' "he wore away last night," they'd say, or else "went over". Many died that way, hunting for eggs or after the sheep. . . .' He tells his hearers that he is the man who raised the stone to Peter Manson's memory. 'I owed him that,' he says. He looks around slowly towards the slopes of Nether-fandal. 'It's the Sabbath to-day and a fine summer morning. Ten years ago ye'd be seeing all the folk on the way to the kirk, the men in black and the women neat and bonny. Young John Isbister would be standing by the gate and the bell would be ringing. . . .'

Slowly the sound of the church bell fills the valleys. Smoke rises from long-cold chimneys. The fields are full once more of waving barley. A long line of men and women in their Sunday blacks is winding towards the kirk, whose lonely graves are once more clean and neatly kept. The island lives again.

The little church fills, the dogs are tethered outside, every soul on the island is there, except old Granny Manson, who sits outside her distant croft in the sunshine; the verses of the metrical psalms float over the loch, while James Gray, with his tuning-fork, 'reads the line'. Peter Manson next reads the lesson, in a dry tone which criticizes St. Paul's sea-manship. The sermon follows. The dogs drowse. The young people fidget. Even Granny Manson nods. At last the con-gregation comes out into the sunshine and the kirk is locked till next Sabbath.

'A grand sermon, John,' says old James; 'one hour and fifteen minutes! Let them beat that in Edinburgh if they can. And mind ye! every sentence sound theology!'

But although this simple life seems bedded on rock, it is doomed. Nature and civilization are killing it. Trawlers have destroyed the fisheries. There is a vanishing market for the wool. Bad harvests and failure of the peat are forcing the young folk to seek work, to marry and to settle on the mainland. Leader of these is Robbie Manson, just back from his job as engineer on one of the hated trawlers. He brings unrest and tragedy. His arguments for leaving the island distress his sister Ruth, and rouse Andrew Gray to anger:

'Man, you've gone over to the other side!'

'Until I went away I said the same as you. But the world's changed, it's bigger, easier to get at. In the old days we were no worse off than anyone else but now we're living in an old world. I've got a turn for machinery, I can do things with it, why should I give that up? What can we hope for, Polly and I, if I drag her back here, like a dutiful son? And because I make you see what's under your nose, you don't like it!'

'That's fair enough,' agrees Andrew slowly.

'I knew you'd see it.'

'But I don't go all the way with you. "One man's meat", you know.'

'It's easy enough for you to be contented. You're the strongest man on the island. You're going to marry Ruth. A king couldn't want more.'

'True enough. I've every reason to stay where I am.'

'But it's not much good being a king without a kingdom. There's enough of them knocking about already!'

Robbie's clever arguments confuse Andrew and their discussion ends in a violent quarrel and a challenge from Robbie to decide the argument in the old way, by a race up the cliff of Wester Hoevdi, the winner to have the way of it. At Parliament next day, by the boats, the Elders at first forbid it, but are soon quarrelling as fiercely as their sons. They launch the boats. Ruth tries in vain to stop them. She watches the race, with the other women, from the cliffs. Granny Manson waits by her croft. All she can see are the cloud-shadows racing over Hoevdi. After an exciting struggle Andrew wins the race. Robbie, in an effort to beat him, takes a dangerous road up the waterfall, gets out on the lip, unable to move forward or back, and, within a foot of Andrew's hand, falls to his death. Knowledge of his death comes to the old lady. She rises to her feet, then falls dead of a stroke.

Peter and Ruth, in their Sabbath blacks, visit each croft, bidding the islanders to the funeral. Against black clouds and falling rain the coffin is carried on three oars to the kirk. The women wail in the houses. Ruth watches from the hill. Across the new grave Peter stares at Andrew in bitter enmity, while James grieves for them both.

The summer passes and the Laird pays his annual visit. The sheep are run down from the hills into the stone pens. Their wool is plucked and weighed. Over the tallying of the tweed and shawls the Laird learns of the feud, but there is no reasoning with Peter. After a tragic love-scene with Ruth, Andrew leaves the island, to find work with the fishing-fleet.

Autumn brings yet another poor harvest. James and John Isbister shake their heads. The peat is giving out. Someone will have to drive sense into Peter. Alone on the cliffs Ruth faces suicide, for she is going to bear Andrew a child. She makes a desperate attempt to send him word by 'letter-boat', but a wayward current brings it back to the island, where Peter finds it and learns the truth. She faces him, expecting his anger, but, instead, he takes her in his arms and they comfort each other.

The child is born early in the spring, before the letters can be sent out, so Peter and James launch a whole fleet of 'letter-boats', with a message of recall for Andrew. One of them is picked up by the trawler on which Robbie was once engineer. The skipper puts into Lerwick and meets Andrew looking for a job. Andrew is at first suspicious, but the skipper wins him round and he begins to see that even trawlermen have to make their living and are none so bad. He ships with them and the skipper promises they shall put into Hirta if they get the chance.

The Edge of the World

A gale blows up from the south-east and in three days is
blowing at a hundred miles an hour. The trawler puts in
for shelter under Hirta, where Ruth's baby has fallen sick
of diphtheria. There is no way of getting it to a doctor, no
wireless to send for help. The trawler puts off a boat and
Andrew arrives in the nick of time. Baby and mother are
rushed to the mainland, where a doctor meets them in a
motor-boat and performs a successful operation in the
cabin of the trawler.

'I've got you both safe, now,' swears Andrew, 'and
you're not going back!'

Peter's knotted hand slowly signs his name to a petition:

To the Laird of Hirta.

We, the crofters of Hirta, petition you to help us in the
evacuation of the Island where life as our fathers knew it is
no longer possible. We also ask you to obtain us a grant of
land from the Government and a steamer to take our
families and our belongings to the Mainland.

(Signed) PETER MANSON

Parliament has met for the last time. Peter puts down the
pen and walks stiffly away, leaving one man after another
to sign away his ancient liberty. Visions of the past cross
Peter's mind; he remembers days on 'the banks', the sheep-
running, his mother's face . . . his son. Then, as the year
closes and autumn fogs roll down over the island, comes
the uprooting of a people from their homes. The three
Elders, James, John and Peter, oversee the Evacuation with
grim thoroughness:

'They'll all be on by noon,' says James.

Peter sighs. 'Ay.'

'What are we going to do about the cats?'

John answers heavily:

'We'll just have to leave them. They'll make a living on
the cliffs. It's the dogs I'm worried about.'

The Edge of the World

Peter looks at his own dog, at his feet. His face sets, if it were possible, in harder lines. He says abruptly:

'They're no good as sheep-dogs, and who's to pay for taking them?'

'Ay, and there's the licences, ye know,' adds James, Postmaster to the last.

'They'd better be drowned!'

John is moved to protest; he is the youngest:

'But maybe somebody on the mainland might buy them.'

Peter's voice roughens. It is not cruelty but a savage resignation to the facts that makes him answer:

'Are you willing to risk that out of your own pocket, for I'm not?'

He turns to James, no longer able to stand by and watch the long lines of men and beasts, stumbling down the quay and over the gangplank, to hear the bleat of terrified sheep being ferried across and the stamp and whinny of puzzled ponies.

'James, man,' he says, 'I'll away up the Kame. One of they daft collectors offered me five pounds for a guillemot's egg I told him of. I know just where it is.'

With his stave and his old rope he goes on up the cliffs and the only eye to see him go is his dog's, who follows far behind. Up past his own croft he strides, up past the last gate, up on to the moor and the great cliffs. With his stave and his rope, he goes over. His rope is frayed; he does not seem to see it. Down and down he goes while his dog peers after him and whines anxiously. He finds the rare egg, but he never brings it back to the upper air. James, hunting in the mist, calls his friend's name. The dog barks and barks. A dull rumble from the cliffs and a broken end of rope are the last of Peter Manson.

The sailor from the yacht, Andrew Gray, stands once more by the stone he raised on the edge of the cliff. His listeners follow his gaze as it sweeps over the sunlit slopes of the island, where only the cry of gulls and the calls of wild sheep are heard. Another hardy, independent people has been forced back from the outposts into the towns.

Chapter X

IF YOU CAN SEE IT AND HEAR IT

*

If the secret of art is compression, then America is a nation of artists. If brevity is the soul of wit, then its spiritual home is New York. My friend, Jerry Jackson, is New Yorker, born and bred. His heart is in the English countryside and he drinks claret; but his voice and his wit remain Manhattan.

During our friendship I have often heard him condense a folio of experience into one wise-cracking line. A sample came zipping over the rail of the *Berengaria* one Christmas, when he was leaving for New York. I was loafing at the time, so had been mobilized to help Vernon make a Grand Guignol film in a little studio which he had off Knightsbridge. It was in a cellar. Vernon's idea was to build most of his sets in scale-model. These were ingeniously joined on to 'flats', against which the actors did their stuff (big actor —big flat; small actor—small flat), by this means giving the effect of a scene in a large room for about two and sixpence. This seemed to Jerry and me to allow an unusual margin of error, so we put some money into it. Not much money. About the equivalent of a million dollar investment to Louis B. Mayer.

As the great liner got under way, Jerry had a last moment of panic at leaving us to our own devices. He made a trumpet of his hands (unnecessarily, for Jerry has a voice which can penetrate teak) and bawled menacingly: 'Remember! If you can see it and hear it, Take One is O.K.!'

This snappy remark reduces the art of film production

to its simplest terms. It was certainly pertinent to our first rushes, because you could neither see nor hear them. The sound crew were not yet familiar with their portable apparatus and fifty per cent of the sound was fogged by light penetration. The other half was pretty terrible, with too much background and not enough top. All the actors had voices in their boots. Then, when we went on the trawler, the sound crew had got out of our way into the hold. They had no more fogging but they were sitting on a few tons of ice for packing fish, for the skipper was off on a cruise to the Faeröes as soon as his ship was free. The cold caused static.

The camera trouble was more complicated.

Ernest Palmer was Rock's chief cameraman; he was an old friend of mine; but he was not available, working at Shepperton on another job. All the studios were as busy as a dog with fleas. The only men available were good, free-lance men, but not what I was looking for. I wanted a genius. Finally I tried to get a Frenchman, with whom I had worked in France. Joe was agreeable but the Home Office turned their thumbs down on it because there were Englishmen disengaged. The Home Office think a camera-man is a man who has a camera. Their refusal cost us a lot of money and nearly cost us the picture.

I have a weakness—only I think it is a strong point; I believe in giving young men a chance. All that our photo-graphers in England need is training and after seven years of good production there is some splendid new material: men like Arthur Crabtree, Roy Kellino, Bernard Knowles, Cyril Bristow, Ronnie Neame, all of whom I had seen come up from assistants. Some of them I had given their first solo job. They were all working, so I cast around. I remembered a quiet, cynical, young Jew, called Monty Berman. I had first met him as camera operator to Palmer at Twickenham, on a film with Ian Hunter and Claire Luce. We met again at Warner's, where he was an assistant.

If you can See it and Hear it

He was a good operator and a good assistant. I never saw him make a mistake. Then he went down to Southend for me on a Bank Holiday, to get scenes for a sequence in *Some Day*, with Esmond Knight and Margaret Lockwood. It was not an easy assignment. I wanted crowds, night shots and day. I wanted the cold dawn breaking over the grey sands and a sticky tide washing slowly in. I wanted distant shots of tired holiday-makers dragging home. Monty stayed down there the clock round and he brought back everything I had imagined, better than I had imagined, composed and shot and exposed like a master. He accepted my praise in silence but his little, pale face had a tinge of colour. He went on being an assistant and doing odd shots.

On the strength of this record I decided to give Monty his chance. Warner's thought I must be crazy but agreed to loan him, first putting him under contract. Ernie Palmer, who of course knew Monty well, was enthusiastic and endorsed my choice, and promised to send us private reports and advice on the rushes.

Monty is a genius. Certain sequences in the picture bear the same unmistakable stamp of quality that was in those shots of Southend—an imagination, a pearly texture, a sort of luminous, almost spiritual quality that seems to be imprisoned in the negative as sunshine is imprisoned in the warm red bricks of an old wall. But that was later, and was his swan-song. His first rushes were bad as they could be. He tried to do too much and overreached himself, instead of staying inside his own experience. I do not blame him for aiming higher than he could attain because that happens to every man, sooner or later; but it cost Joe a lot of money and me a lot of time, and opportunities which could never be repeated.

For those interested in technical matters I will explain where he tumbled.

Monty was a fanatical admirer of American technical efficiency and in particular of the negative quality of famous cameramen like Charles Lang, Victor Milner, Ray June and Joseph Walker. He wanted to get quality in his first picture like theirs, otherwise it might as well be a newsreel, as far as he was concerned. He had nothing startling in the way of lenses on the Mitchell camera. They were just a set of good quality German lenses. Now to get depth and definition in any shot, the lens must be stopped down; but, in doing so, the finer quality is lost. So Monty decided to shoot wide open and control his exposure by opening or closing the shutter, a method of working which is possible on studio work, but on the average exterior shot is impossible; it brings up grain, it throws everything but the immediate foreground out of focus, and it gives no latitude for the action. When, in addition to this, Monty placed gauzes or diffusing disks in front of the lens, the result was awful. Monty got away with certain close-ups, but long-shots were a mess, except when the surface of the sea held enough brilliance to show up detail.

They saw the rushes at the studio, but Ernie was away and nobody knew enough to put their finger on the trouble. They merely sent them on to me with rather disturbed comments. Our plan was to see rushes in the cinema at Lerwick, coming over in the *Vedra* each week-end, but I soon had a projector installed on the island and after some trial and error we were able to give quite a good show in the mess-hut. For the first six weeks there was only the Lerwick cinema. The screen was rather old, which did not help prints which had been made for the brilliantly lit screen at the studio. At our first show, the only persons present were Vernon, myself, the manager and a number of bored rats. My feelings on seeing a sparkling view of Lerwick harbour, which had taken two hours to make, dimly appear through a yellow haze, were unpleasant.

We held a post-mortem and got near the root of the trouble; but the distance from the studio, doubtful projection arrangements, and lapse of time before the next batch could be seen, played havoc. Finally Joe got really alarmed and sent Ernie, who was now free, to take over. We were both sorry for Monty, who had hit his stride; his last work was as fine as anything I have seen. He went home and half the summer was gone and days of retakes had to be allotted.

This constant worry about our photographic quality was a sultry background to the first six weeks. Hand in hand with it were the discomfort of settling in, establishing routines, and getting to know one another's limits, always a prickly business. I regard the Walls Regatta, fiasco though it was as a social outing, as the end of my fumbling and the start of real creation. Looking back upon those times, six weeks does not seem an extraordinary period in which to get confidence, efficiency and twenty-five people working as one; but, at the time, it seemed to go on for ever, like a swamp in a nightmare, and Joe has told me since that he was on the brink of calling off the whole expedition. I can understand his feelings, but he will not know mine, nor realize half of the problems involved, until he reads this book. (Are you reading?)

Other casualties of the Pioneer Period were an appendix —John Behr's; and a collar bone—John Laurie's. The appendix developed suddenly, just before the regatta, in the week of Ernie's arrival. Reports from John Laurie about the dullness of life in Lerwick Hospital had already filtered through and Behr was determined to head for home. He had a hard time escaping from the eager young surgeon but he caught the plane, went straight through to London under will power, and was operated upon as soon as he arrived. He was just in time. The Studio sent us the Professor as a substitute; he took Monty's place in Hut One, Ernie moved into Behr's bed in Hut Two and life went on.

John Laurie had a bad time. He was full of enthusiasm from the start, energetic, quick, friendly, he was popular at once with everyone. He hurled himself into his part. He was growing short side-whiskers. We measured them every day. He tried half a dozen make-ups and costumes. He and Finlay Currie rehearsed their own scenes and coached the others, until MacGinnis, Eric and Belle could go through a long scene without their Scottish tutors wincing at every second word. The accident happened the day before we were to start Laurie's first scenes. He was out with Seabourne and myself, on a walk to the Sneug. We were all in great spirits, though it was a grey day. John tried a tricky jump. To my horror his foot caught in the stone dyke and he went over crash on his shoulder, not in the peat but on the hard road. We had him up in a second, and his shirt off. He said nothing and never made a sound but he looked at the mess of his thin, brown shoulder and looked at us. We started back slowly towards the Haa while Seabourne ran for the stretcher. The *Vedra* was in Scalloway but the weather was calm and the tide high enough to launch the mail-boat. There was an hour to wait while the crew was summoned. We could do nothing for him but rough first-aid. Bill Osborne knew a little and Niall a good deal. It was hurting abominably but all John would do was to curse himself for an idiot. He was a hero.

We slid the stretcher into the bottom of the boat and Syd fixed it there with a brace each side. George went with him; and the last we saw of John for a month was a grimly smiling figure on his back, vanishing towards a distant blue line of land across a calm sea. It was rather sobering.

The last name on our Roll of Honour was the saddest blow of all, coming as it did, in the thick of the final struggle, on John Seabourne. John, the oldest inhabitant of Rock City; John, the best-loved ambassador that ever made ten words do the work of one; John, my right and left hand, tireless aide, fantastic and gorgeous story-teller; I missed him every hour and Hut Three was inconsolable.

At first he seemed a new man; his strength came back with his appetite, his bronzed face and his Viking beard were always in the van. At informal sports he carried off a

174

string of prizes. Then, by the burn one day, he strained himself getting water for the funeral scene; the old trouble started. He fought and he lied. Only Finlay, his staunch friend and bunk-mate, knew how bad he was; and he was sworn not to tell me. Every move must have been agony. I knew he was ill but, in the whirl of battle, I am ashamed to say I neglected him. At last he told me that he must go home and because I knew John well, I was terribly alarmed, for only desperation would have made him admit it. He left and a piece of my heart went with him and my shoulders ached with a sudden burden.

The endless journey nearly killed him and for a very long time he was near death. Recovery was slow and has left its mark. He is the same splendid companion now that he ever was, but his face is pale and his hair is greyer. Yet I do not think he regrets anything. He knows that there is one more place where he is known and loved, where they talk of him daily and write to him every mail-day, talking of the time when the film company was on Foula.

I know what I myself owe to him and in this book I have tried to repay a little of my debt.

Yet, in spite of illness and Acts of God, in spite of hysteria, individual and collective, in spite of triumphs and disasters, loyalty and treachery (or perhaps because of them), my picture was finished. At the eleventh hour? More like 11.59! Suspense was stretched out thin. It was incredible, a melodramatic farce, a comic tragedy. It was living at sixty seconds to the minute, sixty-one minutes to the hour, twenty-five hours to the day. I shall try and do justice to that climax when the time comes.

We arrived in Lerwick before midnight on Tuesday after a grimy passage. I have described our departure through the fog at Aberdeen. None of us slept much that night, Vernon, White and Mac, not at all. But the swell went down as we left Duncansby Head behind us and a brilliant sunrise dispersed the fog and all memory of the night's hardships. It became very hot. We sunbathed and made up for lost sleep. All day we thumped along, at a good ten knots, through the shallow sea over which I had flown two weeks before. It was calm as a lake and the greasiest efforts of the galley failed to spoil our appetites. Certainly, the *Vedra* still rolled, but in a friendly, beery manner.

About midday we sighted the plane from Aberdeen, carrying Frankie and Belle to Sumburgh Head. They were probably on the look-out for a dazzling white turbine-yacht, cutting through the water like a destroyer, with the unit, in spotless ducks, playing shuffleboard. They cut the *Vedra* dead.

Towards eight o'clock in the evening the hot sun betrayed us and brought up a sea-fog as thick as any of the previous night. Once more the engines were slowed to half speed. Once more we groped our way, blind and bellowing. There were signs of panic when everybody realized this might mean another night's 'sleep' on the *Vedra*. But Vernon's navigation stood the test; towards ten we sighted Bressay Light and heard its warning fog signal. We left it to starboard and entered Bressay Sound.

The North Sea Pilot says cheerfully: 'Lerwick harbour has a channel of approach from either end of Bressay Sound. The fairway of the southern approach is deep and clear of dangers, and the land in the vicinity is of a well-marked character, so that by this approach Lerwick is the most accessible harbour of refuge in the Shetland Isles.'

Except in thick fog. The coast is very broken and I have been told that many vessels have anchored in Brei Wick, south-west of the Nabb, under the impression that it was the main channel. However, Vernon avoided this trap. None of us, least of all Wullie Gear, our accredited pilot,

I

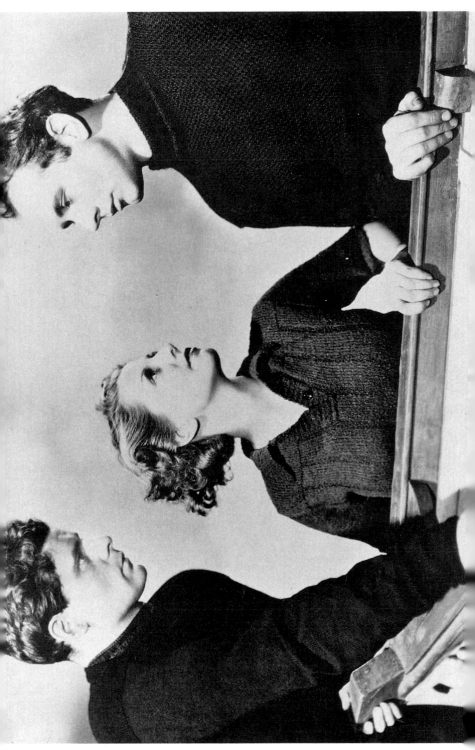

was familiar with the harbour. We crawled in at slow speed. We passed the Nabb, a wild and rocky headland which was one day to save me from defeat, and peeped coyly round Twageos Point. So far we had done creditably but, having accomplished so much, we could not discover where the town lay. There were lights all round us, except where the coast of Bressay loomed dark upon our right. Vernon was anxious to locate the light on Victoria Pier, but the fog was too thick. The proper action was to anchor until morning but not with a party of starved and mutinous gentlemen adventurers, whose beer, generously provided by Mac, had given out. We slunk onwards doubtfully, the town receding behind us, until it was obvious we had over-shot our mark. An unlighted concrete beacon lay dead ahead. We passed with dignity around its north side, while on nearby ships strong men grasped their rails, bit their pipes in two and waited for the crash, for we were passing over Loofa Baa shoal, whose shallowest part has a depth of only one foot. Since the *Vedra* draws nine feet their pessi-mism was justified. However, she fooled them all; we swung around on our course, missed a coal hulk anchored in the channel, hailed it, got our bearings and some tersely expressed advice, edged into North Harbour and let go the anchor in twenty feet of dirty water, just off a fish-curing station, about a quarter of a mile from the hotel, among a crowded and inquisitive mass of shipping. We heard later that the drifter fleet never got in at all that night. 'Where ignorance. . . .'

Frankie and Belle had arrived safely and gone to bed. John had braved a return passage in the mail-boat from Foula and reported for duty. All the huts, except the big mess-hut, were in place before he left. Syd was working like a cherubic beaver; and the whole island was agog.

'There's no other word,' John assured me solemnly,

'agog! From the North End to the Hametoun they are all
waiting with their tongues hanging out for our arrival.
Nobody ever saw the men work so fast in their lives. Why,
the other day Tom o' Gravins broke into a *run*! Their
women come down and watch, all knitting furiously at
socks and shawls for the unit. Do you realize that hardly
any of the young men could afford to buy a packet of
cigarettes before we came? Do you know why people live
to such a great age on Foula and why they take such care
of them? A simple life and kind hearts, of course. But don't
forget that every old man and woman draws the Old Age
Pension. Sometimes that's all the income a family has got.
China venerates their ancestors. Foula keeps them alive.'

'You seem to have learnt a lot.'

'I have.'

'Were you lonely, Crusoe?'

'Until I was out of quarantine.'

'What d'you mean?'

'They are afraid of catching colds. They say that strangers always bring them.'

'They had the same belief on St. Kilda. They called it
"the boat-cold".'

'Every croft I came to, the door would open a crack and
a voice would say: "Hae ye a cold?" When they were
convinced I hadn't, they became as friendly as you please.
And this Jonah said we should have trouble!'

The Jonah referred to was Alasdair, who was staying in
Lerwick, while Moore put the engine in the yacht. He gave
a grin and a shrug and muttered something to the effect
that it was early days yet and poured himself another cup
of our tea.

I think the explanation of this island fear of the 'boat-
cold' is that they lead a very hardy, frugal life, with very
little meat and fresh vegetables, their chief diet being, in
fact, bread and tea. They are not exposed to a constant
bombardment of fumes and microbes, like the lucky dwel-

lers in towns. A stranger, landing on Foula, would obviously be swarming with germs until the gales of Foula had been given a chance to blow them away; I refuse to believe any germ could hang on for long against that prevailing westerly wind.

Skeets and John Behr were sophisticated old inhabitants of the town. They had been lionized and interviewed until their chests stuck out like pouter pigeons. I heard them promising Monty and Karl to show them the town.

'Breakfast at seven-thirty,' I said. 'Start shooting at eight. MacGinnis looking for a job amongst the drifters. Sound, if Tregellas can be ready in time. If not, we'll use the silent camera. George Summers to stand by in costume. Don't shave, George—nor you, Mac! Here's your revised script, John. Is everyone fixed for rooms?'

'Here and at the Grand.'

'You and George will fix them up, then. Good night, everyone!'

I went to bed with my script. John and I were sharing a room at the top of the house. I looked out of the window and the fog was being torn to shreds by a light easterly breeze. The stars were showing and it looked like fine clear weather in the morning. I was asleep by the time John came to bed. My last conscious thought was that in the morning Frankie would be there. I had not seen her for four days.

The sirens of a hundred drifters, racing in with their catch, woke me up and brilliant sunshine dragged me out of bed. We got off to a flying start and the first shot was in the can by eight forty-five. Our trawler, the *Golden Beam*, was moored alongside Victoria Pier. The north-east wind beat down the smoke of the fleet across the town and covered everything with a layer of grit. After three shots of Mac looking for work, talking to various skippers, picking his way along the crowded jetty, I gave up and moved out to the end of the pier which was free from smoke. The sound was ready by then and we made the scene where

Andrew meets the Trawler Skipper and finally goes off with him. It was a tricky shot, involving dialogue and a panoramic shot right round the crowded harbour. The fishermen played up splendidly; we got two good takes and moved in to cover the dialogue scene in a close-up. I had a breathing-space, looked round and saw Frankie watching us. She was dressed in white; and every man on the pier was looking at her. She was quite unconscious of them. She waved to me.

It suddenly hit me, at that exact moment, what I had done. She no longer belonged to me, she belonged to the expedition. It had been entirely my idea. Never, since we met, had she expressed the slightest wish to come and see me at a film-studio. She liked films but thought that the people who made them were boring; they talked nothing but shop. Being Irish she considered food, drink, clothes, gambling, and having to work for a living were the only serious subjects. It was this sane outlook which had been her recommendation for the expedition.

I have always failed to understand a film director or stage producer, who uses his position to give a friend a job. This case was different; there was no necessity for the girl in the prologue to act but she must photograph. Also I must know her well; either through work or as a personal friend. Frankie fulfilled all the conditions. Everything pointed to her as the ideal girl for the part.

So I had promised myself one thing. Not a soul in the unit (except John Seabourne and Vernon, and of course Joe, who approved), not a soul should know that we were engaged or anything more to each other than director and actress. Only I myself could weigh all the reasons why Frankie had to play the part; I was not going to explain them. During production of the film I would treat her exactly as I treated any other member of the company.

The experienced onlooker will smile at this ruthless decision and indeed at the whole situation, for he knows very well what will happen. I know it myself, now. In my anxiety to be impersonal I leant too far backward, over-balanced and was rude. Accustomed to monopolizing all Frankie's attention when I was with her, I could not adapt myself to seeing her made much of by others, while I had to take a back seat. She was an immediate success with the entire unit. As for herself and Belle, they were soon inseparable. Frankie adopted Belle, who is consistently untidy. Frankie managed her clothes, dressed her hair and made her cocoa. Belle repaid her with loyalty and devotion.

My sensitiveness about the situation also betrayed me when we came to do scenes together. (I forgot to mention that I had decided to play the part of the yachtsman myself; partly to save money, partly because the right kind of actor to play such a colourless but ornamental part would be a bore to have around. I knew I could give it just the right impersonal touch, which would build the prologue around the more interesting figure of Andrew, the sailor.) I naturally did not expect Frankie to be a celluloid Bernhardt but I wanted her to be efficient. She was nervous, which I did not guess, and tried to hide it under a cloak of flippancy. Since I was already self-conscious and took my business very seriously, this did not go down very well and there were several incidents. Of course I knew how to make the best of her performance by cutting and a use of close-ups. I had no fear of the outcome, but, for the first time since I was a director, I was in a false position and it played havoc with my nerves—and Frankie's. We drifted further and further apart, gradually losing all sympathy, and sense of humour. On my side this was coupled with the nervous strain of the production, the universal conviction that we should fail and my lonely determination that we should not. I would not care to part with the experience I gained but I would not wish to suffer again as I did in the last stormy days of September and October.

But until the first day of production, on Victoria Pier in

Lerwick, I had no foreboding of this until I looked up and saw Frankie wave to me. I have said before that I lay no claim to second sight, but insight is another matter. In that second I saw the future. I stared frowning, without answering her wave, and I saw her smile die away and her face change. I was called by Skeets to the camera to okay the set-up. When I looked again, she was gone.

As we worked on, I tried to make up my mind to persuade her to return to London, but in my heart I knew I could not do it.

There was an awful catch-phrase, which MacGinnis made the rage of the camp: 'It's the way things break sometimes—and you gotta play the cards the way they fall!' (Said in the sentimental twangy whisper of any American star's big moment of introspection and sacrifice.)

That guy knew something!

I have gone into this personal relationship at some length because, although I shall not refer to it again except as incidental to my narrative, it must be imagined as the leit-motif, through all the stormy orchestrations that follow.

Chapter XI

THE HAAREM AND THE HUTS

★

The *Golden Beam* was costing us twenty pounds a day and we had a lot of dangerous scenes to stage with motor-boats. Charley, the skipper, was ready for anything, and so was Mr. Duffin, her owner, who had come along for the ride, but a trawler takes as long to turn around as an elephant. We worked away, from early morning until sunset, in Scalloway Sound and whenever the owners of the motor-boats sensibly refused to risk their lives Vernon was summoned, would screw in his eyeglass, commandeer the boats, embark John Seabourne as supercargo and deliver the goods, while the owner sat praying in the bilges. On one of Vernon's absences Mr. Smith finally succeeded in stowing his Shetland ponies away on board the *Vedra*. Vernon, once there was no help for it, rose to the occasion and built a double row of stalls on the deck which would have done credit to an Argentine cattle-boat. As usual, mysterious people appeared to help him: a large silent man, who volunteered to come for the fun of it, picked up ponies bodily in his arms and tossed them all over the scenery. He turned out to be the captain of a big liner on his holiday. Another tower of strength was Vet (I never found out his real name), a cheerful young man who as veterinary officer for Walls and Sandness wanted to visit Foula on his rounds; also present was Vet's fiancée (I never found out her real name either) who stood sturdily by his side, roll the *Vedra* never so horribly. They all steamed

Foula-bound past us, as we were shooting close-ups of Belle, so we cheered them heartily and the ponies, too.

Gerry Blattner came up at the end of a week, full of executive zeal. He decided to transport to Foula all the people who were not yet working and were living in Lerwick on the company's hospitality. They were given an hour to pack their things and the first I knew of it was seeing Alasdair's yacht pass within a hundred feet of us as we were setting up the camera in Scalloway harbour. She was loaded with as many people as the *Mayflower*; they all looked gaily out to sea and never saw us staring. They were not so cheerful by the time they arrived. They had a far worse trip than our first to Foula; the engine was very slow, because Alasdair would fiddle proudly with it, there was no wind and they all got very cold and cross. Nobody was expecting them on the island. The camp was finished and Mrs. Rutherford and Buddy were busy preparing it, but not for an avalanche of unexpected, tired, cold and hungry people. Altogether it did much to spoil the happy atmosphere I had been at pains to create.

The last shot of the trawler was made and she steamed for Iceland and the Faeröes, minus the allegiance of her cook and engineer who had promised to enter our service as soon as they signed off at their home port of Aberdeen. For we had no official cook as yet for the camp and had fed in the trawler on epic stews and cosmic doughnuts. Vernon wanted the engineer, for Chief on the *Vedra*. The weather continued perfect. Now that the trawler was done with I wanted the opening sequence between Andrew and the Trawler Skipper, on the quay at Lerwick.

I had planned it for the evening when the drifters have all gone out, the tide is low, the gulls have gone to bed and there is nothing but rows and rows of waiting barrels and an air of expectancy for the morning. Andrew leans on a pile of barrels and stares gloomily at the water. He is evidently out of a berth. It is the first time we have seen him since he left the island so defiantly. He already looks as if the anxieties of the mainland have gripped him. The Trawler Skipper strolls up, neatly dressed, thick-set, a battered old felt hat jammed on his ears.

SKIPPER: Looks empty of an evening.

ANDREW: (grunts assent).

SKIPPER: (eyes him appraisingly). You'll not see the water for drifters by the morning. Looking for work?

ANDREW (cautiously): I might be.

SKIPPER: I need a hand.

ANDREW: Ye do?

SKIPPER: Ay. Two pound a week and share.

ANDREW (buttons coat): Where's your boat, Skipper?

SKIPPER: Over yonder, by Victoria Pier.

ANDREW: (looks and his face falls. He stands irresolute).

SKIPPER: Well, do you want the job?

ANDREW (with a burst): Not on a damn trawler!

SKIPPER: Particular are ye, lad?

ANDREW: Whom I work for.

SKIPPER: Well, then, I'll no' keep you.

He walks off quite unperturbed and after a glare Andrew swaggers off to the quay wall. But most of the swagger is gone from his figure as he leans on the wall and sets himself to wait until morning.

George Summers acted as if he had been in pictures all his life and Mac was splendid. The sequence finished next day when, after Andrew has looked in vain for a berth, he again meets the Skipper, who tells him about Robbie Manson, and about the 'letter-boat' the trawler has picked up.

Nothing further remained to be done on Mainland. Gerry returned from Foula in the *Vedra* and reported that everyone was settling in nicely. On 1st July the last man and the last piece of equipment came on board. Piles of fresh bread were in the saloon. Joints of fresh meat were in the refrigerator. Rows of fresh faces grinned on the decks.

The space between our rail and the quay widened. Except for two brief and unpleasant visits, it was the last I saw of Mainland for sixteen weeks.

I decreed that the first day spent on the island by our united company should be devoted to home comforts. I knew that the first sight of the camp, the Haa, the island, the huts, the camp-beds, the grim washstands and the still grimmer row of sanitary closets would be a bit of a shock to people straight from towns and hotels. I also knew that in a week's time they would have forgotten their first impressions and would have accepted the camp as a home from home. It can be seen why Gerry's kidnapping stunt had so annoyed me. Fortunately he had pleasant people to deal with and, after their first grumble, they had all turned to and unpacked stores, scrubbed floors and cleaned windows. But I arrived to find the first of many burning Public Questions in full blaze. This was the Great Closet (Ladies First) War.

With apologies to John Fothergill and, of course, Chic Sale, who have made the Closet in Literature their special subject, I must devote some space to this, the first of the sweeping reforms promulgated by the Lady Members of Rock City Parliament.

Before I left Elstree, Gerry Blattner called me into his office, where George Black was already standing, looking stuffed with responsibility. I sympathized with his constipated look, for I saw that he had been receiving the full impact of the Blattner personality for about two hours and was so full of injunctions, secret orders, inter-staff memoranda and payment vouchers that he hardly knew whether he was going to Foula or coming.

'Micky,' said Gerry impressively, 'I am Worried.'

'I'm sorry to hear that, Gerry.'

'You and Seabourne will have so much to do that I think that all Management of the Camp and in fact of the Expedition Proper should definitely be under my Authority, that

is to say through George Black, as my Representative.'
(Gerry always says 'definitely', for emphasis, and always
talks in capitals. I think he is secretly saying to himself:
'After all, Napoleon was a Small Man, too!')

I said: 'Of course. Just as you say, Gerry.'

He said, not concealing his surprise very well:

'Then you consider it a good idea?'

I said: 'If it will make things easier for you and George.'

They both looked very doubtful. Gerry fights rather shy
of me as a rule and he could not understand why I was so
willing to have the administrative authority of the camp
handed to another. The plain truth was, of course, that I
knew you can delegate authority, on paper, to any man
you choose but you cannot endow him with the authority
which another man has. Gerry could delegate and George
could administrate as much as they liked, so long as they took
details off my shoulders; but if there was a difference of
opinion how a thing should be done, it would be done my
way. Let George wear a crown, if he wanted to; I could
always play Baldwin to his Edward.

I made this clear on the first night in camp and it stayed
clear, right through to the last night, when it was put to a
very severe test. After our first dinner (a very good one,
which Mrs. Rutherford conjured up with her own fair
hands) I asked the ladies to come from their sitting-room
at the Haa and made the following speech to the full
strength of the company, including Maggie Gray o' Dykes
and Jessie Henry o' North Biggins, who had signed on as
domestic staff.

I said:

'This is no ordinary film that we are going to make and
we are no ordinary film company. Every one of you is
doing several jobs. Every one of you is here because you
were picked as the best person for your job. Every one is as
important as any other to the success of our picture. I have
worked with nearly all of you before. This is not like a

studio, nor like a studio picture, in the very least. We have all got to live together as well as work together and the ordinary rules do not apply.'

I paused and I saw several eyes flicker towards a type-written sheet which hung on the notice-board. It was signed by G. Blattner, Studio Manager, and it vested all authority, spiritual and temporal, of the camp, in George Black, who would be aided and advised by Mr. Alasdair Holbourn, representing the Owners of the Island.

I did not look at it nor refer to it.

I looked down the long room. The four tables were placed end to end, so that I sat at the head of one immense narrow table, covered with oilcloth. Facing me at the bottom sat John Seabourne. Our canvas chairs had been roughly pushed back after the meal; some men leaned against the wall after surrendering their chairs to the ladies. I saw Syd's earnest face, John Laurie's sardonic one; Skeets gloomily fiddling with a piece of bread, Finlay leaning forward to catch every word, Belle watching me with very bright eyes, Frankie listening with no expression at all, Bill Osborne looking efficient, Buddy sucking his pipe, Bill Sweeny looking thoughtful, Bill Martin, like a wiry, dark terrier, whispering to Len, who listened like a smooth, smiling tomcat. . . .

I said:

'I have already had complaints, which have reached me through the heads of the respective departments.' (A self-conscious look passed across the faces of Monty and Bill Sweeny.) 'That sort of thing may be all right back at the studio but it won't work here. There will be a thousand things to complain about, from now until we leave, so don't let us waste time. All of you have an equal right to complain but you haven't all got a right to give orders. I propose that after dinner every night we hold a meeting, like this one—a parliament, with everyone present. First, to hear the Call for the next day and discuss the preparations needed. Second, to hear any complaints and discuss their remedies, said discussion to be open to all.'

'Even to humble assistant cameramen?' asked John Behr impertinently.

'Even to that lowest form of human life,' I assured him.

Belle was bouncing up and down.

'Mr. Chairman,' she cried, 'do Women have a Vote?'

'Safe enough, there are only two of you—I beg your pardon, Mrs. Rutherford—three.'

'Then we want to—we want—Frankie, you tell him.'

Frankie is one of a family of seven brothers and sisters and consequently looks upon the everyday problems of life with an untroubled eye.

'We want a lavatory,' she stated concisely.

Syd, George and I stared outraged. Some person unidentified muttered 'Hear! Hear! Shame!'

'But you've got one,' I protested.

'A beautiful one,' added Syd, aggrieved.

'We agree that it is beautiful, Syd,' replied Frankie composedly, 'but not in its present position.'

A light dawned.

'You mean—in the corner of the yard?'

'I mean—in full view of all five huts. It's a wonder to us', said Frankie bitterly, 'that you and Syd didn't put it on the top of Hamnafeld.'

'I see your point, but that has always been the ancestral lavatory of the Holbourns, hasn't it, Alasdair?'

Alasdair looked shocked. Frankie said:

'But in the Holbourn's time the yard was a cabbage-patch, not a barrack full of gaping idiots.'

'Very well argued. Syd, it must be moved.'

'Where?' said Syd, still aggrieved at the epithets hurled at his pearl among lavatories (painted pea-green by his own hand).

'Yes. That is the point. Where else can we put it?'

'That', retorted Frankie, rising, 'is not our affair; but

until it is moved us girls are on strike, aren't we, Belle?'

'Yes.'

'Good night all,' and they retired, without wasting one round more than was necessary.

I looked down the table at Syd.

'You and I will take a little walk around the neighbourhood and choose a less dramatic site,' I suggested.

'I don't agree . . .' began Syd, sulkily.

'Then you're in a minority.' (There was a murmur of chivalrous agreement.) 'And it has proved beyond question the value of the parliamentary system. Those in favour of a nightly parliament?'

There was not a dissenting vote, not even Syd's.

'One or two more things,' I said. 'We all feed alike, sleep alike and—drink alike. No alcohol of any kind in the camp. The Laird of Foula insists on this, please. The island is dry and must remain so. Captain Sewell extends the warm hospitality of the *Vedra* to all hard drinkers and will get— for cash—anything you order from Lerwick. But it must stay on the boat. Or you can save up for the week-end, when the *Vedra* goes to Lerwick for supplies. Hot baths will also be available on the *Vedra*. Bring your own towel.

'Then there's the Haa. Half of it is under Mrs. Rutherford's command, particularly the kitchen and the storeroom; the other half belongs to the ladies. ["What about me?" said Alasdair.] Oh, yes, I forgot. Alasdair sleeps in between. [Cries of "Well done, Laird," "The meat in the sandwich," etc.] The sitting-room belongs, then, to the ladies. The rest of the cast are welcome, of course, but please remember it's really their room. By their own request, they will have their meals there. [Cries of "Oh! Oh!"] Yes, I know this is a communistic experiment, but women are no longer in an experimental stage, except perhaps to Bill Martin and a few others. They are a refining influence on you roughnecks. Since they are in such a small proportion, we must take care of them. Any more complaints?'

'Yes, why not get more women?'

'I must have five months' notice of that question.'

John caught the Speaker's eye.

'Mr. Speaker, the wash-basins are ridiculous. I would hesitate to describe them as basins. I suggest they be turned over to the kitchen for the soup-plates that they are and that decent army-pattern basins be purchased, *sine die.*'

'I agree. Will you order them, George?'

George made a note. There were one or two other items, then parliament rose.

That was the highly successful beginning of the Rock City Parliament, which sat without a break from 1st June until 20th October, passed many hundreds of decrees, saved thousands of order-forms, call-sheets, inter-office memos, circular letters, carbon copies and all the flub-dub of a normal film production, and abolished altogether several million feet of the red-tape beloved by Gerald Blattner, Studio Manager. The procedure was always the same: the whole unit was there (unless Len and Bill Martin had gone fishing); a proposal was made; the people concerned spoke their piece; if it was condemned, the proposer knew just why; if approved, a committee was appointed to carry it out and report next night.

It sounds simple; it *was* simple. It produced results. There was never any trouble or dissatisfaction, from first to last, because everyone knew that they had an equal right in discussion. I agree that they were a remarkable group of men and women as well. I was very proud of them; and the more I look back on those full days, the prouder I become. I hope when they see the edited, orchestrated, manicured, spit-and-polish result of our united labours, that they are proud, too.

I forgot to mention that the Ladies' Convenience was shifted *to* their convenience, on an eligible site overlooking the sea, with desirable view towards Strem Ness. It was exposed to all the winds that blew, but season-ticket holders no longer had to run the gauntlet of Rock City. (But in rainy weather they had to wear gum-boots.)

By act of parliament tin baths were bought for each hut; a washhouse and huge copper for hot water were installed; linoleum was laid (a particularly florid pattern in No. 3 hut); mouse-traps were supplied to the ladies, who complained bitterly of the Foula Mouse (Apodemus fridariensis thuleo), reporting that it thundered about the Haa, as if it were wearing sea-boots, not realizing, being shrinking unscientific women, that the Foula Mouse is celebrated in the 'muscular' world for its large feet. It was act of parliament that installed the radio telephone on Foula, that imported the first car on Foula, that provided the first motion-picture show on Foula and (its only failure) that introduced the great Streeter Daylight Saving Bill, only to have it vetoed by the Island Vote, after Peggy the Cook had pressed the matter to a division. The first meeting, when I made my maiden speech, was as successful and as memorable as the last, when Walter Ratter made his, speaking for the Men of Foula. Many men in many countries have cursed the parliamentary system, but in its simplest form, I have nothing but good to report of it.

At first we had a fixed time: dinner was at eight, parliament at nine. This was no longer popular when the unit had made itself at home, when the sound crew wanted to be off fishing or the Professor to help with the harvest, when the financiers were playing 'Monopoly' at one table and a shove ha'penny tournament was on at another, when the poker party were playing close to the chest in the Haa and Mac was out on the cliffs with a gun under his arm and Bill Osborne was having trouble with his bladders (all right Bill, I will explain this later). So when the plates were being cleared away and everyone was too full to do anything more active than light a cigarette (if there were any), George

would catch my eye and murmur 'Parliament?' I would
nod and a minute later the bell would ring. With the speed
of an adder through dry grass, intending absentees, usually
Bill Martin, would be demanding dispensation at my elbow
—given, as a rule, unless I had something to say which
would affect them directly. Then a subdued commotion
heralded the lady members; if the weather was bad, an out-
and-out stampede across the open courtyard; later in the
year, the strong light of an acetylene lantern, shining out of
the dark night, would be their herald. Sometimes, through
the wide window which Syd made at the eastern end of the
hut, I could see the riding lights of the *Vedra*, shining from
Ham Voe, and Captain Sewell and Mr. White would be in
the Strangers' Gallery. More often, the boom and crash of
waves on a lee shore would be in my ears and Tom Sullivan, at the radio telephone, would be sending out his call:
'Hullo! Hullo! This is the Isle of Foula calling the steam-
yacht *Vedra*! Hullo! Hullo, *Vedra*! Can you hear me? This
is Rock City calling the *Vedra*! Over!' He would switch
over his batteries, the dynamo would die down and out of
a black, noisy void, full of the scratchy voices of trawler
skippers exchanging gossip about fishing and the weather,
would come: 'Hullo-o, Foula! Hull-o, Foula! Hull-o,
Foula! *Vedra* talking! *Vedra* talking! *Vedra* talking! Captain Sewell of the *Vedra* talking! I can hear you! Over!'
and Tom would read him a list of stores from Mrs. Rutherford and give him the Orders of the Day. Sometimes a
brilliant moon or bright swinging lanterns would light the
rough paths, the steps of shaly rock, the loose stone walls
and the steel guy-ropes of the huts. More often, a blackness
that could be felt, like a velvet curtain, faced the wary
traveller from hut to hut, so that, though he knew every
loose stone and every booby-trap, he suddenly found himself flat in the mud, or jarred by such a sudden descent that

his tongue was nearly bitten through. Sometimes a steady, soaking rain made a swamp of the yard, so that a step off the straight and narrow path brought instant retribution; and sometimes the wind blew; it blew till tongues of flame a yard long shot out of the door of the red-hot stove, till the steel guys twanged like harpstrings and the roofs drummed so that only a shout could be heard, till a touch on the door handle tore it from your hand and slammed it back against the wall, while a burst of wind and rain set the lamps swinging and every man grabbing at plates, books, papers, counters, suddenly endowed with wings.

But in light and darkness, warmth and cold, wind and rain, Rock City Parliament sat regardless. On rare days, when they had no complaint needing instant redress, the ladies of the city sometimes failed to occupy their seats on the front bench; then their call, if any, was delicately transferred to them by Buddy, George, John Seabourne and myself, usually in that order, each subsequent messenger being greeted by a scream of 'We know! You needn't tell us! Call at seven-thirty for the Sneck. Why are we always in the first shot?' The invariable answer being, 'Because, if you're wanted for the first shot, you've got no alibi; and *unless* you were called for the first shot, you'd never turn up at all. Buddy will drive you up to the Roundabout at eight-fifteen; thence up the Daal upon your flat feet. Don't be late!'

We had no 'lights out'. People were free to go to bed whenever they liked. The hour varied, by huts or by personal inclination. I used to stroll around the Voe late at night. The camp and the black shape of the Haa would be above me. The new wireless mast towered by the sea. I could hear our fishermen calling to one another out in the bay. There would be a blaze of light and a lot of bawdy laughter coming from Hut 5, with Hut 3, respectably illuminated, in decent contrast. One of the camera crew is sure to be fiddling in the camera hut. The Professor hurries past from the laboratory over the Shop, carrying some wet Leica enlargements to show Ernie. Through the sunken windows of the Haa, I can see a grim party of poker-players: Eric innocent, Mac gloomy, Belle pop-eyed, Buddy cheerful, Frankie impassive and the air thick with smoke. Len, the brilliant financier, is amassing enormous wealth at 'Monopoly' in the mess-hut. I can see a string of little red hotels on the properties in front of him, whose ground-rent alone is worth a fortune. Ernie, his only serious rival, sits watchfully opposite. The others pay up stolidly. There seems to be a cocoa party in the dimly lit kitchen; Mrs. Rutherford must have gone to bed. A dark form shoots out of Hut 5, rapidly crosses the yard and dives into the storeroom; it is probably Hamish 'on the scrounge'. A distant hoot sounds from Hametoun and presently the headlights of the car appear at the crossroads up by the School House. Presently it comes chuffing down the narrow road, swings round the Haa and comes to rest by the Shop. George, who has been on a payment round, climbs out and, after a word to Tom Sullivan, who is charging his batteries in the lean-to by the Shop, he enters the mess-hut. As I turn back to Hut 1 and bed I hear footsteps come swinging over the path from Sloag. I stop and call:

'Is that you, Bombardier?'

'The Rocket Has Gone Up, Sir!'

'Where have you been, John?'

'Ristie and Blowburn. We want Jimmy and Tina for the evacuation sequence and Peter Manson has promised to send his family.'

We fall into step.

'Did you find out about John Isbister's gravestone?'

'Yes. I forgot to tell you. I saw the Archdeacon. [John's name for old Robert Isbister.] It was his uncle, you know. He said it was all right. But afterwards he thought I had better get permission from John Isbister of Breckins, too.'

'The same name.'

'Yes. I thought he might be a bit difficult, so I went down, dodged that wall-eyed cow, and told the old man that I wanted to borrow the stone to put over the grave in the film.'

'And——'

'He thought it over and he said: "Maister Seabourne, yon man canna object and I willna." '

'Old sportsman.'

'Ay. They're a grand people.'

We were standing outside Hut 1. The door of Hut 3 opens and Finlay's genial bulk fills the doorway.

'Is that yeself, John?'

'The same.'

'Then come to bed, ye wandering soldier. I've a cup of hot tea ready for you.'

'I'll take that invitation, too, Finlay.'

'Hullo, Chief? Are you there? Come in at once, we'll be proud to have you under our humble roof.'

I enter Hut 3, the pride of the camp. Two old soldiers and the Admirable Streeter account for this. Everything is on hinges, pulleys and racks. Their aim and ambition is to have everything off the floor. There is not a thing that does not let down or fly up. The walls are a mass of gadgets, ropes and shelves. Every bed has two mattresses: ask any old soldier how this is arranged. John has made his bunk wider with pieces of three-ply. By the door is the Blot on the Hut—Eric Berry's bed and belongings: no hooks, no ropes, no nothing. Eric believes in the simple life. At first they used to badger him, now they have given it up. They have provided him with a large box. Into this are crammed his belongings. Eric is relieved, considers it an ideal arrangement. When he wants anything he turns the box upside down on the floor, selects the article and goes off, blinking mildly. He knows that one of his bunk-mates will cram everything back into the box again and push it into its corner. They know that he knows and they growl and do it.

The Haarem and the Huts

I stay for half an hour listening to John and Finlay swapping lies, then say good night and go to my own hut. A tin bath, exactly like a deep coffin, is half full of water and quite full of MacGinnis, whistling dolefully. His gun is on his bed and four brace of pigeons, enough for a pie. He grins slowly and happily and soaps himself all over. Presently I help him carry out the water and we both go slowly and happily to bed.

Chapter XII

THE NEGUS IS NOT SUCH A FOOL
AS HE LOOKS

*

It was Vernon who gave him the name. 'Alasdair' was too formal for everyday wear; it was only at special catastrophes, punctuated by croaks of 'Didn't I tell you?' that he was referred to as 'the Smallie'; 'the Laird' was popular with the rank and file but inaccurate (and, while Campbell Robson was with us, confusing); 'the Negus' was just right: a certain dignity, a certain absurdity, short, topical and vaguely pathetic. Vernon took a bow.

Alasdair accepted his new title with a grin. He could take a joke on himself, as I have said; besides we had been in production a few weeks by then and he had become quite human again.

I date his transformation from the day we tried to drown him, with his own consent, in the Blow-hole. During the first weeks of production he was unbearable; he filled the air with troll-like mutterings. I suppose that, in his eyes, I also suffered a sea-change: I had seemed harmless enough (in fact, Money for Jam) in the early days but, before he could say Mucklegrind, I had brought forth a swarm of carpenters, production managers, supply ships, and strange machines, turned him out of his bed, condemned his house, remodelled it, criticized his yacht, subpœnaed his population and turned the ray of decent, faintly glamorous lime-light, which had hitherto bathed the distant shores of Foula, into a glaring, sizzling, million-candle-power arc-light.

The Negus is not such a Fool as he Looks

Naturally he did not like it. Later on he began to enjoy himself and consequently became quite popular.

But at first he was quite phenomenally unpopular. We were innocents abroad and made a lot of mistakes; he pointed them out. We had our own ways of doing things; he had opposite ones. We took some time to get order and organization into our unit; Alasdair was always happy to point out our shortcomings.

First of all he was upset by the departing catechist. Then he disapproved of John Seabourne being left unsupervised among the islanders; he worried lest he should be tactless with them and, when he knew John better, lest he should alienate their affections. At Sunderland he instantly disapproved of Vernon and, as can be imagined, that sentiment was returned with interest by the Commodore. According to the log, Alasdair spent his first voyage on the *Vedra* crouched Cassandra-like in the cross-trees, only descending to take four hearty meals per day. At the building of Rock City he ran foul of the town-planning committee and got his head bitten off by Syd who, though mild as a cherub, becomes like a roaring lion at any breath of destructive criticism.

So altogether that made—not counting Syd and Walter —three men plus, say five, crew of the *Vedra* (though it is true they all left in a body as soon as the ship reached Aberdeen) and sixteen men of Foula (who, for the first time in their lives, were being paid by the hour, and liked it) and of course George Black and also John Seabourne— unless I have already counted him—and naturally Buddy— in all, twenty-nine (or twenty-eight) members of the Rock expedition, whose opinion of the Negus was low.

More was to follow.

When we arrived that foggy night in Lerwick and stumbled, chilled, hungry and dirty, into the hotel, Alasdair was waiting for us, with comments on our organization that were justified but offensive. I can remember now the

incredulous look on Niall's grimy face as he sat by me in
the little glass and pitch-pine lobby, with the potted plants
and copies of the two Shetland newspapers, and studied
Alasdair's expression of gloating superiority. Before we all
went to bed that night, twenty-nine had swelled to forty-
seven.

Yet I liked Alasdair and we all became very fond of him.
I trace a lot of his pessimism to his very real love for Foula.
When I had made my proposal at Penkaet, he had accepted
it as a business proposition. When he saw what his consent
brought in its train, I think he was a bit appalled, as anyone
would be. I am afraid I have too often seen the look on the
faces of proud owners of historic mansions, who have given
me leave to shoot in their grounds and been rather gratified
by the request, when they saw a stream of plain vans dis-
gorging a modern movie unit, with all its formidable
apparatus. The expedition to Foula was only an enlarge-
ment of this, but to Alasdair it must have looked as if the
island would never be the same again. He shrank back and
murmured, like Caliban:

> *This island's mine*
> *Which thou tak'st from me. When thou camést first,*
> *Thou strok'st me, and mad'st much of me; would'st give me*
> *Water with berries in't; and teach me how*
> *To name the bigger light, and how the less*
> *That burn by day and night, and then I loved thee,*
> *And showed thee all the qualities o' the isle,*
> *The fresh springs, brine pits, barren place, and fertile,*
> *Cursèd be I that did so!*

Looking back on those days I can sympathize with the
emotions of the Negus. At the time I had as little sense of
humour and proportion as any pioneer, in the throes of
establishing a Protectorate.

Alasdair, too, had the whole responsibility of his family
upon his shoulders. With his two brothers at Oxford, and

his mother at Penkaet, he had to grapple with a lot of problems whose solution he knew by hearsay but which he had never actually had to solve himself. His knowledge of the island, the people, the coast, the yacht, the weather were all equally vicarious. He was in the position of a man who has been, all his life, a member of a well-controlled household, accustomed to an ordered and accepted routine and who is suddenly called upon to run the house for the week and prepare the meals: he knows that bread, butter, boot polish and washing soda are in the house, are part of the scheme of existence, but at first he finds it hard to put his hand on them when they are wanted; he vaguely knows a great deal about the routine of the establishment but finds he has to modify many ideas in actual practice. In fact, at first, he is often confounded on his native heath by perfect strangers, which annoys him very much. I think Alasdair will agree that this reconstruction of his psychology is a true one.

The Elder Brother

His elder brother, Hylas, was held by Alasdair in considerable awe. I must say that I share his opinion. I have never had the pleasure of meeting Hylas Holbourn, but he is evidently a considerable personality. Each time that he manifested himself, it was by the briefest and most illuminating flash of lightning. To me he will always be a brusque, abstracted figure, at the end of a telephone line, emerging from a sea of calculations—he is an experimental research physicist—to concentrate his piercing eye for a brief moment upon Foula and the suspicious behaviour of his younger brother alone in charge of that film company. An occasion that leaps to my mind is the Levitation of the Kirk Roof, for the Church Sequence.

This apparent miracle was one of the major Streeter Projects, of which the others were the Sneck Bridge, the Sloag Railway, the Evacuation Bridge and the Daylight

The Negus is not such a Fool as he Looks

Saving Bill. Ever since Syd had seen the disused church he had burned to use it as a set. It was the sunken windows which attracted him; and, of course, the perfect proportions of the whole and the beautifully made pews and pulpit, which were as strong and good as the original pine-planks, brought from the mainland, when old John Gray was a boy. There were two windows behind the pulpit, where the round bulk of the Noup and the stony waste towards Stöel and the Daal showed through the small panes. In the north wall were two long windows, with hinged panes. The congregation, seated in the pews, could see the whole sweep of the island watershed and the valley of Hametoun, with the crofts rising out of the sea of barley and the long, white grass. All the windows were recessed the full two feet thickness of the wall. Through the open door to the east the burn could be seen wandering down the valley until the waves of yellow iris met the Atlantic at Grisigarth. A blue line on the horizon was Shetland. Along the south wall of the kirk there was no window; only a solid barrier of stone, fronting Helliberg and the southerly gales.

When at last I went with Syd to see the interior of the kirk, I agreed with him, but I doubted that it could be done. The roof was of small slates. They would all have to be carefully removed and as carefully replaced. Then the wooden roof must be opened up, wide enough to let in plenty of general light and leave room for overhead reflectors. There was a three-sided plaster ceiling, forming a hexagon with the floor and walls. This would have to be cut away for at least half the length of the room. All this seemed too ambitious to a layman like myself. But Syd knew no bridle to his ambition and disposed of all obstacles by invoking, in the Homeric manner, a phalanx of minor deities, such as Ballistics, Suspensions, Joists and Mortices, all his familiars, not to mention Walter Ratter and Bobbie Isbister, and especially the Archdeacon, which so powerfully swayed myself and Alasdair that we became as enthusiastic as he was. John Seabourne approached the Shetland Representative of the Established Church who answered suavely that it was an interesting idea but that it would have been better to ask permission after the deed had been done. This statesmanlike reply was greatly appreciated and we then proceeded to our next step which was to wire the Elder Brother for *his* permission. After considerable thought and sparing no expense (since it was ours) Alasdair concocted a telegram which seemed to him to give all sides of the case, and Tom Sullivan sent it off. That evening Alasdair received the Elder Brother's reply. He showed it to me. It is chiefly upon that telegram that my admiration for the eldest Holbourn rests. It had no signature and was exactly nine words. It read: 'HOLBOURN FOULA WIRE UNINTELLIGIBLE REPEAT AND STATE WHAT CHURCH.'

Alasdair seemed more gratified than offended by his brother's terse reply. 'Ah, that's Hylas all over,' he remarked with pride; 'never wastes a word and knows his own mind. Pity he couldn't come here this summer. You wouldn't have got much change out of *him!*'

I was inclined to agree with him. Ever afterwards Hylas was referred to among us by the title of the Elder Brother —his own name did not seem to do sufficient justice to a man who never wasted a word.

Alasdair accordingly repeated and stated what church. In due course, on the principle that two doubtful negatives make a possible affirmative, Syd attacked the church and had that roof off in record time. I believe that Peter Gray of Burns was the slate expert: anyway hardly one was broken. We made all our scenes and they were the most successful in the picture. To-day the church stands as sound as it always was, empty and unused after its summer of brief stardom but still a monument to the fine craftsmen that built it long ago.

The Negus is not such a Fool as he Looks

The Three Yard Limit

Alasdair had one chief worry. Callous people may ask, what is one amongst so many? But if the same worry was sufficient to plunge a great nation into an orgy of crime, who can blame him for worrying about his little world? I refer, of course, to the enforcement of Prohibition on Foula.

He had an ally in me. None of my people were hard drinkers but, in a bunch of hard-working young men who are all friends, there is bound to be too much 'standing treat'. I saw at once that if I could keep the thought uppermost that all alcohol was illegal, any serious trouble was impossible. It did not matter to me how much liquor was smuggled in, *so long as it had to be smuggled*. Speaking for myself, there were days towards the end of the production, coming in from Soberlie or Back of the Noup, my thick clothes stiff with water and my eyes sore from rubbing the salt out of the lashes, when half an enamelled mug of pale whisky, produced with a conspiratorial grin by Niall out of a battered suitcase, was the only thing to bring me slowly to my feet again when the bell for dinner rang. But although, after Bill Martin's birthday party (of which more later—much more), the restrictions were considerably relaxed, yet they were never repealed and, to the last day, liquor was contraband and tasted all the better for it.

In my maiden speech at parliament I touched on this point and mentioned two possible alternatives. I shall now relate how Theory differed from Practice.

The *Vedra* and her skipper were expected, from the first, to have a busy time. Our only positive link with the world for two months, the ship naturally got a lot of attention, not all welcome, and her duties increased every day until Vernon began to complain bitterly. First of all she was our supply ship, bringing fresh meat, bread and vegetables, chocolates and face-flannels for the girls, bigger and better bladders for Bill Osborne (sooner or later I shall get around to this), a string of cooks, male and female, ranging from bad to awful, exotic woods for Syd, haggis for my birth-day, transit-cases of rushes, raw film-stock, old cameras for new, new cameramen for old, Sunday newspapers on Wednesday (though not necessarily that Wednesday), daily papers weekly, a box of pears for the old gentleman at Blowburn, tin baths, card tables, a motor-car, a Marconi radio telephone, a portable projection outfit, two Scout tents, Gerry Blattner, Campbell Robson, Gerald Boyne, Mr. Greenaway, and endless telegrams from Joe Rock.

Next—a department in itself—were the orders of beer, whisky and sherry, given to Vernon by thirsty exiles, on the strict understanding that the goods were only to leave the *Vedra* in their owner's—and their guests'—stomachs.

Third, there was the grim, metal compartment next to the engine-room, with its aggressive iron manhole adorned with huge jagged screws in the floor, which made every movement a horror and which looked a cross between a cell for solitary confinement and the torpedo-room on a film submarine—by which I mean the bathroom; a place of pilgrimage, so intense and jealous, that chivalry and fair-dealing ceased to mean anything and even a perfect lady was capable of kicking a gentleman in the face in order to get first wallow in hot salt water.

Fourth, there was the Marconi radio transmitter, operated ostensibly by 'Sparks' but more often than not by Vernon, for whom all mechanical gadgets sit up and beg.

Fifth, there was the anchor of the *Vedra*, a full-time job in itself.

Sixth was the fact that steam had to be kept up all the time, so that the *Vedra* could clear out for Shetland in case of a change of wind.

Seventh was the fact that there always *was* a change of wind.

And, finally, there was Black Jack's Boudoir and the Social Life.

The Negus is not such a Fool as he Looks

Black Jack and the Invisible Ship

Vernon's official position on the expedition was Technical Supervisor, which means All Round Genius When Anything Goes Wrong With The Works. In our original plans, which were considerably more modest than Joe Rock's, he was to make the wheels go round, Seabourne was to keep them moving and I was to direct their energies into the right channels. The command of the *Vedra* was only a sideline, essential to our plans because we had to have a steam-yacht registered in Vernon's name; but the *Vedra* was to take her place as a regular supply ship with the mate in charge, as soon as her main work of establishing the expedition upon the island was done.

Two things changed this set-up. One was that Joe Rock insisted on complete sound and camera units, also on discarding Vernon's own sound system and buying a portable [*sic*] outfit of an established make. This naturally implied a Sound Department, consisting of Bill Sweeny and The Puffin, assisted by Bill Martin and Len; and Monty (later Ernie) on camera, operated by Skeets Kelly, assisted by John Behr (later the Professor) and Karl. All these experts not only looked upon Vernon's comments with suspicion (particularly since his first reports on the rushes were, quite correctly, corrosive) but had little need of his help, once they had found their feet.

The other contributory cause was that it became evident that the command of the *Vedra* was a whole-time job, equivalent to running a cargo 'cross Channel in the days of the French wars. Add to this the fact that Vernon, after one look at Rock City, flatly refused to sleep ashore and proceeded to turn his cabin into a stateroom, which seemed almost sinfully luxurious to our beauty-starved citizens, particularly the female section. The *Vedra*, when present, became a social centre. Vernon gave little dinners, chiefly for the aforesaid female populace. The sound of polite laughter, the clink of glass, the scraping of plates, the sophisticated melody of Vernon's piano-accordion, were wafted across the dark waters of the Voe to the wistful ears of the rude citizenry, seated at their oilcloth and enamel, bringing a subtle flavour of the decadence of Deauville to the sterner pleasures of this northern settlement.

However, it will be noted that I say 'when present'. There was little chance that Black Jack Sewell (as the autocratic skipper was generally called) would corrupt the morals of our simple womenfolk, for both he and his ship were so seldom there that they became a standing joke. At all times his crew were in a semi-mutinous state at the uncertain hours and extra work attached to the job; it was as much as the skipper's life was worth (a purely nominal sum, according to his detractors) to lie off Foula for any length of time, with an all-night watch and steam up and usually a change of position at dawn with the wind and tide. It was quite a common thing to go to bed with the *Vedra* moored fore and aft, a cable-length from the jetty, only to find her in the morning a distant, grumpy black shape, heading determinedly for Scalloway and a safe harbour.

There was one morning, never allowed to be forgotten, when Bill Paton came out in front of the Haa to look at the weather, after lighting the kitchen fire, before the rest of the camp was awake. The *Vedra* was moored a quarter of a mile out and on her decks he saw signs of frantic activity. This was unusual enough, for the weather was clear, but as he lingered, he was sighted and hailed in a low voice by Vernon himself. What he heard doubled him up with laughter.

It was Tiger again. After several disheartening attempts with professional seamen, who usually deserted as soon as they received their first week's wage, Vernon manned his ship with youngsters from Scalloway, who were keen enough on the job not to mind its drawbacks. They remained with us to the end. The youngest, shortest, and sturdiest was at once named Tiger Tim. I never knew his real name and no doubt he has forgotten it himself. He was universally known as Tiger. (One of my favourite stories of the *Vedra* is of Vernon waking up, hearing a noise like a sack of coals being delivered down his hatchway, followed by complete and awful silence, and calling out: 'Who's there?' to be at once convulsed and reassured by a deep, husky voice replying: 'Tiger, sorr!') Anyway, in the early dawn, Tiger, on the night watch, had discovered that the lifeboat had come adrift. It was now well on its way to Strem Ness. This was bad enough but tragedy followed. He roused the watch below and Bill White ordered chase to be given in the other boat. The boys rushed to the davits meaning to attach the painter after they had cast off the falls. But they forgot the six-knot current. There was a howl of agony from Tiger, and White turned to see two masterless boats heading drunkenly northwards. The crew of the *Vedra* were marooned. It had then been White's delicate task to wake the skipper and report. Fortunately for Vernon's sanity it was at this juncture that Bill Paton appeared on shore. He put off in Alasdair's boat, took a salvage crew on board, was at his own request put back on the rocks by the Haa and, having waited to see the frantically overloaded dinghy disappear round Taing Head, returned solemnly with his story. That morning there was an hilarious breakfast among the civilians of Rock City.

The crew found the boats undamaged but nearly on the rocks, where they would soon have been stove in, for there was a swell running. One was in Hodden Geo and the motor-boat had got as far as the Stack of the Gaads. After that they put a rope on Tiger.

This habit of the *Vedra* of suddenly hitching up its slacks and vanishing over the Hoevdi Grund to the flesh-pots of Scalloway caused a good deal of embarrassment to the bath-conscious members of the unit. Nobody ever troubled to look below or blow a whistle when the wind changed. They were only too glad to scrape out of the Voe with an undamaged bottom, not to mention bow, stern and sides. I do not think I have mentioned the *Vedra's* actual size; she was about 230 tons, 115 feet long and drew 9 feet. This was about the size of the Voe, and it was a small hell to get out of in a hurry. To make things easier the yacht of the Negus was always moored in the centre of the channel and both skippers would refuse to give way an inch, Alasdair saying 'Why should he?' and Vernon bawling 'How the devil could he?' with the result that somebody usually ran foul of somebody else and anyway the yacht's deck, sails, sheets and owner would be inches deep in clinkers. Meanwhile, as I have said, some Rock citizen, probably Frankie or Eric Berry, would be having a tremendous wallow and would suddenly discover that he or she felt sick (movement and heat of bath). She, or he, would rush up on deck and find that they had been shanghaied. After the third member of the unit had been carried off to Shetland in our travelling bath, I imported hip-baths, installed a copper and made the unit independent of the Hell-Ship.

Alasdair got on pretty good terms with the unit, as I have said, but with the *Vedra* and its skipper, never! For one thing he was unable to forgive Vernon for not wrecking his ship, preferably on the Hoevdi Grund. The wreck of the *Oceanic* is wearing a bit thin these days. It is twenty years ago and has been told many times. The piling up of the *Vedra* was just what Foula needed to justify its reputation. Alasdair never wearied (he mentioned it to me only the other day) of telling how Vernon sailed clean over the reef on his first arrival at the island, cheerfully discounting all Alasdair's frenzied warnings. Every time that Vernon put out from the Voe or hove in sight from Scalloway, Alasdair would down tools wherever he happened to be and run down to the Voe. If anyone was near he would start a monologue in a tone of gloomy fatalism: 'That man bears a charmed life, him and his ship! I wouldn't sail with him for a fortune. It's a mystery to me why he has never wrecked his ship—look at that! He's heading straight over the Hoevdi! The tide will carry him down. Look! He's being carried south! Aha! Mphm! Ay! This time he's gone too far! He'll hit! He'll hit! There's not a chance in a million that he'll clear it. He'll be right over the *Oceanic* now. Well, he can't say I didn't warn him!' and he would stand there with his clenched hands in his old overalls and his mouth set, waiting for the crash and the bodies to come ashore. It never happened.

Fish, however, was a subject where Alasdair's pessimism made good. In our innocence we had assumed, in planning our commissariat, that fresh fish would be plentiful on an island. We already felt a little bored by the amount of the fish we would be expected to eat. In the general turmoil this was forgotten, but after about three weeks, we awoke to the fact that we never had fresh fish at all, unless Lerwick kippers counted. The question was brought up in parliament and Alasdair took the floor. So we had thought that fish could be had for the asking? Well, we had a lot to learn. Nobody on the island ate fresh fish any more.

'Then what are the boats out after, every fine night?' asked Len, who, through constant handling of the mike on the end of the portable boom, had developed a supple wrist for fishing.

'Piltock!'

'What's piltock?' said everybody.

John rose to his feet, with an air of courteous learning:

'It is the intermediary stage, gentlemen, of a fish called the Saithe, or Coal-Fish, locally known as Black Jacks. In their infant stage they are called sillocks. In their interim stage, piltocks.'

He resumed his seat amid applause.

'Why don't we eat them? I suppose the islanders do? Or do they stuff them and put them in cases?'

John rose again.

'According to my information, they salt them, dry them and store them against a rainy day. Nobody ever eats them fresh.'

'Why not?'

'They taste like blotting paper, Mr. Speaker.'

'Well, what are they like salted and dried?'

'If you would care to try, I could borrow some from Andrew Manson.'

'Where does he keep them?'

'In the rafters.'

'What? Those mummified looking things, that hang in bunches by the salted mutton?'

'Yes.'

'I thought they were plaster of Paris?'

'No. Shall I ask for the loan of. . . .'

'Don't bother!'

John sat down with the air of a Prime Minister who has steered his party through a crisis. I turned to Alasdair.

'Are there no other fish on Foula?'

'Not since the trawlers cleaned out our banks. Why, you've got all that in your film play.'

'That's true. But I thought there'd be enough of different sorts of fish to supply the unit.'

Alasdair was enjoying our discomfiture. It was seldom now that he got a chance to tell us how little we knew about anything.

'Well, you know, now,' he said. Then, rather rashly: 'Try yourselves and see!'

'We will!' said Len and Bill Martin and that evening went out with him in his boat.

They had a grand time and caught about a hundred fish in an hour, with three rods, but they were piltock, sure enough. They showed their catch and it was much admired and Mrs. Rutherford undertook to cook it, but John was right. Piltock taste like blotting paper. Very good blotting paper, but—blotting paper.

Nobody was anxious to repeat the experiment, but Len and Bill went grimly on, every fine night, occasionally catching a haddock or a whiting among their mass of piltock. Sometimes they got mackerel, but that was not a popular fish either. John scored one triumph by going out with Alasdair one night, and, although very sick, getting forty-eight large dabs. But, on the whole, our staple diet remained corned beef.

The *Vedra* caught sea-trout in the Voe, the best of which they kept for themselves; and some of our fishermen took brown trout from the burn, which was well stocked; but, all in all, Foula, for variety of fresh fish, is not a patch on Piccadilly.

Bill Osborne and Auntie

The alternative to the *Vedra*, usually preferred by the rank and file, was to save up their energies, on a diet of cocoa and pure spring water, and then go on a tremendous spree in Lerwick, reporting unsteadily for work on Monday morning. After one or two such explosions the attraction waned. The desire to let off steam and absorb large quantities of alcohol was a relic of a civilization which was soon left far behind. The picture became the thing. People got used to soft drinks, simple food, and finding their own amusements in the evenings, just as they got used to knobbly beds (those mattresses were like tennis balls to sleep on), Primus stoves and rather sociable sanitary arrangements. I do not suggest that they would not have rather been elsewhere, especially in the fifth month, but at least the camp had atmosphere, people felt at home, and were happy (except Eric), they did not openly rebel (except John Laurie), and whatever they said or thought at different times, they one and all supported me (except, of course, the Crêpe-Hangers) with a loyalty which was beyond gratitude or praise.

But in the first weeks, up till the Walls Regatta, which was our Rubicon, the associations of civilized life still clung to many of us, particularly to Bill Osborne.

He had joined my unit from British International Pictures, who had just shut down for the summer. We had worked together before in the old days and I remembered his face. It was long and sober and serious, ornamented with horn-rimmed spectacles, earnest and clean-shaven; like most faces of that kind, it belied its owner, as anyone listening for a short while outside Hut 5 could easily judge. Bill is a good mixer; and the motto of Hut 5 was 'Mix or be Mixed!' The hut contained officially Bill Osborne (Props), Tom Sullivan (Sparks), Hamish Sutherland (Ham to you!), Bill Paton (The Eye that Never Sleeps) and Bob White (Syd Streeter's right-hand man). They were all good mixers and they mixed every night—come one, come all!

As far as I can judge, everyone came, every night.

Bob White only joined a month before the great storm. Other birds of passage rested a day or a week in Hut 5, were taken to its bosom and passed on: George Summers (twice), Campbell Robson, Bill Sweeny (on his return visit), Gerry Blattner (but he finally honoured Hut 1, dispossessing the Professor), one of the trawler cooks (the one who only stayed two days), were all alumni of Hut 5, whose four permanent inmates took them or left them alone and went on serenely playing a murderous and never-ending game of solo, while people argued, brewed, undressed, sang, ate, drank, crawled, climbed and jumped over, under and across them.

The moving spirit of the hut was Bill Osborne. First, because he was a prop-man; second, because he is a moving spirit, as witness the Walls Regatta concert. Scarcely anyone who had seen at Elstree the slim, serious figure in the dark brown suit, with the list of props in his hand, would have recognized on Foula the wild apparition, with the gleam in its eye, draped (one cannot say dressed) in buttonless shirt, jersey, antique sports coat, rakish beret, enormous boots, obscene shorts with scalloped edges converted with a clasp-knife out of a pair of flannel trousers, Shetland stockings and bare, purple knees, bent earnestly over a dozen horrid-looking cow-bladders (I have got around to this at last), inflating them into unprintable shapes with a bicycle pump and repairing (with an inadequate puncture-repair outfit, stolen from the car) the ravages of the Foula Mouse.

There are many things to blight a prop-man's life but few can equal a dozen evil-smelling cow-bladders. They were needed for the two sequences with the 'letter-boats', principally that one in which James and Peter are seen sending out a miniature fleet from the Voe. Bill made an ally of the butcher at Scalloway and was soon well equipped, but unfortunately we had to wait two months for the right conditions of wind, tide, sun and opportunity. There were half a dozen false alarms. At parliament I would sometimes add: 'And perhaps the scene with the boats and bladders.' Bill would prick up his ears and dash out and fetch the box from under Hut 5. Three would have shrivelled away, four would be half eaten by mice. Frantic repairs and attempts at resuscitation. By nine o'clock next morning eight distended bladders would be paraded, while six more would have been radio-ordered by Tom Sullivan. The day would pass. Slowly Bill's hope of getting the sequence done would shrink. So would the bladders. At last he would put them gloomily away until the next time and would wear an injured look for the next twelve hours.

But if Bill Osborne was one of the more prominent citizens of the camp, how much more was he renowned in his frequent sallies to the mainland! The wise man, in the jungle, watches the flight of birds to discover fresh water;

in a film company, it is more prudent to follow the prop-
man (substituting for water, beer, with steak, onions, fried
potatoes and tomato sauce). Bill had hardly been in Lerwick an hour before he had met the local bootlegger,
followed by the discovery of 'Auntie', a figure who, to me
at any rate, became almost legendary during the next few
months. Auntie was the manageress of Mrs. Henry's café,
the Ciro's of Lerwick, the haunt of the man about town, a
home from home for the tired prop-man. So many were
the references to Auntie, whenever corned beef appeared
for the sixth time in one week, that I finally made a pilgrimage there during the last agonizing week of waiting
and watching in Lerwick. The half was not told me.

The Walls Regatta

I now approach the turning-point of the expedition.
When George was over in Walls with John Laurie and his
collarbone, he made friends with Mackenzie, the young
and popular doctor of the place, who was also Medical
Officer for Foula. MacKenzie told him of the regatta which
was to take place in a few weeks and invited the Rock Film
Company to be guests of the township and to take part in
the concert which always followed the day of sporting
events. At least that was how George understood it. He
consulted me and, as we both thought that a riotous outing
would do everybody good, we suggested it at parliament
and it was received with enthusiasm. A committee was
formed at once to organize talent. Vernon was warned to
have our flagship decorated, spat and polished for the day.
The Negus beamed wintry approval, announced that he
would sail his yacht across, and called for a volunteer crew.
The only unenthusiastic person was myself, not because I
doubted the day would be a success, but simply because I
had no wish to leave Foula even for one day until the film
was finished.

The great day approached. Things had been going as

badly as possible for me. John Laurie was in hospital. Ernie had been sent out to take over from Monty and, since I had not seen the last batch of island rushes, I had not decided (nor had Ernie) whether the change of cameraman was justified. We both had a soft spot for Monty, and Ernie hated to supplant him on his first picture, especially when he himself had endorsed his selection. For the present, at Ernie's own suggestion, Monty was still in charge and Ernie was only supervising, in the same way that Sweeny, who had returned at the same time, was overhauling the sound apparatus with 'Puffin' Tregellas. I arranged to see the rushes in Lerwick, on the Regatta Day.

The week before the holiday, John Behr developed his appendix trouble and it became unmistakable on the very eve. We hastily packed some of his things and he went with the rest of us between eight and nine in the morning; he was to go straight to MacKenzie for a diagnosis. It cannot have been a cheerful trip for him but he never turned a blond hair and his manner was as unflurried and impertinent as ever. The Negus left with his crew after breakfast; Niall, Belle, Eric, Frankie and Hamish were with him and there may have been others, all boasting how they would make a spectacular arrival into Walls harbour. They did.

Besides the whole unit, dressed in unfamiliar suits and ties, resurrected from dusty suitcases, there were several islanders, by special invitation. Jessie and Bessie were there, beaming all over; Lizzie, who helped at the Haa; Mary Henry, sister of Mrs. Gear, at Mogle, both of them very pretty girls; Jimmy Isbister of the Shop had come along; and Jimmy Gray, now an accredited member of the camera crew; and Peter and Wullie Gear, who were to play the fiddle; and in a corner, giggling like a soda-water factory, was Edith Gray, a blonde, roly-poly figure in a tight brown tailor-made, and I think I remember the red face of her sister Louisa, alternating tempestuous bursts of laughter with the shocked calm of a waxwork's figure.

The Negus is not such a Fool as he Looks

The Negus crammed every stitch of sail on to his yacht, including his topsail, foresail and any other piece of canvas that was around, and he came down Easter Sound and round Rams Head as if it were the Horn. They made a fine sight as they tore down Vaila Voe, and experienced sailors on the quays at Walls admired the show and laid bets whether the yacht would run right up into the village street or else copy the recent manœuvre of a coasting steamer and go slap through the wooden jetty. Meanwhile, on the yacht, was taking place one of those frenzied scenes of naval mishaps so dear to Lieutenant E. G. O. Beuttler, R.N. The reference, to those who have admired the work of this genius in the *Bystander*, will conjure up a vivid picture. To the uneducated I can say, more simply, that there was hell to pay. Nobody in the amateur crew knew much about sailing or anything at all about Alasdair's particular rig, which was highly complicated. He tried to strike the topsail in a hurry, which simply cannot be done. It stuck. He shrieked to Hamish to lower the mainsail. Frankie helped, which did *not* help (Niall, who was the only one who knew anything, merely got trampled underfoot by the others). Alasdair tore at the jib and foresail and fell to the deck enveloped in yards of canvas, and eventually they fetched up, across somebody's bows, but with no damage other than moral, Belle having escaped the boom by the breadth of a pig's whisker.

'Well, here we are!' said Alasdair.

The *Vedra* had made a less spectacular arrival two hours before. A race was in progress as we came down the channel and the Voe, which is very wide, was covered with small craft, all Shetland models, speeding over the water as lightly as a feather, until it hardly seemed possible that any of their keels were below the surface. I have never seen anything more delightful or seaworthy than those light, shallow, wide Shetland models; big and little boats, they are all made on the same lines and have been since the Viking galleys came stealing westward to the isles.

John Behr went off to see MacKenzie. I gathered up all the people concerned with the rushes, piled them into a waiting car and tore madly for Lerwick, where the cinema manager was waiting for us. Bill Osborne and party, bound for Auntie, followed in another car. The rest of the unit wandered into the village with friendly smiles, wondering why there was no address by the school children, or floral archway with Welcome to Walls. We had expected to be rather mobbed by grateful admirers. Instead we hardly seemed to be welcome. And already an awful rumour was spreading that *there were no drinks!*

I came back from Lerwick with a heavy heart. The majority of the rushes were quite impossible. There were dozens of retakes. The sound on the yacht scenes was poor. Frankie had not been well photographed. The last trawler scenes were only passable. There were out-of-focus shots, owing to the awkward blimp on the Mitchell. . . . It was awful.

Poor Monty looked white. Ernie talked to him in low tones. Skeets, the loyalest of friends and assistants, was sunk in gloom; and Skeets, sunk in gloom, is gloomy. Vernon, who had seen the rushes two days before and had warned me what to expect, remained tactfully silent. John had given way to the fit of awful depression which attacks most light-hearted people, when faced with adversity. I pondered. We must have looked a pretty party.

Half-way to Walls we met John Behr in a car. We both stopped. It was certainly appendicitis. He was on his way to Lerwick Hospital, for further examination and attention. He looked pale but as imperturbable as ever. We wished him luck and he vanished down the road and out of the picture for good.

That brief meeting did not cheer us up. In death-bed voices we discussed his probable successor, and composed a wire to the studio.

The Negus is not such a Fool as he Looks

We arrived at the ship to find an indignation meeting. There had been no welcome, no excitement, no entertainments and *no drinks*. It really was a little too bad. It turned out that MacKenzie had issued the general invitation but had made no effort to follow it up. Nor had he imagined we would need entertaining. He was not a very imaginative man.

We calmed the meeting and had lunch. Afterwards things started moving. Sports started and we all took a hand. Frankie failed to win the Ladies' Sack Race but showed form and got a hand from the crowd. A football match, six a side, was played between Walls and Rock City; George and Skeets were our stars; we lost but it was a fast and dirty game.

We also had an event of our own which had been preparing as long as the concert. This was a race between a Shetland boat, coxed by Belle and rowed by Hamish, Buddy, Alasdair and Niall; and another, coxed by Frankie, with Bill White, George Black, and two of the *Vedra's* crew. John Laurie, fresh from hospital, umpired. After two false starts, the rival crews shot from the *Vedra's* side, their course being round a little island and back again. The race was full of incident. Shetland boats are not fitted with effete Southern gadgets like rowlocks: instead they have a kabe, which they stick into the ruths; round the kabe and the oar they twist a hommliband—and are all set. But to row with a kabe needs practice and I need hardly say that one after another of the oarsmen broke their hommlibands. The remainder nearly broke their ribs laughing. Bill White then got down to it properly and smashed his oar. There was a tendency to call it a day but, spurred on by their screaming coxswains, they struggled home, White using a wooden boat scoop with great effect. Frankie's boat was first across the line and many half-crowns changed hands, while White was the hero of the hour.

It was like Frankie to put her money on a sternly professional crew, rather than bask in the adoring smiles of gifted amateurs.

The day passed and got more cheerful. For one thing a secret store of drink had been uncorked; for another, the exploits of our athletes had attracted the attention of several Shetland maidens. By the time the concert arrived the morning was forgotten and the village hall needed elastic walls. The first half was local talent: all I remember is a Shetland sketch (one tall, thin woman was a born actress) about some old man who thought he was ill, or maybe he was dead, anyway it caused a lot of laughter and the dialect was immense. Then there was a short pause and a grey-maned, huge, spruce, agile figure loomed upon the platform. It was Finlay Currie and in three minutes he had that audience, like ten thousand others, in the hollow of his expressive hands.

For the next hour Finlay compèred our show and in a miraculous manner preserved continuity as:

Hamish sang 'The Gentle Maiden', in a pure baritone;

John Laurie recited 'Sir Patrick Spens', with gloomy fire;

Niall sang 'Frankie and Johnnie', to the speak-easy born, and 'Cockles and Mussels' as only a Dubliner can;

Peter and Wullie Gear fiddled 'The Foula Reel', with variations;

Bill Osborne did a comic recitative and brought down the house;

He himself played the piano and sang in a duet with Maud, his wife, whom he had fetched across from Lerwick;

Maud sang 'You are my Honeysuckle, I am the Bee!' and had them lifting the roof off; and

Syd Streeter sang 'Trees'.

I arrived too late to get a seat, for I had been talking to Monty, leaning on the rail of the *Vedra*, in the dusk. After what we had seen in Lerwick we both realized that he had to go back. However good his last work was (and it was perfect, we knew later) he could never live down that beginning. He would have no confidence and I could not take further risk. It was better to hand over to Ernie and go. He knew I was right. He tried to tell me how sorry he was for letting us down. But I knew already and, better still, I knew it was because he had aimed too high, and I made him understand that that is more than you can say of most people.

I went round to the back and got in the wings and saw the show from there, squashed by performers and anxious producers. Bill Osborne was a revelation to me. Until then he had been just a good prop-man. I can see him now, leaping on to the stage, clapping one hand on the other and swinging off into a gorgeous comic ballad, with his bottom stuck challengingly out and his whole person keeping time to the rhythm—then Niall, his dark face bent absently over his guitar, while his liquid Irish voice sings scandalous little songs—Maud and Finlay doing their stuff with the exquisite carelessness of Big Time—Maud, her cheerful mouth in a friendly grin and her body poised nonchalantly as she calls: 'Now, *all* together! YOU *are my* HON*ey*-HON*eysuckle*!'—and Syd, very straight, very earnest, very blond and very clean, a thin mist forming on his round spectacles, as he sings, in an uncertain tenor, 'TREES'.

Last of all the male voices of the company mass on the platform and lead community singing, which would be better without Monty, who has been drowning his sorrows, and Len, who has been helping him. They are not only off key, they are singing different songs.

And so slowly back to the *Vedra* in the dark. There seem to be a lot of female voices around to see us off. I remember one rather unexpected lady on the bridge. Then Hamish, mutinous:

'Mr. Powell, George says you want me to stay with the Negus and come back with him when the wind changes.'

'Yes, Hamish. Somebody must. Don't you want to?'

'Well, I don't. No.'

'All right. Buddy shall stay. But don't let him know he owes it to you.'

'I won't. Thanks.'

Buddy accepts the news with his usual angelic resignation. At one-thirty the *Vedra* sails. It is cold and a wicked swell running. The wind searches the boat like a customs officer. The short night is greying and the spray of the changing tide blows over the deck. Foula seems very far away. Little groups huddle together for warmth. Frankie is muffled in Skeets's overcoat. He tells her the story of his life. Belle is asleep in Vernon's bunk. As daylight comes, the anchor thunders down into the Voe.

The Master of the Horse

The regatta took place quite soon after our first south-easterly gale, when the Negus was nearly drowned in the Blow-hole. It was a narrow 'geo' down on the rocks near the Haa, very long, shelving and very deep. When wind and tide attempted to force about a million quarts of Atlantic into this pint-pot, it was a fine sight. It was comparatively safe for the camera, owing to the formation of a breakwater of rock. We all got very wet but were only once in real danger from a granddaddy of a seventh wave. At other times the backwash occasionally swirled round our waists.

Skeets and the Negus, neither of whom had the slightest fear of anything, made good allies. I am afraid I took advantage of this, for I soon found out that I had only to suggest that some deed was impossible, for Alasdair to sneer violently and insist on doing it. I was busily assembling a collection of startling cuts, with no particular continuity, with which to build up the big storm sequence which occurs in the film before the baby's illness. I had a very clear idea in my mind of how I proposed to present the storm, from the first change of wind and 'towering' of the clouds, and the sea and the barley starting to swell and move uneasily, to the final scream and senseless violence of a wind at a hundred miles an hour, with every second a crowded drama of detailed happenings.

Incidentally, it is in such sequences that the real point of direction lies. That is why 'director' is such an accurate title. He takes the genius available to him, in the experience of an actor or the path of a storm, and *directs* it into the firm channel of his imagination. In this particular instance I imagined the effect I wished to create on the screen, long before I ever saw Foula. After that I had only to remain true to my conception, to snatch opportunity as it was disclosed and to present those moments as dramatically as I could, at considerable risk to my cameramen, my friends and myself. Those who read this book and also see our film will find it amusing to examine consciously the pattern of the storm, from the opening shot of the starred cloud in the sky to the slow dissolve of the lantern ceasing to swing.

In pursuance of this policy, after inspecting the Blowhole in full-blast, I decided that, if we launched a boat into the boiling sea immediately near it, something spectacular would be bound to happen. Alasdair agreed and even suggested that he go out in it, but I drew the line at that. An old boat was bought for five pounds from Andrew Gray, of North Harrier, one of the victims of melancholy of whom I have spoken (he showed me the Norse stones at Netherfandal, when Michael killed the lamb). This was his only contact with the production, he refused to work for us, so John and I were pleased to have made this connection with him. It was a large boat, apparently sound but really full of dry-rot. It took all our men to carry it over the rocks and it was John Seabourne who, at considerable risk, gave it the final push down the shelving rocks. A wave took it. For two minutes we all watched breathless and two cameras shot: it swung upon the waves like a bubble, turned broadside in the trough, shipped a sea but still floated, drifted out, then a huge wave carried it to the mouth of the Blowhole. We held our breaths. It was all over in a second. Before the boat could escape a mountainous sea crashed over it, we saw it turn like a whale and *the next second* it was being carried up the 'geo', in pieces no bigger than a cigarbox. I have never seen dissolution so instantaneous. Skeets followed the wreckage up and down with his camera. The rest of us stared with our mouths open—even Alasdair, who was no doubt imagining himself in the brief supporting role which would have been his as the crew.

I got several storm shots, then moved in closer to try and get the violence of the impact of the tide, which was rising. I found this difficult to put over without some comparative medium. When Alasdair understood the point he volunteered again, this time to venture right down to the edge of the Blow-hole, on a line held by Peter Manson, in the foreground of the picture, who was in his turn held off screen. This seemed unpleasant but safe enough. I was wrong. As we were setting up, the waves did no more than dash spray over all of us, while Alasdair picked his way over the rocks which were knee deep in swirling water. But as we started shooting I heard an awful yell from all the spectators above. I glanced seawards in time to see half the Atlantic rear up into the sky. There was no time to move. The wave crashed down right over Alasdair, who vanished like a seal into the Blow-hole. Peter Manson, brought to his knees, also vanished in foam and spray. The backwash surged up to the lens of the camera but Skeets kept on shooting. Peter Manson struggled up, spitting like a cat. The rope held. The Blow-hole boiled and threw up Alasdair, clawing to the rope, his sea-boots ripped clean off him but his hat still on his head. We pulled, Peter pulled, Skeets went on shooting and Alasdair was with us again.

The Negus is not such a Fool as he Looks

There was a deafening cheer, half relief and half applause, and we decided to call it a day.

Alasdair was made much of, as he deserved to be. For perhaps the first time in his life, he was surrounded by a score of contemporaries who gave him their frank admiration, for his courage and his coolness. I watched with approval as he expanded. He found he liked to be popular, as who does not? From that moment he was a changed Smallie; and, what was more important, the attitude towards him had changed. His warnings, his mutterings, his prophecies, his troll-like grimness were no longer tiresome but an accepted part of that complex person, known affectionately, even to casual visitors, as the Negus.

He proved to have a gift for handling animals and he was the only person who could do anything with the ponies. For weeks a gang, headed usually by Bill Sweeny, who is very horse-minded, and can be seen galloping over the fields of Elstree in his lunch hour, attempted to pass the evenings by a rodeo. Headed by the pinto, the ponies resisted to the smallest foal. But they gave themselves up in batches to Alasdair, perhaps because in his working clothes, unshaved, crouching, with his thatch of hair flopping over his forehead, he looked like a relative. He handled them well, too. He broke them in to draw the clattering water-tank, on its never-ending path from burn to water-butt. He loaded them up with pack saddles and transported gear to the outlying camps. He even harnessed one to the camera truck (which was the cause of the chariot race at Blowburn). Apart from the yacht and his now accepted position as Chief Critic, it became his special job and he was formally installed as Master of the Horse.

He became a necessary part of the camp. When the wind changed in the middle of the night and the sound of the sea altered from broken surf to a steady drumming surge as the tide rose, lights would spring up in the house and heads would come out of the huts to see a headless figure—Alasdair struggling into a brown trawler smock—lurching down the path.

'What's wrong, Negus?'

'What's wrong!' would come in muffled tones. 'Have none of you any ears? It's a run in the Voe. I must double the line to the mooring!'

'What's up?' a sleepy voice would call from inside.

'The Negus and his blessed boat!'

There would be a sleepy chuckle. Then after a pause Niall, or perhaps Buddy, would murmur:

'Suppose we must give him a hand.'

And they would step into sea-boots and oilskins, dive out into the streaming darkness and strive mightily in tossing cockleshells, fending off from the heaving wet side of the yacht, as the slow surges of the run lifted them all high in the air, level with the top of the jetty, silently as the hands of a giant and with the same potential of destruction.

He was seldom wrong about the weather, though that is really an instinct mixed with local experience. By the end of our stay I knew Foula as well as anyone, and a look at the sky in the early morning told me what locations would be possible. But I never arrived at the long forecasts which Alasdair indulged in, and which nearly always proved to be correct.

All through the summer he continued to hold Sunday service, for any that would prefer a simple meeting to a locked chapel. He was supported by Finlay, who played the little organ with overwhelming virtuosity, and by John Laurie, whose beautiful voice transformed the Lessons. But Alasdair's sermons were the chief attraction. I went to hear one and came away, my head spinning from an overdose of metaphysics. Nobody understood more than a word here and there, I doubt if Alasdair did himself, but if the function of a sermon, to the average congregation, is to be unlike anything they are likely to hear on a weekday, then he succeeded beyond his wildest hopes.

I do not know whether it has been gathered by the reader that I am fond of Alasdair. The statement may arouse violent resentment, even incredulity, in his breast, but it is true. I have tried to present all sides of his complex character. But I leave it to himself to supply his own final judgment, by recalling an incident midway through the production, after there had been a good deal of quiet rum-running, chiefly, I fancy, by the party in the Haa. We were all in the big hut one evening, it was either before dinner or after Parliament. Alasdair appeared at the door with an empty whisky bottle in his hand. He waited until all eyes were turned towards him, then he placed the bottle on the shelf by the door. The bottle had a white label attached, with writing on it. With a trollish chuckle he withdrew.

There was a rush to read the label. In a scrawling but definite hand was written:

'THE NEGUS IS NOT SUCH A FOOL AS HE LOOKS.'

Chapter XIII

CADDY THIS AND CADDY THAT

*

Scribbled upon John's private call-sheet one evening I noticed: 'Mem: must get Tom o' Gravins' cracked caddy for first scene in morning. See Tom. If difficult use Blowburn caddy.'

Now this requires explanation. It is not a cryptogram, though if Sir Richard Hannay had found it during a flying visit to Foula (about the only place he has not been since the War, though he came near us when he was in the Faeröes last year) he would undoubtedly have chewed over it for half a dozen chapters. Nor is it anything to do with golf. It refers to caddy-lambs.

A caddy-lamb in Shetland—and, for all I know, in Scotland, also—is a lamb whose mother has died or who is too much a sheep-about-town to suckle it, and which therefore has to be brought up on a bottle. When I was little we always had one to look after every spring. It lived in the boiler cupboard in the kitchen and used to butt with its bullet head when it wanted to come out. It would empty a bottle with the ease of a vacuum-cleaner, which made one sympathize with the mothers who had refused to come across. When the cook began to complain about having a great sheep underfoot, the pet lamb was turned into the little orchard with my pony and would come running at the sight of a brandished bottle, until at last such childish things were put away and he went out into the world.

Nearly every croft on Foula had such caddy-lambs. All

the caddies were loved and cared for, and consequently thought a great deal of themselves and regarded any human being who approached them without a bottle as a cumberer of the earth.

Caddies were featured heavily in the evacuation of the island, either led or carried in arms. The Blowburn caddy attained stardom, with John Laurie, to its own considerable annoyance, in the scene down the cliff at Simmond's Head, where John, with his stave and his rope, goes over after a lamb which has strayed into danger and brings it to the top on his back. The Blowburn caddy is a lamb (now sheep, or mutton, I suppose) of considerable force of character like its owner, Peter Manson, the uncompromising figure made of teak, who has already been encountered in the gloom of the Shop and, again, at the Blow-hole. Peter Manson took some knowing: he was not called Baron Blowburn by myself and John for nothing, any more than Robbie Isbister, at the other end of the island, was called the Archdeacon. Peter was a man of violent temper and he expended a lot of energy when we first knew him, in exhibitions of it. But once he really knew and trusted us he was invaluable. He did not know what fear was, he was exceptionally quick and intelligent, and he made a first-class actor (he sits beside Finlay in the Parliament scene). I liked the Baron and, with reservations, the Baron approved of me but I think Niall was his favourite; their characters had points in common, though all Niall's reactions are overlaid with a thickish slab of Celtic twilight, a contrast to the clear light that beats upon Blowburn.

The Blowburn caddy, then, when first called upon, trotted willingly on a string up to the top of Soberlie, no doubt expecting an enormous bottle as reward. Its face, when pounced upon, trussed up and lowered over a beetling cliff into the waiting arms of its traitorous master, was a study. John swears that the lamb, all the way up the rope, when not relieving its feelings on his shoulder, was positively grinding its teeth with rage. The sequence was not completed for two more days. Each day the caddy was called. But no more trotting to location. As soon as it saw Bill Osborne it lay down, became a prop and had to be carried every step. A lamb, as I have said, of considerable force of character (now, no doubt a vicious-looking sheep, or, if mutton, excessively tough mutton).

Foula sheep are in a class by themselves. To start with they are capable of practically every colour of the spectrum except pure white (like the new Technicolor process). The general run are a kind of cinnamon and, as chubby lambs, are exceedingly handsome. John swears he saw a blue one on Wester Hoevdi, but John sees and hears so many outrageous things on oath. At all events the lambs are attractive but when they grow up it is a different story.

There are no sheep-dogs on Foula. The people say they would frighten the sheep over the cliffs or else rush over themselves in their excitement. This is borne out by Lord Dumfries who told me that he imported dogs to round up the famous, wild little sheep of Soay (Gaelic: Isle of Sheep) in order to transport the stock to the main island of Hirta, where they could be properly supervised. He only succeeded at the cost of all his dogs and a great many sheep, whose wildness has already been described (Chapter II, page 11). The St. Kildans, according to MacGregor, employed dogs, but not to drive sheep; they filed their teeth to sharp points and set them after individuals. The dog would rush at his quarry, get his teeth in the wool of his throat and bring him down with a bang, very like bull-dogging a steer. These heroic manœuvres are not practised by the Foula people whose method is equally individual but more humane, at least to the sheep,

Dotted about the island in certain strategic spots are sheepfolds, called krös. (Dr. Jakobsen, who is my main authority on dialect and spelling, writes this word 'Krø', the third symbol being the one he always uses to indicate the liquid Shetland vowel, similar to the 'ö' in the German 'schön'. But since it is almost similar I have used the latter. It is more simple and Miss Curtis and Miss Page have already had enough headaches with words like Nebbifeld and Hellibaa, dragged into the script to provide colour.) The krös are stone walls arranged in an arbitrary fashion, usually in the rough shape of a lock, thus:

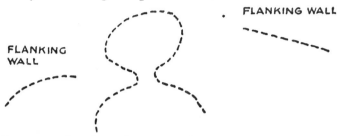

They are placed with an excellent eye to country, the habits and pasture of the sheep, natural hazards, idiosyncrasies of ovine gang-leaders and a dozen other possibilities. They are often changed, for Foula sheep know a thing or two and may be trapped once, with difficulty twice, but not a third time in the same krö. So great is the respect of the islanders for the intelligence of their flocks that they take care to build the krös in secret and at the breeding season when a sheep's time is, so to speak, not her own.

In August come the Sheep Runnings. They are communal affairs and each division of the island is run when the chief owner of that division gives the word, always depending on weather and mail-boat day. In 1936 a film company was an additional nuisance. Comes a propitious day, the procedure is as follows. All the elderly men and young girls (and such young men as are not at the fishing nor at that perilous age when they have attained dignity, but not had time to realize its waste of time) start out early for the hills. They sneak along in a casual sort of way, leaving vedettes and forward listening-posts at key positions. They pretend to extreme aimlessness but the sheep know better. Sooner or later they are spotted by some cynical-eyed matron, whose mass of dragging tangled wool, half on, half off her back and shoulders, gives her a horrible similarity to the leering semi-undress of a mid-Victorian brothel and show that she has avoided 'rooing' for two seasons and will be got into a krö only over your dead body.

She gives the call to arms and more and more sheep stop grazing, stare jeeringly and start a crabwise retreat. Soon there is a definite movement of escape. But the runners have now neared their objective and can throw aside concealment. With a wild yell Robbie Isbister breaks into a gallop which would not disgrace a man fifty years his junior. Swooping down on the flank hurtle Edith and Aggie Jean, their bare feet covering the ground in giant leaps, their shawls waving in the air, which is already humming with their shrill war-whoops. Head of a flying column which has cut off the main retreat is Jimmy Gray (Up the Grays!) running like a stag and bellowing like a bull. The Run is on!

A Foula sheep's one object in life is to avoid being run and rooed, and to achieve it they will scramble, double and dodge in a manner that would bring tears to the eyes of a football professional. They short-cut down the cliffs like chamois, are as cynical as goats and as clever as monkeys. As an instance of their efficiency, there is a certain kind of seaweed, of which they are fond as a cat of valerian, which only comes ashore at the back of the Noup and then only when the tide and wind are in conjunction in a very special way. As soon as these conditions arrive, before ever a piece of seaweed is within miles of the coast, the sheep can be seen drifting down over the banks and lining up like housewives at a bargain sale. And they say sheep are dumb!

Such animals are not likely to submit tamely. The Run, which starts as a rout, soon develops into a guerilla war. Old hands (if I may so describe a two-toed quadruped) dash for the gaps in defence and, unless they meet with determined resistance, will break through, followed by others. Many go tearing down the banks, where it would be a hasty death to follow. Others stop dead and lie down, preferring to be charged over, rather than rooed. All the time, the Run is sweeping down the chosen route, on a gradually narrowing front, till, if the division-leader has placed his defences well, two or three hundred sheep, out of a thousand or so, are being forced into a natural bottle-neck. This can be seen in the bird's-eye view which precedes the closer shots of the Run in the film. Here they are art-fully being driven down to the Sneck, across it by the only bridge of rubble which exists and down the other side on to a path along the face of the cliff, which has sheer sandstone above, and below a broken precipice to the sea. The only exit is on to a small ledge, formed by a landslide, about half an acre in extent, with, in its turn, only one exit up the cliff, which is firmly blocked, first by the older women, second by Skeets and George Black, with the Mitchell. Ernie, with the Debrie, is in the Sneck, shooting the bridge. I am in hiding on the cliff below the path, getting the long, winding line of sheep up the narrow track and hanging on to myself and the Newman camera. The last stragglers down the cliff are shooed up again, the line of runners closes in, waving sticks, coats, and shawls, there is a sudden rush and the krö is full.

Now the older women each grab a hundred pounds or so of struggling adult sheep, yank its legs off the ground and start to roo it. It is then quite evident why the sheep go to such lengths to avoid this process. The short, fine wool is pulled off the hair in quick handfuls, the overcoat separat-ing from the undercoat like the husk of a ripe walnut. They never touch the fleece with shears on Foula (nor in most parts of Shetland), which is the reason for the soft, warm Shetland wool, famous all over the world. In ten minutes a sheep is stripped and allowed to bounce indignantly away up Hamnafeld. Next year it will be a good deal harder to get that one into the krö.

I was determined to get the sheep-running and rooing into the film, although I was without any clear idea of where it would fit dramatically. I knew that it would work in at the time of the Laird's visit to the island, but it was not dovetailed into its proper place, as it is in the film and in my synopsis. It is not particularly necessary that this point should be clear in the reader's mind but it is an interesting one technically and shows why the silent film had more elasticity than the present form of talkie.

In the film, as the last sad shot of the funeral fades away, the audience is suddenly transported to a different world. The sun gleams on the sea, there are distant cries and the bleat of sheep and rapid movement of tiny figures. It is the perfect contrast. Hardly have the audience seen enough of the Run, but enough to see that every soul on the island is busily engaged, when they are switched to the meeting between the two lovers, a tranquil, glowing scene among running waters and yellow iris, another contrast but a part of the Run, for soon the scene shifts away to show the rooing and then returns to the lovers, with the delight of the secret meeting over, and the black future before them.

The Run has now a definite purpose. It changes the tempo at the proper moment, it creates unique atmosphere, it provides a shield for the meeting of the lovers, by its contrast of busy action with complete calm. It is no longer only pictorial and instructive, it is dramatic—and a necessary part of the film.

This was done by cutting the two episodes together. I brought back from Foula two good but sharply different episodes, one dramatic, the other documentary. A casual observer, an unskilled technician, a bad cutter would have recommended either cutting the Run to a minimum or losing it altogether. ('No time for a lot of sheep; they've seen sheep before.') A cutter of genius, like Derek Twist, conceives the idea of combining the two sequences.

This is a long digression but has given me great pleasure to write, for, although I knew what I have just explained, I had never analysed it; and it is fair praise for Derek Twist who will never get a quarter of the credit which is due to him on the editing of the picture, any more than Bob Walters, who toiled night and day assembling it, who worked through Boxing Day, New Year's Eve and an influenza epidemic, and who alone of everybody connected with it, except myself, believed in the picture from start to finish. These are the unsung heroes who really make the films.

While I was up in the Hooses of the Burrie, with Belle and a mob of ponies, John and Monty were down by Broadfoot, getting close-ups of the rooing and of the milling sheep. This was our first encounter with the calm, matter-of-fact poise of the Foula folk when facing a battery of cameras, and especially of the women; for in less civilized parts of the world, it is generally hard to persuade women to be natural. All the people of Foula are natural actors. I would tell them what they had to do and why they had to do it: they would nod and do it. It was as simple as that and, to anybody resigned through much suffering to the other kind, it was Heaven.

None of them were in the least self-conscious, although the Grays (Up the Grays!), when Thomas and Mrs. Gray, with Jimmy, Edith, Louisa and Maggie, joined up with Mary (Mrs. James Morrison) and Aggie Jean (Mrs. Bobbie Isbister), were as a family prone to startling bursts of giggles which would suddenly sweep through a scene like machine-gun fire.

But all poise vanished when the islanders saw themselves upon our little projection screen. The sight of their friends or themselves walking about and talking proved irresistibly comic. When we started officially to project rushes in the Mess Hut with our newly arrived portable equipment,

Skeets started the rot by pleading to be allowed to bring Jimmy Gray in with the camera crew. (Jimmy was officially attached to the camera department who had, unofficially, become very attached to him, for he was an enthusiastic mechanical putterer, like all true cameramen.) This consent naturally meant that, as soon as the rumour spread, all people who were in the current batch of rushes also asked permission, which was hard to refuse. Finally, a sort of convention was observed in the matter, whereby the favoured few came in and took seats with an air of importance and, as soon as the lights were put out, the entire island, who had massed outside in the dark, would creep silently in. The first intimation I had of this was to find my chair rising up into the air under mysterious pressure from all sides, much as the weaker oxen in the herd are forced up on to the backs of their brothers. Mysterious figures would cross the room, suddenly find themselves in the projection beam, blocking the picture to a general roar of disapproval, and would hastily duck down again, only to reappear under your feet.

All through this I was attempting to view the rushes in a constructive spirit and to dictate notes to John and George Black, who were both craned over notebooks lit, at intervals, by pocket torches. Meanwhile the show went with a roar. Chaplin himself never got more laughs to the foot than I did with my most serious scenes. It was impossible to hear any dialogue for the continuous screams of merriment as the Archdeacon addressed a portentous grunt to John Laurie or Mrs. Henry of North Biggins tied up Fanny (who rejoiced in one brown eye and one blue one) to the hitching rail outside the church.

Finally we put our notebooks away, abandoned ourselves to the general mood of appreciation and had our post-mortem later, in the decent obscurity which must shroud such grisly matters.

The only native of the island who really penetrated the

mysteries of film-making besides Jimmy Gray (who was overheard by John explaining to Willy Smith the technique of the overlap in action and its use in cutting) was undoubtedly Bob, the Dog Who Made Good. I must take a little licence—dare I say dog-licence?—at this point, in imagining his more intimate dreams, but no more than is taken by most ghost-writers, substituting for a star incapable of placing one sentence after another.

It is not a new story, you have read it a thousand times, but its hero gives it a touch of novelty which others lack and which justifies its telling.

Bob was one of four industrious brothers. (A classic opening, and he is a classic hero.) They were all industrious in different ways. Vic, of Leirabach, spent the twenty-four hours chasing birds off the Isbister demesne, in particular an Allen Richardson Skua, a personal friend of Dodie, who was to be seen in the spring peering hopefully out to sea every morning until the bird checked in, as it had regularly done for several years. Through constant practice, Vic, who was a long black streamy sort of dog, as light as a feather, had arrived at a new mode of progression (for a dog) which resembled levitation. He could be seen, on the Leirabach skyline, flying through the air behind the birds for an appreciable distance, falling eventually to earth and immediately rebounding without visible effort. When the grass grew longer, he bounded higher. I have never, before or since, seen such a rubber animal. He was known to the camp as the Bouncing Dog.

Lion, of South Biggins, was ordinary by comparison but he was the good-looker of the family. He had an immense head, with large liquid eyes and a tousled mane, and he bit anybody who gave him the chance.

Bill, of Gravins, was kept tied up all the time, like most of the Foula dogs, and spent the entire summer, from the day we landed till the smoke of the *Vedra* vanished for good over the horizon, in a perpendicular frenzy of emotion, which expressed itself in astounding bounds (for they were a family eccentricity) up and down, to and fro and occasionally round and round, when Bob happened to trot by with his nose in the air.

Bob was from Ham. Therein lay his first advantage, for it was the nearest croft to the Haa; and, because he was allowed to play with little Ivor and his brother, he was often loose. Early in the production he came sniffing round the City. Undoubtedly he found a script (probably Niall's, for he was always leaving his copy under boats or in boots). It must have been a great moment for Bob, for there, in black and white, was a part, whose every bark might have been written with him in mind. He crawled around. As far as he could smell, no effeminate dog-star had been imported. If only he could make a test for the part or catch the eye of the director!

In those days Bob, who never knew about his next meal, except that it was unlikely, had about as much body as a spider-monkey. He was all hair, curly, wavy, sort of flowing hair, which made him look like those elaborate pieces of scroll-work that one finds on old figureheads of ships. The fact that he had no stomach enabled him to make himself flatter than Miss Joan Crawford and to worm his way under huts, beds, chairs and carpets with ease. His method was simple. He started at the bottom and worked up.

First he haunted the huts. When everybody got tired of continually kicking him around, he was allowed to stay. He consolidated his position until people started to pat him, then invaded the Mess Hut. Same kicks, same lethargy, same consolidation, and he then moved into the kitchen. Same process. The passage in the Haa followed. Then the parlour itself; the girls were easy game but not the others! It was the toughest fight of the lot, but he won through and Eric had to cede him a portion of the sofa. He was inside!

The rest was easy. The director's eye was already caught

Caddy This and Caddy That

(I had intended using a Shetland collie and it was George who acted as Bob's agent), Bob got a test, Bob got the part and Bob was a wow! He was signed up at once by Bill Osborne, who took him back to live at Elstree. After the trade show of the film, he was the first of the actors to get an offer, and the last I heard of him he was supported by Charles Laughton, to the tune of £15 a week and all found!

Two of Bob's brothers, Vic and Lion, appear in the film, for a short scene with their more successful relative. It is at the church, when all the dogs are tied up outside, listening to the sermon. It is only a brief flash of three bored dogs in a tangled heap, but it tells a story. Look closely at Bob's expression. He is suffering. His expression is poignant with agony, the other two are merely bored. This is not because he is so much the better actor. It is because this little scene was made after all the big scenes, where Bob was the centre of attraction and continually being petted and rewarded—the Only Dog in the film. Suddenly he found himself, one morning, turned out of his dressing-room, forced to do *crowd-work*! Now you know the real secret of Bob's expression. He couldn't take it!

Before I leave the dogs of Foula, I must say a word about the church sequence. The script called for owners, with their dogs, among the churchgoers. The dogs could not, of course, have a place in church (though I believe that has been customary in some parts of Scotland, perhaps in Galloway, with the shepherds). A rail was to be fixed outside and the dogs tied to it in a row. So far, so good. It made an excellent scene. But consider the feelings of the dogs.

I have explained that Foula dogs are kept tied up, or in their crofts, all their lives. This is because of the sheep. It limits their activity but stimulates their imagination. Occasionally a dog would clear its throat and do a bit of barking, just to keep in practice. As he paused for breath, he would start! Faint and far would come an answering bark from Hametoun! He would try again. Same reply. He would meditate, then growl to himself: 'Either that is an echo or, by St. Bernard, there is another dog on Foula! If ever I meet him I'll tear out his lungs and liver! Bow-Wow-Wow! etc.' until somebody gave him a clout on the head.

Dawned the Day! Each Foula dog was unleashed by its owner! taken for a walk! and tied up, nose to nose, tail to tail, staring eyeball to quivering nostril, next to eight other dogs who, to this moment, had only been an evil dream. There was an interval of pure amazement followed by one of the finest mixed fights ever seen outside a totalitarian state. Nurse Dodson's Danny, who was giving a good deal more than he got, was removed by Nurse and could be heard shadow-boxing all the way back to Hamnabrach. And the Show Went On.

I have drifted (a habit of mine) rather far away from the caddies, with which I commenced this chapter, and I realize that I have not yet explained Tom o' Gravins' cracked caddy. He was only called 'cracked' for the sake of alliteration. In plainer speech, he was nuts.

He was a handsome lamb, and allowed the run of the place, to Bill's barkless fury. He loved scouting round people. Frankie and I would be passing and she would say: 'Oh, look! there's the cracked caddy—oh, he's gone!' She would still be looking in the byre, where he had vanished, when I would glance up and see him glaring down at us from the chimney. I would say: 'Frankie, he's up—blast, he's gone again!' We would continue past Gravins, turn the corner and meet him face to face, usually chewing something. We would attempt to fraternize. He would give us a dirty look, bounce up and down on stiff legs, like a Noah's Ark lamb, then turn and make off 'with a dirrel upon him'. ('Dirrel' is Shetland for a sheep's tail and when used in this sense means a swaying walk to show the person is offended: cf. Minnie Mouse leaving Mickey flat.)

Caddy This and Caddy That

Caddy became rather a favourite adjective with the unit. The girls had caddy kittens (they were presented by Mrs. Smith). Frankie found a caddy calf. Its name was Pansy and it lived in front of Leirabach. It was a dear little calf and liked being made a fuss of but, for half an hour after its patron had left, it would moo its heart out and spoil all the sound-shots. Peter Manson had a caddy guinea-pig (it was murdered by Bob, who in his turn was nearly murdered by the wrathful Peter. An hour later, to everyone's surprise, the guinea-pig arose like Lazarus and went on eating where it had left off). Robina, Dodie's sister, had a caddy water-lily on Mill Loch. It has a close-up in the film when the psalm is being sung about 'quiet waters'. Ernie (unique honour) attained to the dizzy status of 'Caddy' Palmer and stayed there to the end. Finally and triumphantly there were the caddy rabbits.

They lived in a pile of great stones from the breach made in the wall for the entrance to Rock City. They appeared to have no mother and were therefore doubly caddy, and were the smallest and boldest rabbits I have ever seen. They sat about, all five of them, not one bigger than my fist, all over the camp. When Bob passed they would vanish, only to reappear as his tail went out of sight. (This took some time, for Bob's parents were collie and spaniel [Michael], and the collie had also had Pekinese forbears, so that Bob's tail was a sort of Three Power Conference.) All through the summer the caddy rabbits amused the camp; and they never seemed to get any larger; they were very popular, especially with Frankie, who would crouch near them for hours, extending a tired lettuce-leaf, hoping they would take it from her hand.

In addition to possessing the one official pet (the cataleptic guinea-pig) Blowburn also boasted the sole fruit-tree on Foula—a pessimistic-looking raspberry cane. Nineteen thirty-six was a good year and it bore fruit, which was proudly presented to John Seabourne who, as proudly, ate it. In return he imported a basket of pears for old Mr. Manson. I never met the old gentleman, for he was bed-ridden and over ninety, but needless to say John had made his acquaintance and had several talks with him.

'What do you do all day?' he asked at their first meeting.

'Just lie in bed here, dying by inches,' was the snappy reply, delivered in a cheerful, matter-of-fact voice.

'Do you read much?' parried John, recovering.

'Oh, yes, I like to read the paper whiles,' said the valiant warrior; and he insisted on John handing him a paper which was on the bed and, holding it firmly in front of his failing eyes, he rattled off a leader about the fisheries. John looked closer. The paper was upside down. He had learnt the entire article by heart.

John became a great confidant of his after that. One day he told John that the only thing he fancied any more was a nice, ripe pear. He had not had one for years. So before we left John got some in by the *Vedra*. They were delayed and some went over-ripe, but John was able to take half a dozen fine ones up to Blowburn.

When Dodie and Walter came down to London a year later to see the opening of the film they told me that old Manson had worn away at last, during the winter.

Healthy as an oak, except for his rheumatics, was old John Gray of Burns, father of Peter. He was the only man on the island with a real, white patriarchal beard. It would take a prize anywhere. Shetlanders do not go in for beards much; which is odd, considering their Norse ancestors, and the piercing winds. John Gray highly approved of the film unit. He privately thought we were all daft but it did him good to watch other people work so hard and every time he got paid for crowd-work he nearly burst himself laughing. One day, as he laboriously signed his chit, he said:

'Maister Seabourne, I'm eighty years to-day. I've been a

ride across the isle in yon car o' yours. I've had a close-up taken by your camera—and now I'm getting paid for standing on the jetty and smokin' of me old pipe!'

I have no doubt that, at intervals during the winters, he takes his old pipe out of his mouth and shakes with laughter at having got away with murder, that year the film company infested the island. When I go back I shall ask Peter Gear.

Peter is the Postmaster and J.P. He lives at Mogle, the croft by the bridge over the burn at Ham, into which Syd nearly somersaulted with the overloaded car (Belle, Hamish, Bill Osborne, Tom Sullivan, Bill Paton and himself, all in a Morris Minor) in his haste to turn the corner and also avoid the Mogle dog, an impossible combination at all times. The dog, whose territory had to be passed nearly every day, resented the car bitterly. Not so Peter Gear, for he felt that at last he had justification for dusting off five hundred copies of the Highway Code, which had been sent to him a year before, with compliments of the Ministry of Transport.

If every salesman of a Morris Minor could overcome half the difficulties which faced us, when introducing a car to Foula, I suppose Lord Nuffield would be able to found a complete university as well as pay off the National Debt. After three schemes had been tried and abandoned, Syd constructed a raft and, on a calm day, the car was lowered on to it. Raft and car promptly started to sink, owing to the number of people aboard. There was a frantic scramble for the *Vedra* and the car remained submerged only to the hubs. In this condition it was towed into the Voe at low tide, giving the shock of his life to the old seal who patrolled those waters. The raft was dragged on to the sand and the car pushed off, the first car to leave its tyre-prints on Foula! But it was not yet in circulation. Pulled by ropes and pushed by hands it was driven up the rocks by Syd, who succeeded in burning out the clutch. For two weeks we continued to pant up the road with batteries and cameras. Then Vernon and a mechanic from Scalloway repaired it and, for the rest of the production, that poor little car moved mountains every day. After Syd and Skeets had had their licences endorsed by special act of parliament, Buddy was put in charge and nursed its failing strength with tender care. Peter Gear's son bought the remains when we left and, by some means, restored life to the shattered corpse. Walter told me that he carried peats with it last year. But I think that the Morris will be the last touring car on Foula as well as the first.

In the photograph of the Voe and Mill Loch, which I took from the top of Hamnafeld, near the place where the Lum is supposed to be, the road up from the Haa is very clear, with its sharp fork, one to Blowburn, by way of Gossameadow and Burns, the other to Hametoun, past Leirabach. It is plain, too, how near Leirabach is to Mill Loch, and its wheeling kittiwakes which Robina loved.

It was Robina who first told me of the Lum of Liorafield, that dreadful abode of trolls. I have referred to it several times but it is only now that I can pluck up courage to deal with it, and if the printer refuses to set up and the publisher to sponsor such a tale of horror I cannot blame them.

All the trolls (except the Smallie) and all their evil influences and the bad luck they bring are crammed into the Lum, so that, even though its depths are fabulous, even though its dark shaft extends from the top of Hamnafeld to the bottom of the sea, it is so full of swirling poisonous vapours that the flagstones which cover it must never be lifted, especially by a stranger to the island. Many daring men have climbed to the Lum and tried to measure its depth. But who can measure the immeasurable? Bad luck, death and the trolls have always followed them to an early grave.

When it yawned open on the moor there were many sheep lost, and once a dog disappeared into it, whose body was found in the sea by Ham Little. After that the Laird of those days caused it to be covered over. The coarse grass and the heather grew above and now no one knows the site of the Lum of Liorafield, or, if the older men do, they keep their own counsel.

I searched for it many times, without success, though there is little doubt of its existence. Sir Walter Scott talks of it in *The Pirate*; Liorafield means chimney-mountain, and the whole of Hamnafeld is a great hollow tank whose water pours out, winter and summer, into Mill Loch through the fissures in its sides.

Robina has a love for every kind of flower and animal, but she is very shy and suffered silent agonies of embarrassment when I persuaded her to appear in the cradle scene at Sloag. She prefers to do good by stealth or to stuff her guests with cakes and scones and bread and jam and tea until they are fit to burst. But she will talk for hours, in an apologetic voice, of the flowers and plants of Foula. She lent me a slim little catalogue, compiled by a botanist who spent the year there. He refers to her again and again, for supplying local sayings and the beloved old names which children and their children's children give to flowers. I wish I had space to print it all; but there is one note which deserves special reference here.

Mrs. Traill was what is termed a fine managing woman. I believe that she had acted as Factor to the previous owner of Foula. According to eye-witnesses, she was tall and wore flowing garments of double-weight cloth which swept her along like a ship in full sail, a square-rigged flat cap on her main-truck, and a square bearded chin, thrust out to meet the weather. When Professor Holbourn took udal possession, thirty years ago, she continued to live in her stout little wooden house, which was built on the flat ground, between Gravins and the school-house. Nor did she change her character, and the fact that she had so little scope to exercise her talents very soon caused friction. The Foula people are independent and conservative. They are also polite; they contented themselves by referring to her, behind her back, as 'the Captain'.

One stormy day, when Mrs. Traill was on the mainland, a sudden gale struck Foula, and down from the top of Hamnafeld swooped one of the dreaded 'flans', which I can best describe as an air-spout. It passed over Mill Loch, hurling the whole lake into the air, swooped down the burn towards Gravins, passed by a wooden outhouse and some packing-cases, picked up Mrs. Traill's cottage bodily and hustled with it towards the Voe. Not unnaturally the floor dropped out and the contents of the rooms were strewn all over Ham. The house crashed down near the Haa and exploded into fragments which were whisked out to sea and disappeared. There was nothing left but the cement foundations. Small wonder that the islanders, thoughtfully examining the damage, were heard to say that 'there was more than wind in yon'.

The epilogue to this saga is in Robina's plant catalogue, which contains the following item:

'56. URTICA DIOICA, or Common Nettle: One only *found on the ruins of Mrs. Traill's cottage.*'

Which shows how Nature can beat Art at its own game.

I—and the whirlwind—have continually passed over the school-house. For very shame I can do so no longer. Nor would I wish to, if I could be sure of seeing Mrs. Smith and her husband, Willy, once again. Of Mrs. Smith I can only tell you this: she is a darling. It has been often remarked that a successful wife must be both wife and mistress. Willy and her school children will assure you of Mrs. Smith's success in both roles.

The school, in the film, ·had bad luck. So had Mr. Greenaway though he kindly does not blame me for it. Perhaps he was a little relieved. I have told how I met him at Walls after my first visit. I wrote a school sequence, to be played on the shore of Mill Loch, with the intention of intercutting it with the grown men's parliament. When I returned to Foula I found to my dismay that Mr. Greenaway had returned to Edinburgh, fearing lest Foula should be overcrowded. I wrote to him and, as soon as he was reassured, he returned.

I had written a scene where he reads to the children from *The Discoverer of the North Cape* and tells them:

'A fine tale! and never forget, children, that it's those same old Norsemen who discovered Shetland and put up the big stones yonder by Netherfandal.'

He points up the valley. Then he drifts off into Burns and reminds them that there is the only poet for Scotsmen . . . a hand shoots up.

'Well, James Andrew?'

'It's only yesterday', says James Andrew, without taking a breath, 'that we were reading in the history book that the Islands never rightly belonged to Scotland because they were given as mor-r-rtgage against the dowry of the Princess of Denmark which was never paid and so we're not rightly Scottish or so the book says!'

He is reproved by a crushing: 'There's a deal that's contradictory in books, James Andrew of Mucklegrind!'

John held an audition in the school one day and there was never any doubt about the winner. Gerald Umphray, of Brae, son of old Robbie, was formally given the part and received a copy of his lines. Besides the 'mor-r-rtgage speech', he had to rush down the brae and scream: 'Andrew has taken Robbie's challenge an' they're a' goin' doon to the boats the noo!' I had a rehearsal in the school-house and he was splendid. He was at once promoted to the post of bellringer at the kirk and also to tie up Bob in the evacuation. But this is all that is in the film. The school had to wait for more essential scenes, until it was too late to think of doing it. But if anyone wants a gr-r-rand little actor, every freckle on Gerald's face can be had, *pro rata*.

Mrs. Smith not only runs the school but contributes to

its success and continuance with her own attractive daughters, Stella, Nanette and Jessamine. Stella laboured mightily in the evacuation scene, in a variety of disguises, but principally in a Shetland wool helmet pulled over her head and framing her face. (Belle wears one, when she takes the baby through the storm to the trawler.) Jessamine has a scene to herself, packing kittens; and also passes by in a kesshie, on her mother's back. She has her mother's looks but has yet to show if she has got her brains. Nanette is shy and dark and very domestic, her mother tells me.

The evacuation is full of pictures and memories for John and myself: the Biggins ram, trotting sedately up and down beside Aggie Jean, its gentle yellow eyes undisturbed; Jimmy Henry, one hand full of ponies, the other straining at the Ham ox, who refuses to budge; Tom o' Gravins drifting by with his caddy, a gentle smile on both their faces; Dodie and James Ratter, solemnly trying to make a huge box look as if it weighed a couple of hundredweight; Shirley Temple running in and out of everything; and, trudging here, there and everywhere, serious, solid and superb, the Dumplings from Stöel.

The Dumplings have a big close-up together, by the cradle at Sloag, in the lullaby scene. They are looking down at the baby with a smile. I have never seen the film with an audience without overhearing: 'Oh, look at those two!' Other people have told me that the shot is like a Dutch painting, which I suppose they mean for a compliment; but they really only mean that there are two faces which God loves.

Chapter XIV

THE FOUR WINDS OF FOULA

★

The *North Sea Pilot*, a romantic but cynical publication which makes an excellent bed-book, observes drily of the Shetlands and Orkneys: 'The wind is generally regarded as the outstanding feature of the climate.'

For subtle under-statement Noel Coward has nothing on Captain C. M. Gibson, O.B.E., R.N., the editor of the eighth edition, which is deservedly one of the Admiralty's current best-sellers.

Later, he adds: 'The general tendency to gusts and squalls of wind in the vicinity of high ground should be borne in mind.' You observe his technique. No build up, no purple passages, no under- or overtones—but he gets there just the same.

I admire his style but cannot imitate it.

When you have attained to that stage of navigational detachment when you can describe a series of horrifying gales in which the wind backs and changes all round the compass in the twenty-four hours, as "an unusual series of barometric depressions", then I should imagine that you can no longer care about sharing your experiences with other people. You have arrived at a serene level, usually attained only by income-tax inspectors. Colour, drama, struggle— you care for none of these things.

I am different. I want to make your flesh creep.

The Four Winds of Foula

The Prevailing Wind

The prevailing wind is westerly. This gives plenty of scope for unpleasantness, for to the west of Foula is nothing but the North Atlantic ocean, full of icebergs, whales, magnetic disturbances, compass variations and swirly lines upon the chart. When I first went to Foula the direction of the wind meant nothing to me. I was the complete innocent. If I had only had the sense to study a meteorological report, to learn a little navigation, to read Captain Gibson's admirable work, I should have saved a month of heartbreaking struggle and disappointment, a whole month during which I would have been better employed in emptying Mill Loch with Jimmy Isbister's forty-one egg-cups.

I have always found that technical experts are quite useless when attached to a film company. I have an anxiety, amounting to morbidity, not to have any serious howler in any film of mine which deals with a technical subject. Invariably there arises an occasion when, even to my ignorance, the scene incorporates a piece of action which must be wrong. An example was a scene in the set of the shipyard on *Red Ensign*. Men were heating rivets in one corner of the set and hammering them into a plate in another. I said to my expert, who was standing by me with the pleased and fascinated smile of a studio visitor to any big set:

'Surely the furnace ought to be near the holder-on? The rivets would cool off if they were carried that distance.'

He said: 'Yes, of course.'

I said: 'They ought to be near each other.'

He said: 'As near as possible.'

I was annoyed. I said: 'You're supposed to put us right on these things. That's what you're here for.'

He looked hurt. He said: 'But it's all right in a film, that sort of thing.'

He was telling *me*!

A variant of this same attitude was adopted by the people of Foula, even by Alasdair. Every child on Foula knows that the North Wind brings dry, sunny weather; the South-Westerly Wind brings high clouds; the South-Easterly Wind brings gales; the Westerly Wind brings rain.

This is an arbitrary division, near enough for practice. Another piece of lore, so obvious that a Foula man would have to consider deeply if you put it into words, is that, except for the north wind, which is a law to itself, you can roughly count on good weather on the opposite side of the island to which the wind is blowing. There is a reason for this. Say, for example, that a great fat cloud, all swollen up with its own importance (like a caddy-lamb) and not quite sure whether it isn't going to be a storm in a minute with a little encouragement, comes rushing at Foula from the south-west. It is followed, all day, by clouds of similar views. What happens? They loom over the horizon, blot out the sun, throw the whole south end of the island into shadow. The shadow creeps towards Ham. Suddenly the leading cloud runs head on into the Noup and into the perpendicular fountain of wind which is continually being hurled up from the foot of the cliff. There is an 'Ouch!' and that cloud either bursts itself in a shower of stinging rain (which is old stuff) or separates into apologetic lumps. This continues all day. The south end and west remain in deep shadow, but Ham and the north end have ten hours of sunlight.

All Foula people know this, as I have said, but I doubt if they have ever put it into words or whether anyone else (perhaps some unsung Captain Gibson) has done it for them. It certainly never entered the heads of any of them to take me or John on one side and give us a five-minute lesson on planning locations. For the first month they watched us trudge up the Daal nearly every day to Camp 1 at the Sneck of the Smallie. Every day the wind still held steadily in the south and west and every evening we came wearily home with a few minor scenes, snatched from the clouds. It was not until I gave up concentrating on one location, abandoned the hope of shooting every scene with a sound-track, listened to the astonished remarks of the Base-campers: 'What? No luck to-day? It's been marvellous here!' and started to send out scouts and make my own observations and conclusions that I made any progress at all.

I selected the Sneck for the location of our most difficult scene—the dialogue sequences on the cliff-top between Andrew, Robbie and Ruth—because I had been influenced by Alasdair's praise of that part of the island and impressed by the Sneck itself. But although the background was certainly splendid (Wester Hoevdi and the Wick of Mucklaberg to the north and the blunt precipice of the Noup to the south) it was a bad mistake. First because it was on the west, second because the Sneck cannot be photographed. The combination of these two circumstances was very serious. I estimate that only two days' work, out of that first month, appear on the screen. The Sneck, which featured twice in the script, does not appear at all; and the dialogue scene is cut to a minimum. I tried to retake it in the studio but it was unconvincing and we cut it.

The Sneck beat us at every turn. We got well away from it and it looked like a shadow; we moved in close to it and it looked like a cellar; Skeets and I got down into it and water poured into our lenses; we crawled below it, among the cormorants, and it looked just what it is, a big crack in the hill where the cliff is coming away, but nothing more. Finally Syd built a bridge across the sea-end, a triumph of alpine engineering. It was two hundred feet to the bottom of the Sneck and two hundred bumps into the sea after that. We sat in rows on the creaking structure and spat on to the backs of puffins but we still failed to make the Sneck look at all impressive. The Smallie won. He is probably chuckling to this day—he and John Gray.

The unforgettable thing about the Sneck and Hoevdi

locations was the trudge up the Daal and back. The photograph shows what a great, desolate curve this valley is. When the wind is driving across, it seems endless. Each group had its favourite route. My own method in hill-walking is to fix an objective and to get there as directly and quickly as possible. I usually took the Heather Route, high on the side of the valley, gradually working higher until I plunged over the shoulder of Hamnafeld and down the other side into the road. In this I was imitated by optimists, actors, etc.

The pessimists (i.e. people carrying heavy equipment) preferred the Swampy Route, where there might be mud, but it was flat.

The Stony Route, along the side of the Noup, was exclusive to the Sound Department, who kept their batteries and camera at Stöel, to the great awe and gratification of the Dumplings who, says John, used to pat them every night and tuck them into their blankets (the batteries, not the Sound Department).

From the Daal to Hoevdi Burn (Camp 2 and headquarters of the cliff-climb) there was also a choice of routes.

The He-Man Route soared up Hamnafeld from the chapel, took the shortest line across the broken ground of Tounafeld, passed perilously near the Lum, and dropped down 500 feet to the burn. This was not popular except with Alasdair and Bill Martin, who had lungs like seals and the agility of unrooed sheep.

The Alpine Route was via Mucklaberg, a grand way in dry weather. You slid down the cliff and took a sheep path, which rose from sea-level up to the burn again, a thrill a minute, but faster than over the top. In wet weather it was dangerous.

The Resigned Route went over the top of the Ufshins and then down again the other side.

The Maniacs' Route was straight across the Ufshins, innocently taken by the Professor, followed by Skeets and

Karl, heavily laden, who all, most unjustly, lived to tell the tale.

The Ufshins are, or is, a green, grassy bank, about half a mile long and nowhere more than 400 feet wide. At its top is a small cliff, along the top edge of which is the Resigned Route. At the bottom of the Ufshins, invisible owing to an overhang, is the 500-foot precipice of Mucklaberg. This innocent-looking bank has been responsible for more fatal accidents than the rest of the cliffs put together. Its danger is this:

At each end it is of moderate steepness and pastoral appearance. Sheep graze all over it. Soon it grows steeper and, in the centre, the slope is about 65°. The grass is cropped short and very slippery, wet or dry. But it still *looks* safe to an inexperienced climber. On the path, which is only a sheep-track, a foot wide, he is safe so long as it is unbroken. If he leaves the path, every step is a danger and likely to be his last. He will slip, quite slowly but quite inexorably, down. There is nothing to catch hold of. He may slow up, but he will not be able to stop. At first it is exasperating, then annoying, at last terrifying. There is no edge of the cliff to catch him. One moment he is still sliding, the next he is falling. . . .

And the Professor carrying the Newman, Skeets carrying the Mitchell, and Karl carrying everything else, trudged gloomily across it on a wet day!

At Wester Hoevdi the burn, which flows through peaty, narrow banks down the brae from the Sneug, spreads out over a broad sandstone ledge and slides, in a smooth, sinister manner, into space. On my stomach I investigated. I found that, ten feet below, was another ledge, protruding like a shelf and, below that, yet another. After that the burn leapt into the air and very little of the water reached the bottom, 500 feet below. I saw that this was an ideal spot for the climax of the cliff-race. I showed it to the rest of the company, in particular Eric and Niall. At first view they blanched, also crawled on their stomachs. Within a week the entire company was frolicking about on the lowest ledge of all, carrying cameras, choosing angles and dropping stones into the void.

Eric had to climb up through the waterfall. I decided this was not spectacular enough. Syd organized a dam-crew and, at the word 'Camera!' they let a ton or two of water over the top. Of course we all, especially Eric, got wet, but the scene undoubtedly had more punch, especially when small boulders and half the dam came over into Eric's open mouth. The rest of the climb was shot on various locations between Hoevdi and the Sneck. The method was simpler than it looks. On bad days I scrambled round the cliffs and found nasty spots that were also effective on the screen. Eventually we all arrived there. I demonstrated the climb. Niall said to himself: 'Where he can go, I can!' Eric, fortunately, was short-sighted and I do not believe to this day that he knows half of what he did. The only thing that put him off was surf below him. To his eyes, without glasses, it was a dizzy, white gulf full of noises far below. He was not far wrong, either.

Hoevdi burn was our worst location to get at, but once there it had its attractions. We were miles from any house, in a cup of the hills. The sea sparkled far below. A column of smoke, or flame, marked where the two Bills argued with the Primus. Grey slabs of sandstone protected us from the regular squalls of rain, between bursts of sunshine. The porters were happy, all they had to do was play at waterworks. The Sound Department were far away, sufficient excuse in itself for contentment.

The only depressing day at Hoevdi was when the boats came round from the Haa. I wanted shots of them, from high above, approaching the base of the cliff, watching the climb; also in the same shot as Eric, visible far below, like toy boats, as he climbed the waterfall. The previous night John and I arranged an 'infallible' code of signals with Bill

Osborne, who was to be in the boats below. I forget the details but I know that flags, gunshots and swear-words played a prominent part.

The day was fine. We landsmen disappeared early up the Daal. Ernie and the Professor were in the mail-boat, to shoot the two Foula boats from sea-level. The mail-boat was also to tow them round into position. John Laurie and Bill were in one boat, Finlay and Hamish in the other; Bill was doubling for Eric, Hamish for Niall. Everybody was ready on time. The mail-boat panted to be off. All Nature smiled. Then they made a fatal mistake. They took the Sound Crew along for the ride.

On the cliff we were working hard. Presently the boats appeared round the Noup and took up position. The mail-boat sheered off. Bill answered John's 'stand-by' signal. Everything seemed grand. It was not.

To us, far above, it was almost a flat calm, 'a wee swell, maybe', said Jimmy Gray, who is a humorist. According to John there were 'bloody great rollers, Michael'. Hamish was so sick that all he could do was thresh the water blindly with an oar, muttering doggedly: 'I can take it!'—a statement which he disproved by presently announcing he was going to jump overboard and swim to the shore. As he still had several scenes to do this was not permitted. Somebody sat on his head and the Show Went On.

After a few takes the signals got at cross-purposes and never came right again. John waved, swore and fired gunshots, Bill waved politely back and nothing moved. I passed through all the directorial stages of patience, suffering, open impatience, sarcasm and callous brutality. John and I almost came to blows which would undoubtedly have ended in us hurtling over the waterfall together, like Sherlock Holmes and Moriarty. Finally, the mail-boat came in the picture and would not move out. We will now cut back to the boats.

The sound-crew had been fishing! A simple statement unless you knew Len and Bill Martin. Their lines had got round the propeller. The mail-boat was stuck!

Somebody relieved somebody else on Hamish's head. The Show Went On.

Far above, we had lunch—and wondered.

It was a beautiful day.

John Laurie was sick.

At last, long last, we saw the mail-boat move.

'Good,' I said, 'now we can get on!'

John leapt to his signals. Nobody replied. The mail-boat had the other two boats in tow. They set off at a good pace for the Noup. They kept on going. We watched dumbfounded. They became three specks. They vanished round the Noup. They never hesitated and they never looked back. *They had had enough.*

When we got over the shock we went on shooting, with pained faces. We had quite a good day. But the row at Parliament that evening. . . !

Hamish was particularly noisy and had three fights before dinner. We never tried it again. But John and I argue about signals to this day.

One other use of the Daal I forgot to mention. It provided two interesting holes of golf for Buddy who, incredibly, had brought his clubs, and a supply of balls which seemed inexhaustible, until he invited me to play with him.

South-Westerly Gale

The women of Foula were delighted to act with Belle but were afraid to go anywhere on the cliffs. It made them feel head-light, they said. This ruled out the west side; besides the location had to be easily reached. I finally fixed on a rocky tower, standing up from the rubble of old landslides at the back of the Noup. It was called Skirvidle. In the background was the long, black South Ness, and Helliberg's Wick, with the long rollers creeping up the sloping shelves. Below the tower was a sheer drop to the sea. All around it were sheep-paths and giant piles of rock, which provided good camera positions. The short grass was slippery. Above us rose the Noup.

This was the setting for Belle and the women watching the two boys climb.

The cliff-climb, regarded as a film proposition, consisted of nine cutting-points: (1) Eric; (2) Niall; (3) The boats; (4) Finlay in his boat; (5) John in his; (6) The grandmother and her view; (7) Hamish in the empty church; (8) Belle and the other women; (9) Belle.

Each one of these subjects represented a complete sequence to be done: a complete reaction, from the landing at the cliff to the final catastrophe. Individual tragedies had to be emphasized. Each sequence was shot from many angles to heighten its suspense, variety, surprise. Continuity of thought as well as action had to be preserved over a period of months, so that each cut, being assembled later, should take its place in the mounting suspense of the climb, which reaches a very high natural level.

This natural, or story suspense, was further heightened by every cut being real and every cut having its personal history. If each person, taking part simultaneously in a dramatic incident, reacts in a different way or for a different reason, it is evidently more effective than, say, a dozen people screaming. The climbers, who are the focus of interest, are still only part of the dramatic pattern. Even the most effective shots of the climb are less important than the recurring shot of the cloud shadows darkening the Ufshins, all that the old lady can see from her chair; or the close-up of the blank eyes of the catechist in the empty church; or the dark figure of the girl with quivering fingers, and the slow Atlantic rollers far below.

Skirvidle was possible in a south-westerly wind and at its

most dramatic after a gale. Then the whole of Helliberg, which shelves for a long way into the Atlantic, was a procession of huge rollers, half a mile in length, stretching across the bay from the Noup to the Ness, whose 100-foot cliff disappeared regularly, like the black head of a seal, as the waves broke high over it. Nearer to Skirvidle a wave would gather speed until it curved below us, broke in thunder, swept up underneath the cliff out of sight, only to stream back down the shelves in acres of foam.

We never tired of watching the Helliberg rollers. I spent hours scrambling near the surf until I found places where the waves could almost break over the camera without danger. Then I would reappear on ground-level and bellow, and soon another wave-shot for the storm sequence was in the can. One horrifying place I found, where the rock made a perfect breakwater to a deep, round geo. Underneath the overhang was a shelf; it was possible to get down there and be inside the wave as it shot overhead and dropped like the sky into the boiling geo. The only danger was that the backwash of a big wave would sweep the climber off. This did not deter Skeets who spent a happy half-hour down there with the camera. I must admit it was a wonderful feeling to be under a huge roller—when you got used to it.

One morning the waves were absolutely mountainous. Skeets's late perch was a seething whirlpool. We decided that on the lee side of the geo it would be safe. We accordingly descended there, with Niall and Jimmy Gray. We set up above the tide-line. Niall and Jimmy waited with a plank of driftwood while I watched for a spectacular wave as background.

'Here's a big one!' I exclaimed. It was.

I shouted 'Action!' and the camera turned. I kept my eye on the wave. Karl sheltered the lens from spray. Skeets had his eye to the finder. Ernie stooped by him. To my amazement the wave suddenly doubled in size. It broke late and it broke big. It shot up into the air, surged right over the geo (which was sixty feet wide and thirty feet to the water-level), crashed on to the near side and was on us. Ernie said 'Here!' (an inadequate remark); I yelled 'Damn!' (better, but still an under-statement); Niall (I think) exclaimed 'Jasus!'; Jimmy is not recorded; Skeets, as always, went on shooting until Karl was hurled into him and the camera, and Ernie grabbed him by the collar, yelling: 'Let's get out of here!' On the screen, once the wave breaks, it is a scene full of water, violent movement and Karl's legs. We use every frame.

As the wave subsided I combed the water out of my hair and looked for my camera crew. They were half-way up the cliff, a small waterfall tumbling down out of the camera and their clothes. They climbed hastily, without dignity and without a word spoken. They did not look back. They vanished over the top of the cliff and I looked at Niall and Jimmy, and Niall wiped his nose thoughtfully and Jimmy looked politely away. Finally I said: 'They've gone!' There was an awkward pause, then I said: 'I suppose we'd better follow them,' and with a wistful glance at another huge wave, we did.

We found them wrapped in blankets at South Biggins, huge cups of hot tea in their hands. They looked at me and grinned sheepishly and Skeets went on wiping out his beloved camera and Ernie handed me a cup of tea, and that was all that was said of the matter, until now.

There is not much point in reciting all the trials of Skirvidle. We started to shoot the sequence—about thirty shots altogether—in August. I got the last shot in the middle of an October gale, when Belle could hardly keep her feet, but earned the admiration of the other women for her freedom from 'head-lightness'. Aggie Jean and Bessie were also without nerves and stood on the edge of the world with a calm that was not shared by their anxious relatives.

The cabbage-patch scene, between Finlay and Hamish, is another of my favourite scenes at Helliberg. It is a romantic sequence; and it pleases me intensely to have turned cabbages into romantic and decorative objects. Recipe: Take a south-westerly gale, throw it in the air, mix with sunshine and mist in equal quantities, high-light the cabbage with this mixture, over-expose slightly and develop in slow bath. Even Max Factor would be surprised at what this treatment does for a somewhat plain vegetable.

But the high spot of the south-west location was the church.

There were three physical changes which had to be managed. These were: (1) The derelict building (in the prologue) with weed-grown yard, buried grave-stones, battered roof and forlorn old belfry, and a fragment of frayed rope where the bell once hung; (2) The church in the story, trim and neat, a path worn by the years from the gate to the door, the bell clanging as Gerald pulled the rope; and the row of dogs sitting peacefully (!) by their rail; (3) The interior of the church, sans belfry, sans roof, sans ceiling and especially sans warmth.

It is hard to believe, but the whole of the church interior was shot in half a gale. It was as cold as Christmas. When making close-ups of Hamish, Finlay and John, we had to place oil-stoves all round them, to warm their patch of glacial air so that their breath should not show. Alasdair, Bobbie Isbister and Syd worked the reflectors, roosting on the rafters in the full force of the wind. They had to nail their reflectors. Themselves, they froze to their seats. The orange cellophane, on the doors and windows, crackled like a bush-fire as the gusts caught it. The clouds sailed over at such a pace that we never had more than two minutes of sunlight. On three days we had to drop everything, all rush out and make fast tarpaulins before a squall hit us. The actors were beyond all praise. They had to be ready, like racehorses, to get off to a quick start and cram as much action into a short period as possible; and all the scenes called for subtlety and sincerity. It shows to what a pitch of efficiency we had attained by then, that those sequences were the best in the film.

No mention of the church could be complete without the North Biggins road-house. (Prop: Mrs. Henry.) For days on end we crowded her out of her kitchen, perched all over her furniture (about eighteen of us, in a room eight feet by twelve feet), boiled her kettles, borrowed her saucepans to cook her blue potatoes, sang songs, munched bread and butter. Through it all moved dear Mrs. Henry, her kind, square face wreathed in smiles, her gaunt graceful figure bending over the fire, stopping by me occasionally to ask me about the work and pat me encouragingly on the shoulder, quite unperturbed at the wholesale occupation of her kitchen. Bless her!

Biggins blue potatoes are—unlikely though it may seem—bright blue. When not blue they look plain bad. But they taste wonderful, like a heavenly vegetable bred from royal chestnuts and humble tuber. To the very end, Belle refused to touch them. I admit they looked terrible, but then, so do oysters. Their only drawback, of course, is that you cannot tell when one really is bad; but that is merely splitting hairs, as well as potatoes.

I forgot to mention that the long meadow of South Biggins provided a further two holes in the Farr Long-Distance Handicap and, any grey day, Buddy was to be seen tramping doggedly to and fro, trailed by a bored but persistent gallery.

South-Easterly

Most of the low-lying ground on the east is Bonxie territory, both Allens and Great Skuas. The road to the Haa makes a rough division; north of it is exclusive to the Allens; south is genuine Bonxie land, particularly between the War Memorial and the Chapel.

The two families are as distinct in their habits as in their appearance.

The Four Winds of Foula

The Bonxie is a big bruiser. He ought to wear a check cap. He already has a striped sweater. He bullies smaller birds. If he can get away with murder, he will. He is a cannibal and a racketeer, who lives by hi-jacking his friends. He is Public Enemy No. 1 of Foula.

The Allen is more of a lithe apache. He is cunning, attacks from behind, and pulls the old disabled-wing gag. He is not so crudely obnoxious as the Bonxie and, for that reason, will probably last longer.

But they both attack savagely and tirelessly if their nests are in danger; and they were actually in the middle of several locations. The only way to ward off attacks was to shoot one's arm into the air as they dived, for they were afraid of their legs being grabbed, and towered. Unfortunately I was unable to work into the script an adequate reason for the actors suddenly and repeatedly giving the Nazi salute, so I had to change the locations. It was a pity. It would have made the picture a riot in Germany.

The scene of the most ambitious sequence in the film was Sloag, a thatched croft in a brae north of the Haa, only about two hundred yards away. A burn ran down into the sea from Rosie's Loch, up in Allen territory. The three hills of Foula were all visible from Sloag, one behind the other, Hamnafeld like a black wall, the Sneug over its shoulder and, beyond, the top of the Kame. All around the croft were smooth grassy mounds and fields of oats and barley. In front was the brae running down to the sea. At the back was a noble cabbage-patch. It was a place to dream about.

I had two big sequences to make there: the lullaby scene and the dancing of the Foula Reel.

The lullaby opens with a shot over the sea; white pools of light are falling from a stormy sky and waving grass is in the foreground. The camera starts to swing, round past the fields, over a field of oats bent in the wind, black and white and uneasy like the sea, round and farther round until a wooden cradle appears among the corn and the camera stops on a close-up of the baby asleep.

The cradle is gently rocking. Belle is seen, bent over it, the Dumplings and others around her. In the distance Hamish plays the violin. The hills are black against the setting sun. The wind blows the smoke of the chimneys out in a long ribbon.

Other people are arriving. It is an unofficial gathering as the light fails. The elder women sit busily knitting in a row under the corn. Mrs. Isbister's gentle face; Mrs. Gray's firm one; Mrs. Henry's square old jaw on her worn hand. Tommy Gray listens solemnly, the Archdeacon fills his pipe, old John Gray puffs away composedly (he is being paid to do it, mind you!). Robbie leans challengingly against his door at Brae.

Out of the shadows walk Finlay and John Laurie. It is evidently the first official visit to his granddaughter. He walks stiffly and self-consciously. Hamish walks down to the cradle. Belle looks up. The others wait to see the outcome. John looks at the baby. He steals a look at Finlay and finds him smiling. John is embarrassed. He looks again for help. Finlay is laughing. The baby stirs and smiles. Something snaps in John's heart. He smiles too and even pokes a tentative finger at his granddaughter.

In a flash, the scene changes. Night has fallen, lanterns are lit, there is dancing on the green. Hamish leads a dashing group of fiddlers in the Foula Reel. Wullie Gear is hitting it hot and strong. Jimmy o' the Shop is striking sparks. Peter Ratter lacks fire but makes the grade. And who is that light-footed capering figure, his bow flashing, his elbow jigging, his leg bent in a dashing manner, music flowing from the tips of his fingers, his eyes sparkling as he leans over, still fiddling, to whisper a piece of scandal to Wullie? That, gentlemen, is Andrew Manson, of Veedal, who in Chapter VIII was suffering from melancholia! An awed voice from the crowd remarks: 'A' never thocht in this life to see Andra' Manson dance again!'

John and I reach across a couple of heads and shake hands.

Now the Foula Reel is being danced. Down the row of clapping hands gallops a bearded, sprightly figure, spurning the grass in a way to shame the younger generation. An amazing beret crowns his head, a bulky jersey covers a giant torso, his hand is in his slender partner's—Maggie Jean from Skeld, on a visit to her cousin at Punds. In other words, John Seabourne opens the dance!

Back he prances, with a pronounced dirrel upon him, and now it is the turn of Syd, bounding willingly beside the cousin at Punds, also a Maggie Jean and a noted dancer. Bill Paton and Edith Gray have joined both hands and are doing an Astaire-Rogers routine. Jimmy Gray (Up the Grays!) has got a bit tangled up with Bessie Henry—in a choreographic sense, of course. The fiddlers work like mad. The audience, spread about on the grass, clap in rhythm; even little Ivor and Jessamine are beating time. As far as the eye can see the Show Is On.

As John pants down the line for the second time he catches my eye and beams. This dance is the fruit of dark conferences with Bill Paton; of that first rehearsal at Punds, as secret as the Black Mass, when the two Maggie Jeans were sworn in, and Edith stole over from Dykes with Jimmy and his mouth-organ; of the full-dress rehearsal that frosty night at South Biggins, when Bobbie and Aggie Jean got the lino up in the parlour and pushed the furniture and the Archdeacon and Deaconess into the kitchen; when Hamish played his fiddle and the reel was danced till Biggins shook and Hametoun rushed wondering to its doors, until at last the dancing master and pupils fell upon a huge supper and an official trying-on of costumes, chief item of which were rivlins; this then is a moment of suspense to every balletomane, until, as the dance proceeds, murmurs are heard of 'Magnifique! Viva! Schön! A lightsome dancer is Maister Seabourne! Up the Grays!' etc.

The Four Winds of Foula

What is a rivlin? A rivlin (spelling not guaranteed) is a slipper made from the green hide of a cow and laced on to the foot and ankle by a double line of cord. If worn continually (like Finlay's) they are as comfortable as any shoe in the world; if allowed to stiffen (like mine) they get considerably harder than cast iron.

The dance proceeds. Lanterns gleam against a dark sky. Finlay leaves John and comes up the path. The camera starts to move with him. It follows him along, past the dancers, with a nod and a gay word, past courting couples, on until Sloag and the dancers are distant; there is a halt by a group as he waves his pipe and does a snappy bit of solo dancing, then the camera swings with him until he passes out of sight.

That sounds easy. It is so smooth that, in the film, one scarcely notices that the camera has moved. But behind that smooth movement is toil and care enough to launch a ship. Beside Finlay runs an inclined plane, a wooden railway, one hundred and fifty feet long. On it rides the camera truck with Skeets, very snappish, Ernie, very calm, Karl, breathing stertorously. A rope through a pulley lets them slowly down. Syd and an army of men practise gliding smoothly over a ploughed field, as they walk with the rope. Behind the camera car a worried director hops absently over projecting battens. This is the third and, finally, successful attempt at the Great Track Shot of Sloag!

In connection with the first attempt, there was a slight misunderstanding. It was before we knew the island and its people very well. In particular, Peter Manson meant nothing to us and we meant the same amount to him. Everything went wrong. Syd cried: 'No! no!' 'Blast!' and even, I regret to say: 'Idiots!' There was a certain amount of tension developing. Finally a successful rehearsal was got under way. The truck crept down the runway. Syd watched his mark with an eagle eye. The limit was reached. 'Make Hoff!' he cried. There was a perplexed pause. What did he

266

mean? Syd says he meant, 'Tie Off!' But, again, incensed by inaction, he called: 'Make Hoff!' Peter Manson cast down his rope and stuck his hands in his pockets. 'Come on, what are ye waitin' for?' he remarked. 'Domned fool says "Make Hoff"! Well, here goes!' And he made off and was not seen again for three weeks.

Belle is meanwhile standing on the cliff, while beyond her the moon rises out of a cloud over the sea. You think that is easy? To start with, the sun is doubling for the moon. That means a grisly reconnaissance before dawn by Bill Paton (the Eye that Never Sleeps) and myself. It was September and it was cold. For three mornings Bill woke me in a whisper (or what he thought was a whisper) at five o'clock. I huddled on my coat and boots and went out to the headland. For two mornings there were no clouds in the east and I went back to bed. The third day there was a low bank of cloud. Ernie and Skeets were roused, Finlay was already awake, there only remained Belle. To my surprise she was down in ten minutes. A call is a call to Belle, even at 5.30 a.m. Bill had the fire already going and cups of tea, so what time he got up is a mystery. I don't see how anybody in Hut 5 ever got any sleep anyway.

As we trudged across the wet grass to Sloag, a wild bleary figure presented itself to our shocked gaze: Bill Osborne with the lantern for Finlay to carry. His eyes were tightly closed, but he was on the job.

We had ten minutes in which to set up, then the sky grew lighter. Belle threw off two overcoats and a sweater and drew a light shawl carelessly around her shoulders, clad in a thin blouse (for the scene was a warm spring evening).

'All ready,' I called. 'Don't shiver, Belle!'

The rim of the sun (I beg pardon, the moon) rose above the bank of cloud. Finlay ambled forward with the lantern. He stopped by Belle and put his arm round her shoulders. Together they looked out to sea.

'Thank heaven!' we all said; and went back to bed for an

hour, except Bill, who probably did not know the meaning of the word.

Bill, who has so far functioned more than adequately, without any explanation being offered of his presence, is a native of Lerwick and was imported in the first weeks of production by Vernon, who was under the impression that he was a fully qualified cook—or perhaps that had been Bill's own impression. At any rate, after a third-degree interview with Mrs. Rutherford, who rattles no mean saucepan lid herself, and after seeing what was expected of him, Bill's nerve failed him. (He has an unusual modesty about the things he can do and an equal optimism about those he cannot.) Normally he would have joined the endless procession back to Mainland of incompetent, belligerent, or take-one-look-and-say-no-thank-you cooks. But it had just become clear that the camp needed a handy-man around and that somebody was needed to set out with lunch in the middle of the morning, as soon as our location was settled. This called for someone with the lungs and legs of a Shetland pony, the temper of an angel (as he frequently had to chase us, heavily laden, over half the island) and a certain amount of sex-appeal, to get round Peggy the Cook (last but by no means least of the cook procession) and Mrs. Rutherford. Bill got the job.

He held it to the last. He was assistant producer to John on the Foula Reel. He is now my manservant and has supplemented my memory many times during the writing of this book, also my knowledge of the underworld which had its headquarters in Hut 5.

The owner of Sloag was Peter Petersen. He was a tall, dark man, with the face of an American Indian, which never changed even when he was uttering the most outrageous statements—for Peter is a humorist. His eyes were dark and set deeply in his head. I am told, by innumerable authorities, that he has broken many a heart. I can quite believe it. Of one, in particular, I can speak. I will put my readers—and Peter—out of suspense at once by stating that it was not a female one.

It belonged to a bright young midshipman of His Majesty's Navy, who landed smartly upon Foula some twenty years ago and left it a few days later feeling as old as Rip Van Winkle. He had come to Foula in search of Peter.

Peter was in the Navy during the War. When peace was declared Peter packed his things and silently returned to Foula. Some months later the demobilization authorities arrived at his name and rating and discovered that Petersen, P., Able Seaman, had already demobilized himself without waiting for the untying of several fathoms of Gold Braid (as Red Tape is, no doubt, called in the Senior Service). This was a direct insult to His Majesty, Earl Beatty, the Rt. Hon. Winston Churchill and innumerable other dignitaries. A cruiser was detached from its lawful occasions and despatched to Foula. Mission: to report with body of Petersen, P., Able Seaman, alive or dead, preferably dead, as it would save the taxpayers the expense of a court-martial.

On an overcast morning, with the wind veering into the west, the cruiser's picket-boat came chuffing into the Voe, watched with expressionless faces by several natives of Foula. 'Hi, somebody, make fast this line!' called the midshipman. A tall dark man, with the face of an American Indian, with deep-set eyes, obediently caught it and made it fast to a ring-bolt. He then moved silently and with dignity away.

The midshipman hopped up on to the jetty, his gold braid glittering, his sword clanking, his face shining. His file of men followed, lined up, grounded muskets, sprang to attention, numbered off. Their officer cast a confident eye around him, singled out an informant, probably the Archdeacon, and said:

'I am looking for a man called Peter Petersen. Can you direct me to his house?'

The Archdeacon (though I cannot swear to this) murmured:

'Peter Petersen?' as one would say, 'I have heard that
name before.'

'Yes,' prodded the invader. 'Do you know him?'

'Oh, ay. It was him who made fast yon rope for ye,' was
the answer. The officer bristled.

'Which way did he go?'

'Peter?'

'Ay—I mean, yes, dammit!'

'Well, I couldn't rightly say. They might tell you at his
croft.' After five minutes' cross-examination the search-
party obtained directions for finding Sloag.

'Squad—slope arms! Right turn! Forward march!'
barked the snotty. They arrived at Sloag. No fox's earth
was ever emptier. Peter's sister was pasturing the cow. 'He
went off towards Hamnafeld.' No, she couldn't tell when
he would be back. Peter was a chancy man.

'Double!' shouted the baffled invader. They doubled up
Hamnafeld. On the top was undoubtedly Jemima who
directed them to Soberlie. At Soberlie a solitary figure
referred them to the Noup. At the Noup there was no
doubt someone who had seen Peter Petersen, 'an hour
agone', on his way to the Sneck and down Mucklaberg.
They doubled to and fro, they panted, they scrambled,
they got drenched with rain and beaten by wind, in fact
they went through all the normal experiences of a visitor
to Foula. At long last, on the top of the Sneug for the sixth
time in one day, the midshipman surveyed his command.
They looked like mangy beachcombers. Their rifles were
rusted, their beards had grown, their boots were in ribbons.
His gold braid was tarnished, his sword was snapped off
short, his own mother would not have recognized him. He
heaved a sigh. 'Rejoin ship! Double!' he said.

In silence they regained the jetty. With downcast faces
they took their places in the picket-boat. 'Cast off, some-

body,' he snapped; and, as the propeller started to churn, a tall dark man with the face of an American Indian, with deep-set eyes, obediently cast the rope off from its ring-bolt and moved silently and with dignity away.

Peter was one of the two men employed in carrying water to the Haa; washing-water from the burn; drinking-water from the spring by Mill Loch. For this purpose they had a tank on wheels, such as is common to any large garden, and, after Alasdair had done his bit, they had a pony to pull it along. Day in and day out, Willie (of Ham), Peter and a pony (usually the one whose belly was badly out of drawing) went up and down the road. They were a feature of the landscape—Willie trudging, the pony ambling, and Peter, his head erect, his arms to his sides and in his deep-set eyes a permanent twinkle, gliding effortlessly along over the roughest ground, as if Foula were thin ice, over which he skated.

Between Sloag and the Haa, though not on the direct line, was Veedal, home of Andrew Manson and his coos. It was a big straggling croft, only one room of which was still habitable. It was well situated and had good grass around, but the artist that Andrew proved himself to be was more likely to be oppressed by his loneliness than cheered by negative consolations. I am sure that the melancholy into which he had settled was a fit of artistic temperament, for if ever a man was a born actor and marked out for friendship and popularity, Andrew was that man. He should not live alone. No man should live alone for long, but Andrew, never! It is not fair on other people who have not spontaneous gaiety, imagination and a mercurial temperament. These things are valuable. If Andrew is still living alone when I come back to Foula I shall be seriously annoyed. So will John.

It was in Veedal that we made the interiors of the croft, the scenes when the baby is ill during the storm. They will always be to me the high-water mark of photographic quality under difficult conditions. The actual production quality of the sequence is as good as a studio-made scene would be, with the added fact that it is so obviously the real thing. It almost smells real. The same with the church. No studio set could ever look like that. Or so I thought until the other day when a Scottish lady said: 'Of course the church was a studio set—they would never let you use the real church. What? They did? Amazing! Well, you cannot tell me that the funeral was made on Foula. No Scottish islanders could ever be persuaded to take part in a mock funeral.'

The lady had never met John Seabourne.

The funeral was undoubtedly the greatest triumph of a long diplomatic career, which may be said to have started on Guernsey, when Bombardier Seabourne did not want to go to Malta. (Wild caddy-lambs will not drag this story from me. This book is practically a Seabourne biography anyway.) When we first came to Foula we discussed it with Alasdair, who was (justifiably for once) pessimistic. But he added: 'Well, ye never know. It all depends how it's put to them. If they understand that you're not making a game of it and that in the film it will be a beautiful thing—ah, but it's a lot to ask of people who don't know you from Adam!'

He was right but I left it to John. I admit that I myself could never have done it. Results speak for themselves. One day I said: 'John, how about the funeral? It looks like rain to-morrow.'

He said: 'Whenever you say.'

I looked in admiration. 'All the men?'

'All except the Gears. Peter does not approve.'

'I'm sorry. Any reasons?'

'Just general. I must say, I admire a man who sticks to his opinions.'

I gathered that Peter had put up a stern fight. But the greatest question was to come. I hardly dared to ask:

'How about Blowburn?'

'All fixed, so long as they get notice of our coming.'

'We can stage the funeral procession there?'

'Yes.'

'And bring the coffin out of the house?'

'Yes.'

'How on earth did you arrange it?'

'I explained it all to Peter and made him understand there was no mockery in it and he finally gave us leave,' said John simply, but with a complacent ring in his voice which said: 'Foula—*c'est moi!*'

I often think that if only they would let John Seabourne get together with Hitler, Stalin and Mussolini. . . .

The call for the funeral was made every wet morning until we finished it. The usual procedure was to put on oilskins and thigh-boots, set up the cameras in pouring rain and get everything all ready for the first shot of the procession crossing the bridge over the burn. Then the rain would stop, the sun would burst out and in half an hour we would be shooting the love-scenes at Mill Loch.

This went on for a week. It's an old Foula custom.

It was interesting to watch the reactions of everyone on the call. The men of course were in Sunday blacks, which made them stiff and solemn. Our crew had been warned not to fool about in their usual manner and consequently all looked as if a near relative were in the coffin. Bill Osborne and Jimmy handled the coffin as if it were glass, and spoke in whispers. It was placed, ready lashed to the three oars on which it was carried, on the bank of the burn. Everyone avoided looking at it, made a wide circle round it, spoke in reverent murmurs to one another when near it.

At the end of a week, everyone was sitting round the coffin, drinking cups of cocoa off the lid.

This was not callousness, as Peter Gear would think. It was simply that the men had made an adjustment in their minds. They had realized the difference of the associations; and they had also begun to realize what I was trying to present on the screen and how I was setting about it. They noticed that in an actual take I was quick to notice anything that jarred, to make an adjustment which would increase the impressively simple effect of the funeral. They were no longer onlookers, they were sympathetic members of the company; and they remained so to the end.

One of the critics remarked on the charm of the love-scene at Mill Loch and its natural setting. His actual words are 'the midges dance in an evening light over the unhappy lovers in the reeds'. If he had been there, he could not have picked his words better. He ought to hear Belle on the subject!

It was a difficult scene and a long scene and the first scene made between Niall and Belle, unless you count a few pouncings among the irises. They rehearsed splendidly. We were all lying in a foot of water among the reeds, while the 'unhappy lovers' brooded on ground like a wet sponge, with their feet actually in the brook. Monty was all ready. 'Let's take!' I said.

Niall dried up. Take 2 came on the board. Niall dried up again. Take 3. Niall dried again. . . . The midges danced—some of them—the rest had discovered Belle.

Take 6 was going splendidly. The home stretch was in sight; fifty feet more—'Damn! oh, damn!' screamed Niall. Take 7 was chalked up.

Take 12 was perfect. Belle collapsed in real tears. Her face and her body were a mass of bites and bumps. Tenderly Frankie bore her off to bed. Niall looked sheepish, said: 'I'm terribly sorry, Michael. . . .' 'Forget it!' So he did and went pigeon-shooting instead.

What happened to the coffin after the funeral sequence was finally in the can?

Its fate was a secular one. It had been earmarked from the beginning by John Seabourne and the other members of Hut 3. The second I had said 'O.K.' to the last batch of rushes, it was whisked out of the prop-room and transported to Hut 3. Burke and Hare never did a cleaner job. It was stood on end against the wall, Syd gave a touch here and there and, by nightfall, Hut 3 had a new Compactom wardrobe.

The North Wind

The north end of the island was a privileged quarter, firstly in sunshine, secondly in exclusive tone. Its three principal citizens were Jimmy of Ristie, David of Mucklegrind and Baron Blowburn. At Freyars, near the Boat Parliament, lived an elderly gentleman, his wife (or sister) and his collie. They were not sociable, and seldom even visible. The old gentleman shook his stick at me once and the collie, I believe, was the mother of Bob and his three brothers.

Blowburn only just scrapes into this aristocratic neighbourhood for, commanding though its position is over the whole east side of the island—it is the highest croft on Foula and, but for the shoulder of Hamnafeld, would look clear to Hametoun—Soberlie Hill, against which it clings, is a barrier between it and the true North End.

The road, which falters at Burns and dwindles to half its size and, at Sandvadden, frankly forks into two paths, one to the Harriers, the other to Blowburn, altogether ignores the North End. The north-enders rise above such matters; each croft has its favoured route, one for dry weather, one for wet; in awful weather they stay at home. At one time there were three other crofts. Logat and Soberlie are under the hill, roofless and desolate. Springs was once the home of Andrew Gray. It will soon be a ruin.

Its isolation and its comparative desolation were a double reason for my neglect of the North End in the first weeks of production. If I had shot the Sneck sequence at Maggie Henry's Hoose, as I had half a mind to do after my first tour of the island, a lot of things would have been different.

Ristie is the trimmest, whitest and loneliest croft on

Foula. It stands at the edge of the finest pasture on the island. A little burn runs by its wall. There is a walled garden, crammed with vegetables and more flowers than anywhere on Foula. The walls are white-washed till they dazzle the eye. The ground rises sharply, sheltering the croft, for about a hundred yards, then drops into the sea by the Gaada Stack, a huge natural arch, through which the yacht is seen at the opening of the film. When a party of us came down the desolate slope of Soberlie and stumbled suddenly upon Ristie, John Laurie exclaimed: 'Hah! the man who hates the rush and bustle of Ham!'

Jimmy has the gentlest and most sensitive face I have seen on a deep-water sailor, a face like a wise priest. He sails his spick-and-span little boat by himself and keeps it in the nöst by the Brough Skerry, drawn well above the highest tide into the long hollow, dug out of the turf and lined with great stones. Tina Gear, his niece and letter-carrier of Foula, keeps house for Jimmy. They are both musically inclined and a social evening at Ristie always leads up to Tina performing on her piano-harp and Jimmy playing a selection of beautifully kept records on his shining gramophone.

Tina has to trudge from one end of the island to the other on mail-boat day and is equipped for it with a stout heart and a sturdy figure. Alone among the islanders she asked quite early if she could read the script and meditated deeply for days afterwards. The local allusions and descriptions intrigued her. Finally, when one evening John was at Ristie, and had paused to draw breath for a moment, Tina said: 'Now how would ye describe me, Maister Seabourne, if ye were writing me into the film?' John answered promptly: 'The lady with the thick legs.' Tina looked taken aback. John, not a bit abashed, continued: 'You *have* thick legs, haven't you?' 'Ay, I suppose I have,' said poor Tina, wishing she could look at them herself but not quite liking to. 'I have walked down the road behind you many a time,' said John matter-of-factly, 'and I always thought to myself: "That's a fine strong pair of legs that girl has! and she needs them!"—and you do need them, you know!' 'Ay! Ay, that's so. I do,' said Tina, quite pleased, and she played the Eriskay Love Lilt on the piano-harp.

Only John can get away with social conversation of this sort.

Ristie was the rallying-point for the Boat Parliament scene, which was held round a great flat stone, embedded in the turf by the nöst. Such meetings of course were normally held down at the Voe, but the nöst at the north end was a finer background and we were sure of better weather. In any event these meetings of the men were always held by the boats, a link with the past lives of their fathers who made their living on the sea and chiefly met at the 'haaf' or deep-sea fishing. Twice Jimmy was out when we visited him but on our last day he was at home and beamed silently as we swarmed all over his little cottage, which is as neat inside as out.

It was at Parliament that David first joined the company. We had often seen him walking back from the Shop and noted his dark, thin face, with its high cheek-bones and black eyes, like a Breton peasant, a resemblance completed by his big beret. He had never been on a regular call, for he was over eighty and seemed very thin and frail. He was Jimmy's brother.

But the big day of Parliament fell on mail-day boat and no plea, no bribe, no threat can interfere with His Majesty's mails. We were short of five men, a serious matter when the whole assembly is only seventeen. Chief Whip Seabourne left no stone unturned. He finally persuaded James Henry of Quenister (brother of Magnus) and, early in the morning, was knocking at Mucklegrind. The door was opened by David, in a long nightshirt of a material as stiff and unyielding, John assures me, as corrugated iron, which it closely resembled. John explained the urgency and David agreed at once. When he arrived we took great care of him for there was a stiff breeze and he looked as if he might blow away. As soon as the main shots were done John paid him and suggested that he would like to go home. Not a bit of it. He was interested and stayed the rest of the day, in a thin coat and a bitter wind, without turning a hair.

Presently it clouded over. Somebody found a tin and put it on a big rock and in a second a volley of stones was hurtling towards it. It was a long shot and, though there were near shaves, nobody hit it. After a minute or so David ambled forward and picked up a stone. Everyone smiled and waited for him to move in nearer and try his luck. On the contrary. He stepped back a bit, threw and knocked the tin off with his first shot. There was applause, at which he gave a slow smile. 'Do it again!' said John, as proud and delighted as the manager of an infant prodigy. He did it again.

That is David—of Mucklegrind.

It was in attempting to keep communications with the North End open and in a mobile condition, that Buddy and Alasdair staged an event which I bitterly resent not having witnessed—the great cross-country chariot race. Our only form of transport, other than our backs, was the camera truck, an old motor chassis (an Austin Seven, I believe) to which was bolted a strong wood platform. There was also a rather horrible, floppy iron rod, which was supposed to control the steering and most certainly pinched one's fingers.

Vernon and Buddy had been detailed to bring up this truck and bitterly resented having to drag it over the heather. They hit on a bright idea. Alasdair brought along the big black pony, which he considered his star pupil, and with many ropes they harnessed it to the truck. Buddy lay on his stomach on the platform, the steering-rod in his hand. Alasdair took hold of the bridle of the pony, whose eyeballs were nearly dislocated from rolling rearwards. It was obvious, even then, that their resentment was as nothing compared to the black pony's.

'Giddup!' said Alasdair.

The pony left the ground all in one piece, Alasdair travelling with it, and when it landed was already moving at appalling speed, which rapidly increased as it heard the chariot surging behind—not to mention Buddy, who was yelling his head off. They were on the track to Blowburn but the pony left it and started a lightning tour of the island. Alasdair, touching the ground from time to time, continued to go the same way. A Holbourn never lets go; it is a point of honour, as with lobsters.

The ground all around them was bog, varied with giant peat-tummocks. For all the difference that it made to the pony's speed, it might have been the track at Brooklands. Buddy, who had nothing to cling to but the rod, was being flapped up and down at the full stretch of his arms. Every time his stomach hit the deck he gave a bellow. Alasdair had lost his feet altogether and was being dragged through the bog with closed eyes and clenched teeth. The pony, now completely mad, shifted into top gear and fairly flew.

After some time, Buddy's yells increasing in volume, Alasdair hastily opened his eyes. They were rushing downhill towards a large ditch, about four feet wide and three feet deep, whose opposite bank was considerably higher than the near one. Alasdair hastily shut them again. But he continued to hold on as the pony made straight for the ditch. Buddy allowed them to proceed alone. He half jumped, half rolled off the chariot and went on bouncing for a dozen yards. Through peat-plastered eyes he saw the pony, a second later, take the leap. The chariot hit the near wall, bounced a man's height into the air, came down right way up and struck the bank on the other side. There was a check as the pony did a back-somersault. The ropes held. The pony scrambled up, jerked the truck over and dashed off again, but no longer with any conviction. Alasdair was able to stop him in the next hundred yards. Buddy came limping up. Alasdair was cursing the pony, more in sorrow than in anger, but his only direct comment on the incident was: 'He'll not take it an' it's no use trying.'

Buddy did not attempt to argue the point.

As soon as ever the wind showed signs of shifting into the north everyone, even Alasdair, would beam as if he were personally responsible for it and say:

'There! now you're in for a few days' fine weather, surely, if it holds.'

Unfortunately it seldom did; one day of north, three of east, six of west, was about the proportion. But many a day of unbroken sunlight came with the north wind. Such a one was the great day when we at last arrived at Blowburn and in eight hours made forty shots, completing the entire Sunday sequence at the croft, with all the pictorial angles and, also, every one of Kitty Kirwan's scenes for which she had been patiently waiting twelve weeks. Twelve weeks on the island for one day's work! She has the north wind to thank for that hectic day, which started with her listening to church bells and finished with her dead on the grass!

Kitty was sent for by cable as soon as we had fixed our schedule. She was told to hurry. She caught the night express, grabbed a plane at Aberdeen, raced across Shetland in a car, took a flying jump on to the waiting *Vedra* and arrived at Rock City in twenty-seven hours from Rock Studio, an all-time record. Not bad for an eighty-year-old.

All her first scenes were with John Laurie. The *Vedra* passed the mail-boat taking him out with his fractured collar-bone. We broke the news to Kitty. She settled down for the longest 'wait' an actress has had in history.

As we could not shoot Blowburn we moved the sound to the Sneck. For eight weeks we remained at that end of the island. It was a day's work at least to move everything across the island. I felt compelled to do the church and the bidding in Hametoun first. Kitty tried out make-ups. She collected her two costumes. John Laurie returned but his arm was not strong. The scene called for him to carry his paralysed mother out into the sunshine. We postponed the sequence again and got the roof off the church. We went back to the Sneck. We worked at Hoevdi. Kitty practised screams. She sat 'paralysed' for hours at a time, only using her eyes. Whenever my conscience smote me at her wistful look—she attended all our parliaments and listened to the call—I would order a test to be made of Miss Kirwan, with or without teeth, with or without a wig, with or without make-up. This probably saved her reason and me from being assaulted.

At last we left the south end. We were shooting sound scenes around the Haa. One day the wind changed. I looked up at the sky and that night I said:

'Blowburn to-morrow! John, Eric and Belle in Sunday clothes. Belle change of clothes for watching the climb. Miss Kirwan. . . .'

I was interrupted. The entire table broke into a loud cheer, there was clapping and stamping of feet, congratulations were showered upon blushing Kitty. She went to bed at once, was reported by Dodie to have spent the whole night rehearsing, was out at dawn and first to arrive at Blowburn. I had fixed the two positions of her chair some time before and she had everything worked out on a piece of paper, with dotted lines. The wind held, the sun held, John rolled his r's, Kitty rolled her eyes. She listened to the distant psalms, she slept, she watched the Parliament, she listened to Belle's frantic speech, she watched the shadows on the cliffs during the climb and, when second sight told her of her grandson's death, she died upon the grass in front of her chair, again and again.

Later Twist persuaded me to cut this out of the film. He thought that the funeral would have much more point if it were Robbie's. We could leave the grandmother's fate untold. I was worried lest it should puzzle people. But he was right. Coming, as it did, at a big climax, her figure was never noticed in the discard. She had beautifully served her turn. Not one person has ever asked what happened to her, even those who gave special praise to Kitty's work. So I hope she will forgive me. She is a grand actress and a dear woman.

Being just half-way up Soberlie, Blowburn became our north-western base. Equipment was stored in the byre, hot meals and cocoa were prepared in the kitchen, people dried and thawed out there during those countless days we were working on the high cliffs. From Soberlie to the Kame the cliffs are a level wall, eight hundred feet high, broken at long intervals by corries down which one can climb almost to the sea. One of these was at Simmond's Head, where John 'rescued' the Blowburn caddy. Near the Kame was the slippery grass cup, on the very edge of the cliff, in which stood the 'gone over' stone. Then there were all the final shots of John climbing after the guillemot's egg; the opening sequence of the yacht party with Niall; the passages through the fog of Finlay and John; all Bob's most important scenes. When I look back I wonder how I ever dared to plan those sequences and still more how we ever managed to finish them.

As the Bonxie flies, from the Haa to Camp 3 on Soberlie was about two miles. Three-quarters of that was hill climbing and we were all heavily laden (about 50 lb. per man of mixed gear). Some of us, like Finlay, had a lot of weight of their own to carry and were no longer young, except in heart. Finlay tramped to Camp 3 eleven times before we were able to do his scene there. Never a murmur.

John Laurie had the hardest physical work of his life. With his shoulder still painful, he had to carry sheep, hammer in his staves, coil and uncoil his heavy ropes, as well as carry them (if you think rope is not heavy, try a walk with thirty fathom of new Manila half-inch rope round your shoulders); he had to climb and descend perpendicular cliffs on the strength of his own arms and had to act important scenes on crumbling ledges a foot wide. The way he kept to the true characterization, through all these scenes which required in themselves complete attention, was beyond praise.

But the champion athlete of the unit was Bill Martin. Being small and light and tough, he knew no limitations. The sound crew were only working about half of the time we were on the island, so he had plenty of opportunity for getting about. Alone among the sound crew he sometimes came along and gave the camera department a hand. I remember once, at Camp 3, he became bored with inaction. He slipped away. A few minutes later Skeets said: 'Look at Bill Martin on the Kame!' I looked and finally spotted him, a tiny figure, just arriving at the top of the 400-foot slope, at an angle of 1 in 2. We looked away. In five minutes he was on the Sneug. I became interested. He ran down the ridge to Hamnafeld, came back, plunged down the Sneug on to Flick Lochs and rejoined us casually. He had covered the whole watershed of the island in about fifteen minutes.

After that, I ceased to congratulate myself on being in good training.

On Sundays I collected an unwilling crew of assistants, piled them on to the *Vedra* and spent the day at sea. As we could not work on the island I worked on the *Vedra*. But it was so casual and the surroundings were so different that it was better for us than staying in camp—or so I said, and the others glumly agreed. Our main objective was to get long shots of the island under different conditions. We got them —shots and conditions—never twice the same. Often at sunset fog would come down and the island would vanish while we were still five miles to the north. Then, sometimes for six hours, we would grope slowly round the North or the South End (according to the tide-rip) and creep bellowing up the coast within sound and occasional sight of breakers, while at the camp they would ring the bell, burn flares, bang tea-trays and send up rockets, feeling very useful and romantic.

Our other objective was to land at the foot of the Kame, and on the eleventh Sunday we made it. The beach was formed of perfectly round, white, smooth boulders, from the size of a football to the size of the great stone globe of Tilly Whin at Swanage. Every one was scoured clean by the ceaseless grinding of the winter rollers, which come roaring in from Greenland and toss these mighty weights about like tennis balls. Every day there had been a bad swell along the cliffs, and a bad swell under the Kame means a rise and fall of twenty feet! But on this day it was about six. Our only danger was that the boat might be left high and dry by a wave upon the sloping ledge while we landed, in which case it would certainly have capsized.

We stood at the bottom of the cliffs and looked up. It was even better than looking down. We got an effect of sheer size which was stupendous. Clouds were drifting half way up and around the summit. Any moment as we stared I expected to hear a bellow and see the face of King Kong stare down through the mist. The place was alive with echoes and mournful with the singing of seals who could be seen swimming under our boat and popping up all round us. There was a very neat one, with a shiny black head and a well-kept moustache, who kept staring sadly at me, like Bill Sweeny when I say unreasonable things about the sound department's lack of co-operation.

Finally we put off again for the *Vedra*. We had noticed a lot of manœuvring and signalling going on but had ignored it in a well-bred way. We reached the ship, a long way out, to find John Seabourne speechless (a sensation in itself!). A whale had been circling round the ship, had turned over, sounded, reappeared, blown-off and finally made off (with acknowledgements to Syd and Peter Manson). As satisfying and complete as anything in 'Swiss Family Robinson'! But as we had not seen so much as a fluke, we failed to be very impressed and, though I heard John, only the other day, hold an audience spellbound with his story, I still cannot summon up any excitement. I merely record here that while we landed at the foot of the Kame, John saw a whale from the *Vedra*. After all, he did not *land* on it.

Wind-Up

We have now followed the winds counter-clockwise around Foula and can return to Captain Gibson with our sincere congratulations. The wind is undoubtedly the outstanding feature of the climate; the general tendency to gusts and squalls of wind in the vicinity of high ground has been proved, *ad nauseam*.

Among steam-trawlers, alas, his book, if read, has been imperfectly digested, at least in one case I can remember. It was after we had been a month on the island. It was a fine day and a Sunday (which often happens on Foula if nowhere else). Nobody had a care in the world except myself (old man Care in person) and Alasdair (who was composing a sermon).

A trawler was seen to be standing in towards the island in an indecisive and highly dangerous manner. Alasdair was summoned to witness the wreck and appeared licking his lips, but she shifted her course at the last moment and headed for the Voe. It is quite plain to an onlooker when a ship is unhappy about something; a débutante entering her first ballroom is not more conscious of every move she makes. Finally her captain slowed down and lowered a boat. Obviously both ourselves and Foula were objects of considerable interest, not to say consternation. By this time a small party under John's leadership was down at the jetty to welcome them. As their boat drew nearer its crew stared harder. One man was evidently the skipper, for he wore a felt hat and had a greasy chart on his knee. One of his crew carried a basket of fresh mackerel. The others rowed, their chins on their shoulders, their eyes popping out with interest.

I suppose that what they saw was an odd sight on a barren island. Firstly there were Frankie and Belle, probably in shorts, and shorts that did not pretend to be anything else; John with two months' growth of grey beard, shirt-sleeves and rivlins; Len in khaki shorts and singlet; Bill Martin in no singlet and not much else; Bill Sweeny, nattily turned out in gent's sporting outfit; Alasdair, in grim Sunday blacks, with a theological furrow on his brow, bristling, as usual, at any hint of invasion.

The skipper took all this in and swallowed. He looked at the chart. He looked at the mate. He examined the island behind us.

'He's lost his way,' exclaimed John gleefully.

This was evidently the case.

'Let's pretend we are the Azores!' said someone, 'and jabber Spanish.'

'Do the Azores speak Spanish?' someone asked doubtfully.

'What does it matter? At any rate we don't look like Shetland natives.'

But inspiration, when it came, took another and better course. The boat threw us a line and the skipper and mate landed, with the fish-offering held prominently.

'Good morning,' he was greeted politely.

'Marnin',' he answered, 'care for any fresh fish?'

'Thank you,' said John, appropriating the basket.

The skipper took another look around him and at the island. Then he said, half to his mate:

'It ain't Mainland, nor Yell, nor any part of Shetland, I'll lay my oath on that. I'm damned if I know where we've got to.' Then to us: 'Excuse *me*, but would one of you mind giving us our bearings and telling us where we are?'

There was a second's pause, as a psychic current swept joyfully through his hearers. Then with one voice they replied: 'Sorry, but we're all strangers here!'

Chapter XV

CRÊPE-HANGERS

★

In the mornings Bill Paton rang the first bell at 6.30. That is to say for two months he rang it at 7.30, then changed to 6.30 when the days drew in and stayed at 6.30 when the clocks were put back, although, if you get my meaning, it was to all intents and purposes 5.30 (I am not quite clear about this myself). Anyway, before I go any further I must deal with the Streeter Daylight Saving Bill, which is associated with the whole thing in my mind. By the time I have tried to explain *that*, the whole time-table will be in such a tangle that I can leave it and proceed with a clear conscience.

Syd, like Hitler, sprang his great scheme on a Saturday. Personally I have never quite grasped all the implications of it but then mathematical theory is not my strong point; on the night that the clock has to be altered, I usually find myself two hours wrong next morning.

We were discussing at Parliament the rapid shortening of the days. We were no longer able to work until six or seven at night while, near the Haa, the sun sank below Hamnafeld as early as 4.30. The scene of the peat-cutting, which Monty had shot in the first three weeks, proved impossible to retake two months later. The sun no longer reached there when the light was in the right direction. The light was changing rapidly, too. It was thinner: it had lost its force and heat. After long days, the north was rushing swiftly towards the long nights. I could almost feel the

287

shadows closing round me; and a third of my film was still to be done.

I was in the mood to catch at any suggestion which would cheat the sun. Syd's proposal was simplicity itself, like all great schemes.

His suggestion rose out of a sharp division. The first bell, for two months, had rung at 7.30. Now I proposed it should be rung at 6.30. There was very naturally a roar of protest. I assured the opposition that I would make concessions at the end of the day; that I would not work after six unless it was called for in the script; that dinner should be earlier and punctual. I received sceptical looks and low growls. They knew me.

Syd rose and made a classical speech. He pointed out that association was all that mattered. It was summer time now, anyway. Our 7.30 was really 6.30, yet nobody objected to getting up at that hour because of an accepted convention. Here on Foula we had nobody to worry about except ourselves. Let us put the clock back two hours, instead of one, and continue to rise at 7.30, Streeter Summer Time.

The beauty of this compromise made it instantly popular. The opposition crossed the floor of the house and a Government defeat was averted.

But, among the rabble without, there was murmuring and discontent. It lacked a leader but that leader swiftly arose; and so swift and popular was the uprising that this leader was able to force a meeting with Parliament and repeal the Streeter Bill.

Peggy the Cook was from Hillswick, in the north of Mainland, from where she had been snatched by Vernon, after a wild drive in an old car, scouring Shetland for a cook. She was his seventh attempt and when she met with Mrs. Rutherford's approval, she was able to drive a hard bargain with George, who was in too thankful a mood to argue.

She was young and very good-looking. She had fair hair,

her eyes were grey and her skin was golden. She had a fore-
arm in the Wagnerian tradition and a body to match it. In
a fifteen-round contest between Peggy the Cook and Brün-
hilde, my money would have been on Peggy.

When she said there would be cold dinner on Sunday, a
cold dinner there was; when she ordered Bill Osborne out
of her kitchen, Bill did not stay to argue the point; when
she said No Streeter Bill, the Honourable Member had to
withdraw his suggestion.

We knew by now the way Syd could set his heart on a
thing, and the bitter rear-guard action which was fought did
not surprise us. Peggy and a deputation took the floor at
Parliament, stared me coldly in the eye and threatened to
down tools, unless we abandoned this devilish scheme. The
men of the island were noncommittal, but every woman
backed Peggy. Why, I do not know, unless it was a dim
pagan fear of meddling too much with Nature. But there
was no bluff about it. They none of them would object to
getting breakfast an hour earlier, if I ordered it, but they
would not meddle with Time. She looked me straight in
the eye, a wisp of hair lying across her splendid forehead,
her mouth a firm line and her arms crossed, bare to the
elbow, and I admit I ran for cover.

Peggy went back to Hillswick after we left the island and
I suppose she is there still. So if any young Nordic glancing
in the mirror, seems to see a resemblance to Siegfried, the
boats leave Aberdeen for Lerwick three times a week in
summer.

In the morning, then, Bill Paton rings the first bell. This
is *not* followed by a series of thuds and the dull roar of a city
preparing for the day's work: instead, Bill comes into my
hut with a pail of hot water from the copper; we hold a
short conference on the weather; I yawn, light our Primus
and carefully place a biscuit-tin lid to get red hot over the
flame; Finlay grunts over *his* Primus and makes a pot of tea;
Huts 2, 4 and 5 are as lively as the morgue.

Crêpe-Hangers

In a quarter of an hour the second bell goes. One quarter of a minute later it is followed by a hideous yell from Hut 2. This is caused by George Black persuading Skeets to get up by whipping the bedclothes off him and placing a film-tin, which has been kept outside in the cold, upon his unprotected stomach (for Skeets sleeps raw). A series of girlish squeals announce that John Behr—Joanna to his fond companions—is receiving the same treatment. The next thing is usually a metallic crash as Karl's bed collapses, not unaided.

Hut 2 is now, if not up, at any rate on the floor, which is something. Hut 3, with the exception of Eric, their resident corpse, is soberly preparing for the day. Finlay comes beaming into our hut with two steaming cups of tea for John and myself, a saintly custom which he is developing into a tradition. Niall says from under the clothes: 'What sort of day is it, Michael?' 'Take a look!' I suggest. He sits up, looks at the streaming window-panes, groans and hurls himself down again. His bed immediately collapses.

Monty, the drone of our hut, sits up and gives Niall a sour look. He also grimaces at the weather. 'Why bother to get up?' he enquires of the world. This rouses Niall, who has been lying in a bemused heap. He grunts and rises, draped in blankets. 'Fer the honour of the hut we cannot permit this subvarsive attitude, Monty the Drone!' and Monty's bed collapses.

In Hut 4 Buddy is dressed and going over the call. He makes no attempt to rouse two horrible lumps, which are presumably Len and Bill Martin; he gave up trying long ago. The Puffin is lacing his riding-boots, grumbling in low puffin tones.

Hut 5 is as lively as the morgue.

As the hour strikes, the last bell is rung. Hamish opens a bleary eye. 'Wobbelzatt?' he enquires. Tom sits up with a grunt. 'The last one,' he says. 'What!' yells Hamish. (I can never make out whether this astounded horror of all last-bell addicts is assumed or real. It sounds real. I could always hear them in Hut 1.) In Buddy's hut Bill and Len are hurtling silently into their clothes. Doors are opening and slamming. Feet are crunching down the path. Bowls of porridge and cans of cocoa are being borne by Maggie and Bill into the mess-hut, where Mrs. Rutherford, with a clean starched apron and an enigmatic look, administers the high, the low and the middle helping.

In Hut 3 Eric reaches across absently to Finlay's bed and pulls another rug over himself, as he settles down for one more ******** day on Foula.

Our days on Foula were numbered not only by the precession of the equinox, but by a far more serious thing—the growing uneasiness of Joe Rock and John Henry Iles.

Their visible presences were Gerry Blattner and George Black. George of course was always with us. Gerry would appear from time to time, share our meals, beds and troubles for a few days, try to pin me down to a definite date for leaving the island, finally obtain a qualified statement, hold a secret conference with George and depart with a brief-case bulging with petty-cash vouchers and requisition slips. For the next few days George's shoulders would ache with the new responsibility of a definite finishing date. When it became evident that it would be quite impossible to achieve it, he would cheer up, wash his hands of the matter and send and receive innumerable telegrams.

In the last month, when war between myself and the production heads was quite open, the camp had its loyalist party and its defeatists. Those who supported me were quite open about it. They took the attitude that it was my picture and my story and I was on the spot; I knew what was best to do and it was absurd to ask for a finishing date as if I could control the weather. The other party, having more to lose by quarrelling with the studio, retaliated by pointing out that the film could not go on for ever, but looked like doing so unless I was stopped. Also the winter gales were on the horizon and we were as likely as not to be cut off until Christmas once they took hold. There was a good deal of truth in this.

None of them, of course, could see inside my mind, could see how thin the line was between victory and defeat, between a completed picture and one with impossible gaps in continuity. Very few of them even believed that I had a plan, a scheme of production, a pattern to which I was working. I shall always remember that the people who backed me to the limit on the picture and believed in my authority to the end were not the people who knew me well but those who had come to know me during our struggle together.

My relations with Frankie had become as stormy as the weather. That is the bad thing about an island. The outlook is limited. At intervals we would attempt a friendly walk together, but the trouble had gone too deep. We usually came home by different roads.

The days closed down. Ernie had put away nearly all his filters except the neutral density '5N5' and '3N5'. He used them constantly in the pale, low sunlight of those days and the negatives he got were astonishing, rich and brilliant. He never made a mistake. There were days when he had ten different conditions in one hour. There were fog scenes in bright sunlight, in soft sunlight, in no sunlight at all and practically no *light* at all; they all had to match and inter-cut—and they do. He had new experiences every second, that nothing but a genuine instinct could have solved. I have seen him change the aperture four times during one shot, as the weather changed with it. Glass to eye, long fair hair brushed back over his head, oilskin flapping buttonless, legs well apart, slow grin on his face and slow eyes that never missed a thing—Caddy Palmer!

The equinoctial gales were late that year and, when they came, were soon over. They were followed by a period of dry, windy weather, with high clouds and long shadows.

Crêpe-Hangers

In those days we worked as I have never worked, cramming a week into every day. A dozen sequences had been left, with holes in them that you could drive a herd of elephants through. Day by day we filled them up, we snatched scenes that we had waited three months for, we tore from one location to another, we jumped from the prologue to the finish, to the cliff-climb, the lullaby and back again to the prologue. Everything seemed to be turning my way at last: a south-westerly wind blew and I shot Belle and the women at Skirvidle against the background I had always dreamed of getting; the next day I was on Soberlie completing the discovery of the 'gone over' stone. Often we started our climb of the hill in thick banks of fog, stretching from Foula to Shetland, where the hills stood up, twenty miles away, like islands out of a calm cloud-sea; John Laurie and Finlay climbing up, ever up, out of the mist of the evacuation, while Bob pattered behind, until the sun broke through and rolled back the mist, so that we could kick off our heavy, soaking clothes and work in jerseys, while Frankie and I played scenes in thin shirts and summer clothes. A change of the wind would bring me back to the Voe where at last I was able to remake the ghost scenes of Niall, which had been the first shots turned on Foula; close-ups here and there, shots of the church bell ringing, shots of Belle with the ponies, unloading peat, launching her letter-boat, running to warn the boys; now this sequence was finished, now that; I could see the gaps in my defences slowly closing and, one by one, as in a jigsaw puzzle, the difficult little missing pieces suddenly came into my hand. Actors could start to count the number of scenes they still had to do. Hardly one was ahead of another. Locations had been so evenly split, it was a dead heat. The weather changed so often, I never knew what to expect from one day to another. All the rules were broken. But the whole shape of the film was in my hands now, every problem was so definite that I never had to hesitate and

every day saw twenty scenes added to our bag. The wind
shifted to the east and we made the scene at last of John and
Finlay launching the fleet of letter-boats. It was almost
impossible shooting in the wind and spray. The next day
the wind dropped altogether, soon there was a flat calm
and fog lay around. For the first time for three months
conditions were right for the evacuation scenes with the
Vedra. Vernon brought her in at high tide until she floated
level with the jetty. We had two hours of high water. Syd
was ready with a huge gangplank as strong as a bridge. Up
in the air it went. A rope snapped and it crashed sideways
into the water. Nobody was hurt and they had it out in
five minutes, Syd crimson with mortification. Cameras
were all ready in boats, on the quay, on the cliff. The second
the bridge was firm a stream of animals, people, and
bundles, mobilized since breakfast, poured down on to the
quay and across the bridge to the ship. All the angles on
the ship, with ponies, sheep, boats and people, were prepared beforehand, the final shots being on the ship itself.
As we grabbed the last close-up the *Vedra* bumped on the
bottom. Vernon threw us off, cast the bridge clear and just
scraped out into deep water again. There was never another
calm day.

All this time Vernon was getting more and more agitated.
He saw little and knew less of our work on the island. He
was having trouble with the Customs, trouble with the
Board of Trade, trouble with his crew, trouble with Joe
Rock and worst of all, trouble with me. I would not listen.
He would take me on one side, tell me that we were running a grave risk staying on into October, that all the men
at Scalloway said we were likely to be marooned on Foula
for the winter. He was being warned against endangering
his boat and other people's lives. We were weeks over
schedule. He was bound to report all this to Joe. I said,
'What of it?' The picture must be finished. If I gave in now
—if I had given in and retreated from Foula three weeks

ago, as I had been ordered to do—what would my responsibility be for bringing back an unfinished job, a thing that must be faked in the studio, or patched with bought stock shots, or held over until next year? Short of revolution and mutiny among my people, I must stand by my job, complete every bit of it properly, continue to see the film as a whole, and not let a moment of panic upset my judgment. Nobody else could or would do it; the responsibility was mine.

Barnes had been sent up by Gerry on 15th September, the day on which I had promised to try and leave Foula. He was sent ostensibly to arrange the evacuation of the unit and dispose of all goods which were not worth bringing back. Actually he was to keep a watch on all I did and despatch confidential telegrams to the studio. Except that they were not confidential, his telegrams were a great success. So were Gerry's, Vernon's, and George Black's. To the Loyalist Party these four were known collectively as the Crêpe-hangers.

I often think that the remarkable weather we experienced in that last month was mostly due to the atmospheric disturbance created by the *Vedra's* radio. Those four never gave the poor thing a moment's rest. Hundred-word cablegrams, at threepence a word, describing the latest doings of Powell, the Mad Dictator, were a commonplace. Whole feuilletons of brilliant prose from Vernon would describe the threatening clouds and the ominous swell on the sea and what the ancient mariners had told him. Gerry would pour out his soul to his lieutenants, urging them to combine wisdom of serpent with mildness of dove, recommending iron hand, velvet glove, and subtle propaganda. George, afraid of being left out, would reply with suggestions of his own and ghastly warnings.

Never was such a splendid free entertainment in the history of radio. For every word of these and a hundred other messages, intimate cables, imploring requests, rude replies, orders of film and food, nice long gossipy chats, pieces of juicy scandal, crude personalities and confidential memoranda, were one and all received over the short-wave sets throughout Shetland and proved such a popular item that the B.B.C. had to take a back seat while the populace listened with appreciation to 'the Film Company'.

It was inevitable that such an atmosphere of fierce struggle and taut nerves should produce one or two explosions.

Bill Martin's birthday was towards the end of September, not long before my own. Suddenly the news spread round the city that it was his twenty-first! Something had to be done. Bill was popular. Mrs. Rutherford was consulted. Hasty preparations were made. Bill had been expecting a cake but no mail had arrived for a week.

At dinner he was detained on some excuse and everyone managed to get in before him. A pile of presents was on his plate. Two bottles of Niall's whisky adorned the table and the Negus was gracefully turning a blind eye. The door opened and Bill dashed in. We all rose and he was presented with an enormous cardboard latch-key by Bill Osborne.

He was hustled to his place. Dinner—a real dinner!—was served. Bill sat in a happy, ejaculatory daze, accepting everything pressed on him—presents, food—and drink.

'Whisky when I'm well makes me sick; whisky makes me well when I'm sick.' Whisky made Bill Martin fighting drunk. Soon a shrill war-cry rang through the room—one-third Indian war-whoop, one-third Tarzan's mating call, one-third Haig and Haig.

A concert was soon in full swing. Finlay overflowed with song, story, and bawdy allusions to the guest of honour. Niall and Hamish shook the hut to its foundations with an imitation of an all-in wrestling match, complete with grunts, roars, faked injuries and apelike expressions. Maud sang 'You are my Honeysuckle, I am the Bee!' and Syd Streeter sang 'Trees'.

Crêpe-Hangers

After the concert Bill had to fight someone! It was there and it had to come out. (Yoo-oohoo-ooay!) The Puffin was an ass! The Puffin must get what was coming to him! The Puffin must die the death! Where is the Puffin? In bed? Gimme a bucket of water!

Such are the startling effects of a bottle of whisky when you are free, white and twenty-one.

The Puffin, as may have been gathered, is Lionel K. Tregellas, Bill Martin's boss. He was given his name by John, after one look at his puzzled, fretful expression, stiff neck and way of jerking his head round towards the object of his attention. Before becoming a sound-engineer, he had been—of all things—an acrobatic dancer. Somehow this seemed to clinch it.

He attempted to reason with Bill Martin, with the result that he got very wet. Bill was, by now, out of control. The Puffin kept his temper admirably but a strong right arm was what was needed. His bed was soon floating. He went for help. Bill hurled the whole bed into the yard and danced on it. He refused to come to grips. He shot in and out of the darkness with his piercing war-cry. At last the camp lost interest. Somebody sat on his head. The Puffin took Bill's bed. Bill, still yelling, was rolled up on the floor in a blanket and passed out cold.

At breakfast next morning everyone was in his seat as the door slowly opened and Bill hobbled in. Twenty-two grinning faces and a severely noncommittal one surveyed him. Never was there such a self-conscious entrance or such yellow eyeballs. Bill Martin had attained his majority.

This minor riot undoubtedly prepared the ground for the large-scale battle which took place on my own birthday a few days later. We prepared something rather special, for I had been impressed by the effect on the morale of the company of a little gentle relaxation—even the Puffin seemed to have gained from the experience, he was more popular. There were haggis, two Michaelmas geese and unlimited whisky.

Bill Martin's dinner had been brilliant but impromptu. This one was a city banquet. The ladies were invited to dine with the gentlemen and graciously accepted. Mrs. Rutherford converted the geese into roast Birds of Paradise. (They had flown from Aberdeen, but not under their own power.) The haggis, supervised by Hamish, expressed from the sacred premises of Waugh in Edinburgh, was acclaimed. There were eight bottles of whisky. There was a Pudding.

Speeches followed. Finlay and Maud gave me a Shetland sweater and scarf. Frankie (she admits it was a sop to public opinion) a Shetland rug. There was a gala concert, mostly items 'by request'. Niall and Hamish staged a return match of all-in wrestling (I shall never forget Hamish unexpectedly flying over Niall's head and landing on the stove); Maud sang 'You are my Honeysuckle, I am the Bee!' and Syd sang 'Trees'.

The party broke up, 'having drink taken'. A lot of us went into the Haa, poked the fire and felt mellow and optimistic. As in another world I heard dreamily shouts, distant bangs and splashes and the sound of running feet; but I paid no attention until Alasdair lounged in, dripping wet and grinning like Tommy Brock, and said in a disinterested voice:

'You'd better stop the fight before there's murder done.'

I leapt to my feet and, without asking questions, made for the yard. Niall and Ernie followed me.

It had started—need I say?—in Hut 5.

As in most famous combats, the spark had been struck during a scene of mutual confidence and brotherly love. In other words, Hut 5 had held open house as usual to a number of guests, of whom one was Karl. Over the cocoa and biscuits (for the lavishness of Hut 5's hospitality was oriental) some slighting remark was made. Perhaps some tactless individual mentioned 'Keatings' (tactless because, when the peat dries, it seems to produce a flea almost as large as the Foula Mouse, which makes at once for a more suitable home, which in 1936 was Karl. Other people caught occasional fleas, but on Karl, for some reason, they performed day and night; either his skin was more sensitive or his imagination more lively, but he used Keatings as other people use talcum powder.) The fact remains that direct evidence proved that Karl, having absorbed several cups of cocoa and about half a pound of biscuits, withdrew to his own hut, with a disparaging reference to the quality of Hut 5's hospitality.

This meant War!

With a bucket of water each, Bill Paton and Hamish strolled along to Hut 2. 'Oh, Karl!' they called, 'Karl, we want you! Yoo-hoo, Karl!' etc. Hut 3 was preparing for bed. Karl, who had a pretty good idea of the reason for his sudden popularity, smiled benignly and went on sprinkling Keatings. But, with Middle European sense of humour, he said nothing to Skeets who, having dined well and feeling tired, strode to the door, yanked it open and said: 'For Pete's sake, haven't you two got. . . .' A bucket of water at this point took him under the chin.

There is something very inspiriting about scoring a direct hit with a pail of water, even if you get the wrong man. A howl of triumph rose from the attacking force as Skeets spluttered and slammed the door. What next? They soon knew.

The door flew open and Skeets and Karl hurtled through the air, no more than sprinkled by a wildly aimed shot from Bill Paton. In their hands were empty buckets. Straight as an arrow they tore for the water-butt, with a rallying yell which brought George out of the mess-hut where he had been entertaining Bill White. Skeets gasped out a tale of murderous assault on Hut 2. George and Bill White grabbed buckets from the boiler-room and joined the fray.

Crêpe-Hangers

Back through the darkness thundered the counter-attack. Before the others had time to warn Tom and Bill Osborne, the door of Hut 5 was hurled open, as if the United States Marines had landed. Four buckets swung as one. The two innocent bystanders were struck by a wave of water and bit the dust, which simultaneously became liquid mud. But the enemies' bellow of triumph was cut short by a flanking volley from the original aggressors. The Great Water Battle was on!

Hamish and Bill had learnt their lesson and, after a desperate scuffle, in which Hamish lost his singlet and Bill his pyjama trousers, they gained sole control of the water-butts —a master-stroke, for when immediate supplies gave out, Hut 2 were forced to get sea-water from the Voe, which extended the battle over a wide front and left their base unprotected. They achieved some desperate sallies out of the darkness but Hut 5 held the city. Hut 2 very soon resembled an aquarium. In the darkness neither side could stop to distinguish friend or foe and the civilian population, as usual, had to suffer. A bucket skimmed through John Laurie's hair. Alasdair got drenched and the city began to look as if a cloudburst was passing to and fro.

At this point I intervened. I knew nothing of what was going on and it was dark as a cellar, except where a lantern burned by the mess-hut and light streamed from the neutral huts. Huts 2 and 5 had blacked out. I peered about. Suddenly there was a clash and a roar. Into the light burst a naked figure, his hair streaming water, acres of wet chest heaving, murder in his eye and a battered bucket in his hand. Hamish had gone berserk!

We grappled with him and soothed him down. He gasped out his story, a slightly prejudiced version naturally. (The account here is compiled from contemporary historians on both sides.) When Ernie realized that his hut was the storm-centre and that his bed was the nearest to the door he gave a groan of dismay and, rushing to it, was just in time to receive several gallons of salt-water in the face, hurled by Skeets before he realized that his own boss was the target.

This appalling act of *lèse-majesté* took the stuffing out of the defence. Hut 5 prudently retired and started feverishly to mop up the mess. They were fairly successful but Hut 2 was as wet as the Blow-hole. It streamed with water. Its besiegers had even climbed up and poured a bucket down the stovepipe. Ernie was coldly furious as he sorted his dripping belongings. Each fresh discovery provoked him further and spurred his trembling assistants on to feverish salvage work. When annoyed, Ernie does not lose his temper, but gives out a stream of tight-lipped, bitten-off, vitriolic comment, at regular intervals, like a soured and weary newsreel commentator.

I went in search of the salt-water party and found George and Bill White, somewhat to their embarrassment, crouching in a ditch, surrounded by pails of water—a perfect. ambush. Fortunately I saw them first and, in response to a direct challenge, they came out and fired their ammunition into the air.

We then all went to bed. . . .

The next day—the 1st of October, the month of gales—was fine and clear. The north wind blew steadily, The early equinox, after a short and violent storm, had given way to a period of crisp, cold weather. We worked like madmen. Day after day, Jessie would tiptoe into the girls' bedroom at the Haa with cups of tea and 'It's an awfu' pr-r-retty day, Miss Chrystall,' in her soft voice.

Day after day the days drew in.

Chapter XVI

EPIC, STUPENDOUS, POSITIVELY MEDIOCRE

When it was all over, my friend on the *Observer*, who had unwittingly been the cause of the expedition, provided a charming epilogue. Although, at the time of the Great Storm, it was the last word on the subject, I do not think that the last word upon *The Edge of the World* will be said for many years. When a theme has beauty, integrity and a national, as well as human, importance, it is apt to last a long time, even in such a brittle and ephemeral shape as eight cans of celluloid; and when you add the spirit of an old land and its people, strong enough to influence the shaping of the theme, you have something more. In making our film many of us formed ties of sympathy and friendship that will never be broken, that are stronger than many we have had all our lives. I know that my friends on the island feel this. They cannot express it in speech, nor can I. Several times Walter, Dodie, Jimmy Isbister, Willy Smith, Andrew Manson have struggled to say what they feel; to explain what has been awakened in them by the change and the struggle together and by sharing in the completion of something in which we believed. We knew that it was worth while. My friends have never been able to complete these thoughts except in their hearts, but I have understood. I am trying to write down what I have understood. This is for them to read and I think they will nod their heads and say: 'Yes, that is what I felt, although I could never say it.' They alone will have understood me (torn from one existence and hurled into another which I had almost forgotten) when I said to Herries in Edinburgh: 'It has been not only an adventure, but a spiritual experience.'

Said the *Observer*, when we were all safely off the island:

'The marooning of a film unit on the lonely island of Foula has created more public interest and excitement than the film on which the unit has been engaged is ever likely to do when it is shown on the screen. Indeed, it is doubtful if the story of that film, *The Edge of the World*, can be more stirring than the story of the film-makers' adventures as variously related by them to the Press. They were "epic, stupendous, positively mediocre", as movie magnate Mr. Goldwyn might say. Certainly the wind that left the company marooned on Foula was not ill enough to blow nobody good. . . .'

The *Aberdeen Bon-Accord* (which seems an extraordinary name for a magazine, but whose editor can certainly write) was rather more cynical about us and equally entertaining:

'DOUSED STARS ON FOULA

'Whatever sort of film *The Edge of the World* may be when it comes under the public eye, the producers should go down on their bended knees and thank old Boreas, the newspapers and Sir John Reith for a publicity campaign which has cost them absolutely nothing and yet has been one of the most successful—though unpremeditated—"stunts" on record. We hope no one will think us heartless if we confess that the pitiable stories circulated from one end of the earth to the other of the horrors and privations which the "stars" on lonely Foula were supposed to be suffering while an 80-mile gale roared and blustered all around them, did not provoke us to a single tear. For, though Foula is "lonely", compared with Piccadilly, it most certainly is neither uninhabited nor uninhabitable. The islanders live there in all sorts of weather from lusty childhood to breezy old age, and neither the B.B.C. nor the news agencies trouble their heads about the awfulness of existence on a diet of canned foods and express winds. They live on "the edge of the world" all the year round, hanging on happily by the skin of their teeth; and we hail them as fixed stars of our northern latitudes, in contra-distinction to the wandering lights that shine resplendently in a picture-house but seem to lose something of their splendour when grim old Mother Nature treats them to the best "blow-out" in her cupboard.'

Except for the prodigal display of inverted commas, I could not have put it better myself.

One thing these frolicking pen-men forget, though, is that their 'fixed stars' protect themselves against the winter gales with walls, three feet thick, plastered outside and panelled within, as tight and dry as a cigar-box. The windows are set deep in stone and mortar and are small-paned. The doors of living-rooms are nearly always double, by which I mean they open into a small hall, sometimes no bigger than a sentry-box, where you can close the inner and open the outer door without blowing the house inside out. The roofs are solid timber, with tarred felt, solid tiles or thick thatch, held down by many ropes, weighted with great stones. The houses crouch close to the ground, surrounded by stone dykes and byres, which can be easily reached, if necessary, on hands and knees. The fireplaces and chimneys are as strong as pillars. When the weather is bad their owners stay at home. When the island is cut off for six weeks—as it was from the day we left—they draw in their belts, go on rations and smoke Iceland moss when tobacco gives out.

The 'wandering lights' of the film company (which I take to mean all of us, for I do not see why Belle and Frankie should hog all the publicity just because they were rescued heroines) have, on the other hand, very different quarters. The two girls, whose stories in the Press, retailed to us at second hand, made us realize our heroism too late, were well off in the Haa. (I can hear ghostly female laughter again. It has a sarcastic ring.)

The huts however were on high ground, and exposed. They were made of wood. They were raised a foot off the ground on a platform and were lined with three-ply inside to a height of four feet. The windows were ordinary, flimsy windows, set at opposite sides of the hut. The panes were large and were fixed. At the top, a sashlight opened six inches. The doors were at one end and opened directly into the yard. They did not fit very well. The roofs were of light wood, covered with roofing felt. They projected at each end of the hut in a thin gable. Each hut had a little stove, whose pipe went through a hole roughly cut in the wall, at the end opposite to the door. The mess-hut was across the yard, down some steps and along a path. The Haa and the Shop were equally accessible but you had to get there. They were not all under one roof, as in the crofts, where they do not need to stir abroad for a week on end in a gale. For us, a gale was a good time to get shots. Rain or shine, we had to struggle out to finish the film. Every day was the hardest kind of physical and mental work. Energy needs good food and plenty of it. Also luxuries. The difference in the unit, during the three tobacco famines, was astonishing.

I have said enough to show other differences between fixed and wandering stars. What those journalists said was amusing and true, but if either of them had been in my hut during the Great Storm they would have slept very little. If they had been responsible for the expedition, they would not have slept at all.

Syd had heard enough about Shetland gales and did not

intend to be caught napping. The safety of the camp, in any wind that blew, was a matter for his personal honour. I believe that if we had lost the huts he and Bob White would have committed hari-kari with their chisels. They strengthened the walls, they doubled the roofs, they stretched more and more guy-ropes from the roofs to the ground and across to the next huts, until it looked as if steel spiders lurked in each little alley. It became evident that, if the huts did blow away, they would all go together, soaring into the air like the tail of a kite.

By September he felt pretty satisfied, but the equinoctial gales modified his opinion. They opened our eyes to what Foula could do and showed very clearly that, in a south-westerly gale, the island became a funnel for the wind. That was the day we struggled over the Ufshins when the gusts were reaching ninety miles an hour. I got a shot of the short marsh-grass, in the Hooses of the Burrie, shimmering—there is no other way to describe the effect—under the blast of the wind. It is the key shot for the change of tempo to gale force in the storm.

We reached Hoevdi to find the burn in spate but not a drop going over the lip of the waterfall. The wind was piling the water up in a ridge and as fast as a crest formed it blew it into the air, where it dropped back into the burn; and so on, all day, rushing continually down and as constantly being dammed and turned back on its course by the wind, which was now a hurricane. We made for home, caching most of our gear, and we were glad to get there.

Syd and Bob were already out, strengthening the mess-hut. That night the rain blew through the walls of the huts and up under the floor. Several windows caved in. The steel guys held well but the roofs lost a lot of felting. Then the wind dropped. The clear weather followed and we were glad of the respite and the rehearsal we had been allowed. We knew that the October gales would be something to reckon with.

II

On October 19th, one million, six hundred and five thousand, nine hundred and seventy-one readers of the *Daily Mail* opened their morning newspapers to see:

FILM PARTY MAROONED ON STORM-SWEPT ISLAND

WIRELESS SOS FOR SUPPLIES

Hideous photograph of Belle, looking coy and blonde

From Our Special Correspondent

—

Even worse photograph of Frankie looking like a horse

Wick, Caithness

An unspecified number of *Daily Mirror* readers (when I rang up they seemed shy about their circulation, though

doubtless it is enormous) saw confronting them, in black
type you could hang your hat on:

B.B.C. RADIO MESSAGE
TO PARTY MAROONED
ON ISLAND

The B.B.C. last night broadcast a message of cheer to thirty men and women of a British film unit who have been marooned by the storm and are in danger of starving, etc.

Revolting photo-
graph of John
Laurie

The day before, an equally problematical number of
readers of the *Sunday Graphic* (quite huffy about its circulation, but of course it is colossal) revelled in a meaty front
page with a screaming banner-line:

Epic, Stupendous, Positively Mediocre

FILM STARS MAROONED

CUT OFF BY STORMS ON LONELY SCOTTISH ISLAND

Libellous picture, snatched from the files, of Belle, *circa* period *Hindle Wakes*

'Sunday Graphic' SOS From Party on 'Edge of the World.'

Dramatic seascape of storm-swept island with one unperturbed cormorant in foreground of picture staring idiotically at camera

Thirty British film actors and technicians, their rations running short, are marooned on Foula —'John Bull's loneliest island'—twenty miles out into the wild Northern Atlantic, etc.

This was only the start. It can be seen that 'Observator's' gentle cynicism was well founded.

The parties responsible for this hideous but profitable uproar were Gerard Blattner and Gerald Boyne. Anxiety at the studio had been gradually mounting, as the latest messages from their spies were decoded. Chief Crêpehanger Sewell had got a taste of a south-westerly gale at the time of the equinox and he did not propose to wait for another if he could help it. Undoubtedly his ship was in

309

danger but, inevitably, he found me still unsympathetic. The fine spell was continuing far into October. Of course I knew as well as Vernon that when it broke it would break suddenly and winter would be on us with a rush. It had been easy enough to land our sixty tons of equipment during the summer; getting it off in bad weather would be impossible, but I pointed out that half of it was being left behind. We were presenting the mess-hut to the island for a recreation-hall. The camera department had bought their own hut—a miracle of shelves and boxes—and were giving it to Jimmy Gray for a workshop. The other huts were being bought, either by the Negus or by islanders. Barnes was planning a grand auction sale of timber, kitchen utensils and surplus stores. The camera and sound equipment, the dynamo, the batteries, the projection machine and radio were all that was left. They were heavy, expensive and awkward, but it would be bad luck if there was not one day when we could get them off the island.

I hoped that the post office would buy the radio for Foula. We had spoken to the studio, who offered it to them at cost price. It seemed such a chance for the island. But the plan clashed with the huge scheme which the G.P.O. are gradually carrying out in the Northern Isles, by which in a few years every island will be linked to the mainland by a beam-wireless system. They did not accept our offer—rightly, as was eventually proved—but it caused a good deal of popular indignation at the time and I admit that I too thought that, whatever their main scheme, there was no reason why Foula should go another winter without communications.

All preparations were put in hand for evacuating the unit and equipment. Syd and Bob White replaced the roof on the church, brought in all timber from outlying locations, packed up the portable rostrums, made carrying-cases for equipment, crated up the church bell, the belfry itself, and Shetland boat; Bill Osborne feverishly collected props for close-ups or possible retakes on the studio lot: querns, kesshies, buddies (a small relative of the kesshie), kuddies (still smaller,) rivlins, owsers (wooden scoops for baling out a boat), tushkers (spades for peat-cutting), spans (a high wooden hooped vessel for churning milk), kubbies (hollowed-out stones for pounding grain), and kabes and hommlibands in profusion.

Karl and the Professor spent worried evenings with the film-stock, trying to account for ten thousand feet of negative which had probably only existed in the imagination of some dispatcher. Buddy and George Black were in perpetual committee.

Meanwhile we continued to snatch scenes in the face of the gathering storm. The last shot was made on Soberlie; the last trek was made from the North End, with every man heaving on the loaded camera truck. The third retake of the suicide scene was successful. The ultimate angle on Belle at Skirvidle was made: no more 'head-lightness' for the women. I was feeling almost safe, but for one thing: try how I could and where I could, I could not get the shots of the boats that were needed for the sequence of the climb.

I have explained how the climb was composed; the boat shots were indispensable. Shots were needed of John Laurie rowing and of Finlay, in the stern of his boat. The boys had to be in the prows, stripping off their boots and jerseys as they neared the cliff. Close-ups and long-shots of all this were necessary. The boys had to land at a spot that looked difficult and dangerous, so difficult that it was only just possible; there must be a swell running, enough to make the landing dangerous but not too dangerous. This had to be shot from several angles. The boats had to draw off and wait, if possible in the background of the boys, as they surveyed the climb and awaited the starting-signal. Close-ups with dialogue must be shot all through the climb of John and Finlay; and the angles must be as varied and interesting as their reactions. Finally John must get alarmed, land with a rope and climb to his son's aid.

Altogether about ten main angles and about thirty shots. The camera would have to shift from one boat to another, to the top of the cliffs and to the bottom, all this with a swell running. It is small wonder that I began to despair of ever getting the sequence on Foula.

On the west the swell was always dangerous. We tried three times and nearly wrecked the boats on each occasion. On the north the coast was too broken, a mass of evil skerries. On the east there were some ideal spots but the sun left the coast in shadow after midday. The south, in Helliberg, seemed the only solution.

I fixed at last on the little geo, where Skeets got underneath the wave. It was a perfect place. We had a stand-by call every day. But every day, from that time, the geo was a sullen cauldron of white water. The wind shifted slowly but steadily into the south and as steadily started to blow with increasing force, until, by the 10th of October, the geo, the shelves of Helliberg, the Ness and the cliffs of Skirvidle themselves had vanished into the grey sound and fury of a full gale from the south-west.

It blew until the mess-hut shook and heaved beneath our feet and any minute we expected to see it torn to pieces; it blew the water out of Mill Loch and up into the air, a whirling waterspout three hundred feet high; it blew the camera off its legs with Skeets on top and Karl underneath; it blew until at night sleep was impossible, while every hut tugged and strained at its mooring ropes, the roofs vibrating like drums, the steel guys humming and twanging, and each gust tearing at the boards beside our heads. The yacht in the Voe heeled over until her whole keel showed through the flurry; there she stayed until Alasdair got to her with a rescue party, who made fast a cable, with a breaking-strain of a ton and a half, round her mast. It snapped in two minutes.

Epic, Stupendous, Positively Mediocre

The wireless mast was blown down, the stone dyke behind the school-house was blown over, Frankie, venturing out with me to see Mill Loch waterspout, stepped beyond the shelter of the house and was at once picked up by a flan, hurled forty feet away and rolled head over heels down the hill. I had to go after her on my hands and knees and crawl back to safety with her bumping and laughing behind me.

By the fourth day there were no fresh vegetables, by the fifth day, no fresh meat (except caddy mutton, which means about one joint per person to make a square meal); by the sixth day, no cigarettes left but Woodbines; on the seventh, not even Woodbines; on the eighth, coal and coke gave out and we had to beg from the island's winter store of peat; on the ninth, a famine of everything that makes life worth living stared us in the face; on the tenth, we began to consider seriously a plan of rationing and Ernie, discovering a packet of twenty Players in his oilskin, was nearly lynched. The concert, long planned by Finlay to show the islanders what they missed at Walls, had to be cancelled. It was impossible to hear anybody speak in the mess-hut, the racket was appalling; and tongues of flame, three feet long, shooting out of the stove at all angles, limited our space. It was a bitter blow. (Maud was to have sung 'You are my Honeysuckle, I am the Bee!' and Syd, by request, 'Trees'.)

On the eleventh day, the gale began to drop. Our spirits rose accordingly. We sallied out with Belle and the pony. We had to keep in the brae or in the lee of a croft: the wind was still strong enough to hold a small reflector high on the side of a wall without any need of hands; and the Hoevdi was still breaking; but there was likely to be a lull before the next gale and we no longer had to wonder how twenty-five people in excess of the normal population were possibly to be fed for another week, or perhaps six weeks.

Every day and all day Tom Sullivan had tried to make

contact with the *Vedra*, cautiously hoisting his aerial on a temporary mast in the lee of the Haa. There was no reply. We thought our apparatus must be injured but we could discover nothing very wrong. We decided it must be lack of a proper aerial. Nobody dreamed that the *Vedra*, safe in Scalloway, could possibly be in trouble. But she was.

Scalloway harbour is at the end of a long sound and is 'protected' from the south-west by Burra Isle, which is low-lying and no protection at all against an Atlantic gale. The *Vedra* lying by the pier was pinned against it, while waves broke ceaselessly over her, broke loose a boat, flooded the saloon, flooded the engine-room, flooded the wireless cabin. Night and day she bumped and banged and grinded against the pier. It was impossible to leave the ship and awful to stay on her. Vernon could not get in touch with us and finally his own radio was smashed by a huge sea. He got desperate and wired Gerry: 'Trying for three days to get in touch with Foula but no response. Feel there is possibility their station has been blown away. Weather terrible.'

Gerry now had something real to worry about. For all he knew the huts had gone as well. Our last message to Vernon had been that food supplies were getting low. He could not talk direct to Vernon in Shetland, but he could radio-telephone from Wick, where there is a big station. He jumped into a plane and flew there, stopping at Aberdeen to pick up Gerald Boyne.

Boyne was a young journalist who had come out for two weeks to Foula, stayed at the Nurse's and accompanied us shooting each day. He was delighted with all the details of our life on the island, especially with our parliaments, and he was popular with everybody for his own sake, as well as for the delightful dispatches which he sent out to his papers. Except for telling the world that I wore 'exotic, red leather slippers and a tired look', and was 'worshipped by my crew', two items which I am never allowed to forget, his stories made grand reading, because he was as sympathetic to the whole expedition as we were ourselves.

Even with his heart in his mouth at what he might hear from Vernon when he got to Wick, Gerry saw that here was a great publicity story which it would be criminal to miss. Boyne did not wait to be asked twice. They flew to Wick, they talked to Vernon, who had mended his radio but still had no news from the island and, next day, one million, six hundred and five thousand, nine hundred and seventy-one readers of the *Daily Mail* opened their newspapers to see on the main news-page:

FILM PARTY MAROONED ON STORM-SWEPT ISLAND

And on the main news-page we stayed for the next six days.

III

There are estimated to be some two thousand million people in the world, and in two days' time most of them were reading this sort of thing:

SUPPLY SHIP REACHES LONELY FOULA

FILM UNIT FOUND SAFE

| ARTISTES DE CINEMA DANS UNE DRAME DE SAUVETAGE | SHETLAND ISLES RESCUE |

YACHT RESCUES MAROONED MOVIE MAIDENS

ACTRESSES TELL OF FOULA ORDEAL

AL MARGINE DEL MONDO!

PERILOUS TRIP IN RAGING SEA

LOS ROBINSONS DE CINEMA !

ONE MAN DASH TO MAROONED FILM COLONY

ATTEMPT TO GET OTHERS OFF TODAY

If your eyes can adjust themselves to ordinary print, we will look behind the headlines.

It was really very annoying. Not the publicity but the hysteria that it provoked. On Foula, of course, the only inkling that we had of the world's interest in our fate was a B.B.C. message, which came through to us on Saturday night (the two Gerrys again). Very few of us heard it, partly because there was too much noise and general excitement to worry about the radio. But they heard it at the school-house, and on Sunday night we were all present as the announcer said: 'If the marooned party is listening to this broadcast, we take the opportunity of sending them a word of greeting and, along with it, the hope that the seas will soon subside.' Very handsome.

The seas were already subsiding but there was no sign of the *Vedra*. Monday dawned a clear, beautiful day. There was still too big a sea running to attempt the boat sequence. We could do with some climbing shots. The ladies were left to pack their things. (Belle's final shot—hammering the cover on the letter-boat and throwing it into the sea—had been made on Saturday.) Frankie's last shot had been on Soberlie.

We made straight for Hoevdi Burn, which was fairly roaring over the lip. We lined up the first shot, but I had been watching the sky: a bank of cloud was spreading up against the wind. In ten minutes the brilliant sun had gone and in half an hour we were sheltering from a violent squall of rain. The top of Hoevdi was no place for the day that followed. At noon I sent Bill over to intercept Bill Paton and prepare lunch at the Sneck, where the faithful bell-tent, sodden, covered with mildew and thick with gulls' droppings, was still a home from home. The rain kept on. At lunch time we shouldered our gear and started over the Ufshins. It was pouring with rain, but what was rain to us? 'Better luck to-morrow,' I said.

Lunch was being dished up as we slipped down into the Daal: corned beef and Biggins potatoes. The tent had been flat on the ground all through the gale and smelt like very old, wet tombstones; but after we had all crammed inside for an hour, steam started to rise from the trampled grass and things began to dry off a little. The rain tattooed on the canvas. Presently it slackened. I poked my head out and saw there would be a gap before the next squall. 'Come on!' We charged down Mucklaberg and scrambled out on to a ledge. A narrow gallery ran up the face of the black cliff. On the command: 'Crawl!' Eric crawled up it, vanished out of camera. As I said: 'Cut!' the next squall hit us. We regained the tent and started to dry off once more.

We had just caught Karl out for the third time on 'Spelling B', when there was the sound of galloping hoofs outside. We all listened. They slithered down the bank to a squelchy stop, there was a howl of greeting and the flaps of the tent were burst open by Len, wet as a goldfish. Without waste of words he tore open his waterproof jacket and showered packets of cigarettes into the tent. The next second he had vanished beneath a ravening mob which, in another second, had separated into smiling individuals, each with a cigarette stuck in his face. In five minutes you could not see across the tent.

317

Len reported that the *Vedra* had arrived 'lousy with telegrams', that Vernon was striding about like the captain of a slave-ship, that all the Crêpe-hangers were in a huddle and that Barnes was on his way out to see me. There was also two weeks' mail, and lashings of food, drink, and tobacco —considerably more important.

It must be borne in mind that I had no idea of the screaming front pages on which we were star feature. There had been other storms and other tobacco famines. This one was five times as bad, that was all. If the wind had wrecked the camp, we should have been in considerable misery; but it had not, for which we had Syd to thank. We thought it was very nice of the B.B.C. to think of us and went on making pictures.

I expected a certain amount of wind-up, when the *Vedra* got through, but not the hurricane which was blowing. It was the breakdown of the radio that caused it. Vernon and Gerry had been imagining the worst for so long that they believed it. I was by the Noup when Barnes arrived. He came to look for me, full of importance, in his hands a sheaf of damp telegrams.

I read them and gasped. Vernon was held personally responsible for the immediate evacuation of the entire unit. Barnes was to arrange transportation of all goods, or if impossible, fix storage on the island. Powell was not to shoot another foot of film, was to leave immediately and report to the studio. Black was to arrange brief accommodation for the crew in Lerwick and transportation by first boat to Aberdeen. The ladies and principal actors were to fly down, in order to give out interviews to the Press while the story was still hot. As soon as we arrived at Mainland Powell was to cable complete account of horrors and hardships to gasping, waiting world. These orders were definite, signed, countersigned, irrevocable, final, costly, fragile, perishable, immediate and not to be gainsaid by anybody, which meant Powell.

At first I was furious, then I laughed. The contrast between the onlookers of a storm and the storm's centre never struck me more forcibly.

'When are we all to leave?' I asked.

'To-night,' answered Barnes; it was all serious to him—big stuff.

'To-night? You're mad! It'll be dark in an hour's time. We've got to pack; and anyway there's still the boat sequence to be shot. The girls can go.'

'All of us!' repeated Barnes, in what he imagined was an inexorable tone. 'Mr. Sewell is waiting with steam up. The girls are ready to leave. The rest are packing.'

My smile vanished. This was high-handed, to say the least. I went back to the tent. The crew looked at me expectantly. 'Come on, boys!' I said, 'let's get back to the Haa. We seem to be missing a lot.'

The Daal was a swamp. The rain poured down. Very few of us had oilskins, the morning had been so fine. As usual I wore a flannel shirt and thick sailor trousers, two sweaters and a leather jacket; no hat. By the time I got to the Haa it was dark. I had left the others far behind. My heavy clothes were drenched through and stuck to my body. I found the camp in a turmoil. Some had packed at once, others had waited for me to come. Vernon was hurt by the lack of enthusiasm at his arrival. He had expected to be greeted like the Campbells, his ancestors. His mind was still full of newspaper stories. He was stamping about the place, appearing and disappearing out of the darkness, like a figure in an old German film. I went into the Haa. The girls were sitting by the fire, dressed in unfamiliar clothes, looking subdued and rather scared. Finlay was on the hearth, saying: 'Unless the Chief gives the word I stay right here,' and meaning it. George displayed telegrams like Moses showing the Tablets to the erring Children of Israel. Finlay waved them aside with magnificent gestures. He caught sight of me: 'There you are, Chief, it's time you

were back!' He grasped my arm. 'The man's half drowned!'
Vernon loomed in the background, a dark fidgety figure,
ostentatiously looking at his watch. Frankie helped me off
with my leather coat; it fell with a squashy thud on the
floor. 'Look here, Vernon, it's quite impossible. . . .' 'Sorry,
Micky, old man. I've got my orders.' 'Oh, stop acting like
the Flag Lieutenant. We can't leave to-night. It's. . . .' 'You
can. Everybody here has packed. How soon can the rest of
you be ready?' 'Not to-night, Vernon!' 'Sorry, Micky, old
man. . . .' 'I know! You've got your orders! Now you've
got new ones! The girls are ready and waiting. You
shouldn't be here after dark anyway. Push off and come
back early next morning—and make it early, not tea-time!'
'But my orders. . . .' I lost my temper. 'Damn your orders!
Is that plain? You, Barnes? George?' (They were all there.)
'What do you think this is—a kindergarten? Do you think
we've lived and sweated on this film and on this island to
be pulled off it, with a sequence unfinished, at an hour's
notice, in the dark, with a swell running and the mail-boat
needed? Use your common sense! We'll get ready to-night
to leave the island. If it's fine to-morrow, we'll shoot the
boat sequence off Ham Little. We'll be finished by the time
you get here. Then we'll come with you. If it's bad weather
we'll come anyway. But not to-night!' Vernon looked
irresolute. Even then, of course, I did not realize the week
of badgering from Gerry which he had undergone, on top
of his own anxiety. 'Very well. I agree—under protest,' he
said shortly. 'Make a note of that, George,' I said (rather
unnecessarily), 'Mr. Sewell protests.'

My memory of the next few hours is vague and confused.

I remember going down to the jetty with Frankie and
Belle and a silent, grumpy Vernon. The motor-boat was
rising and falling, even in the shelter of the Voe. Outside
there was a big swell running. The saloon light of the

Vedra, a quarter of a mile out, appeared and disappeared as she rolled. The rain fell in torrents. It was a dirty night.

Three days before, Frankie and I had faced one another in the Haa. Outside the storm was at its height. It swooped and hummed and crashed. Sleep was impossible even if I could have slept. It was very late. Lights were out in the huts. The Aladdin lamp on the table, its mantle broken by cigarette ash, burnt sootily. The peat on the fire was damp and smouldered. The Haa looked untidy and dishevelled. Overhead Alasdair snored, Belle lay sleeping, Mrs. Rutherford slept the sleep of the soon-to-be-repatriated exile.

Frankie was going on the next boat out, her work was finished; I say her work because, without her, Belle would have been lost; she says so herself. That had been the important part of her job. Now it was finished, and we were no longer prisoners together, I was able to say a lot of things that should never have been left unsaid.

The two girls stumbled down the wet steps; there was a little crowd gathering to see them off. Their baggage was dropped after them, there was an inch of water and oil floating in the bottom of the boat, the engine sputtered and turned over, the girls crouched in the shelter of Vernon's patent wind-break as the launch curved out and vanished into the darkness, guided through a waste of waters and skerries by a pocket-torch held by Tiger. 'Good-bye!' we called. 'Good-bye, Foula!' came faintly over the waves. The pocket-torch winked and went out.

I remember a mysterious summons to meet Walter Ratter by my hut. He refused to come into the light. 'What is it, Walter?' He had pressed a roll of paper into my hand. 'It's from the men, Mister Powell.' I struck a match; before it blew out I saw the roll was money, with a paper round it, torn from a notebook, covered with names. Walter was talking: 'We thought we would give you all a dinner, but there's no time for that, so I've brought you the money we collected and you must say what you will do with it.' There was a lump in my throat. 'Walter, you have got to tell that to the boys.' 'Na, na, Mister Powell, I can't make a speech.' 'But you've just made one—I want the others to hear it.' Walter blinked in the lamplight as I told the others, hastily summoned to the mess-hut. The men of the island who had hurriedly held their meeting in the Shop, crowded outside in the dark. Everyone listened to Walter's speech with a full heart. This was the sort of thing that was worth working for, the thing that meant nothing to outsiders but everything to ourselves, the appreciation of the men of Foula and the fellowship that had grown between us, the memories that would always be shared; this deep feeling, more than anything, was the cause of the shock and our instant revolt when ordered to pack up and leave as if our long struggle of eighteen weeks meant no more than an illicit week-end.

'Walter,' I said, 'we'll accept the money, and thank you.' (There was a five-minute interval here for cheers.) 'I'll tell you what I am going to do with it. I am going to have a map made—a souvenir map, in colour, of Foula—with the names of the camps and the places where we've worked and pictures of things we all know; and every man who has worked on the film shall have a copy, so that he can frame it and hang it on his wall and show it to his grandchildren when he tells them what a tough old bird he is, thanks to those days on Foula.'

The proposal was carried without a dissenting vote. The frontispiece of this book shows how I kept my promise.

The formal presentation of the mess-hut to the Island followed and soon after dinner we went early to bed, most of us for the last time.

The last day was no miracle. It stayed grey and stormy. The *Vedra* appeared at noon. All the afternoon we were loading from the mail-boat. The swell was dangerous and there was one nasty moment when our gunwale got jammed under the *Vedra's* counter in the trough of a big sea. We clawed off without much damage. We were all aboard by tea-time, those who were going; there were still nine left on the island. The anchor was raised. The *Vedra* blew her siren. A group of islanders stood on the jetty and waved through the mist. The mail-boat circled round us at full speed; we waved and they waved; there was so much to be done and so little time to say anything. We turned our bows for Scalloway. The faces in the mail-boat blurred. The island dropped astern in the twilight. Soon we were away from the land and could see our home for what it was to the rest of the world—a lonely, desolate island. It vanished in the darkness.

Scalloway post office was full of telegrams from newspapers. I answered them, while cars were obtained for Lerwick. My old clothes and boots seemed out of place. I had not been to Mainland for ten weeks. As soon as I could, I changed.

My immediate job was to persuade Gerry that a skeleton crew and the four principal actors must stay in Lerwick, as the coast around the harbour was suitable for the boat scenes and it was essential that we have Shetland boats and Shetland men to row them. It is incredible, but it took him a long time to see it. He wanted to do the scenes in Cornwall! At last he agreed.

I met with revolt from my actors, especially John. I admit it was hard to be half-way home, within reach of mail and telegrams from frantic relatives. I preached the Old School Tie and he gave me an ultimatum. To-day was Wednesday. A boat sailed. There was another on Monday. Get the scenes before Monday or else. . . .

We got them on Monday morning.

I do not propose to create suspense. I had enough that week to last me for ever—sitting all day in the rain in an open boat. Let a plain statement suffice. We shot those scenes on Monday morning, all thirty of them. On a day when the Meteorological Bureau reported no sunshine *anywhere else* of any duration whatever (it was 26th October 1936—see if I lie), Lerwick in Shetland had six hours of sunshine! It was watery, weak sunshine, but under Ernie's magic hand it becomes vigorous, it achieves contrast. And Skeets! Never shall I forget him. Half the time he had no tripod. His tall body screwed up in the boat, while I directed over his shoulder, he held as steady as the Kame and performed miracles. Thirty shots in four hours—in boats—in a pitching sea—on slippery rocks—with four actors—and dramatic scenes: it was worth eighteen weeks together to show it could be done!

The boat sailed that afternoon at four o'clock and we all sailed with it. Every sequence was complete. Everything planned had been finished. The picture was in the can.

IV

We once had an old cook who was a great hand at elaborate pastries. I watched her in the kitchen putting the final touches to a huge pie—vine-leaves, scrolls, and curly bits of pastry—all brushed over with a feather dipped in yolk of egg. A final flourish, and: 'There, Master Michael, a pie fit for a king!' she said.

Then, as she slid it into a hot oven, the disillusionment of the true artist swept over her and I heard her mutter darkly: 'And then you eats it and it's all done. . . .'

If her audience praised her work, she beamed. If they were indifferent, she would say scornfully: 'Not a bit of good cooking for some folks.'

She is still making pies and I am still making films, but for a long time none can be so near my heart as *The Edge of the World*. I wish I were as sure of its perfection as the old cook was of her pies. At any rate, like her, I can always have the last word.

APPENDIX

CREDIT TITLES

*

Appendices are of two kinds, chronic and acute. Some people regard them as unnecessary evils and ignore them. I will say no more. I cannot force my Appendix on the reader. It is a matter for his conscience.

When a finished film appears on the screen, it is preceded by a long list of unfamiliar names, of people who have helped to make the film. These are called CREDIT TITLES. (Vernon says that *The Edge of the World* should have a special DISCREDIT TITLE: 'This film was made In Spite Of . . . etc.')

The Edge of the World opens with very simple titles, in a graceful Gaelic lettering evolved, after some thought, by Mr. Parkins, the Title Expert.

Title 1.   The slow shadow of Death is falling
upon the Outer Isles of Scotland.
This is the story of one of them—and
of all of them.

Title 2.   When the Roman fleet sailed round
Britain, they saw from the Orkneys a
distant island in the North, like a blue
haze across a hundred miles of sea. They
called it—
ULTIMA THULE

Title 3.   THE EDGE
of the
WORLD

Title 4.   A
JOE ROCK
PRODUCTION

Title 5.   STORY AND DIRECTION
by
MICHAEL POWELL

Title 6.   MUSICAL DIRECTOR   CYRIL RAY
Choral effects by
THE WOMEN OF THE GLASGOW
ORPHEUS CHOIR
Conductor:
SIR HUGH S. ROBERTON
Orchestrations:
W. L. WILLIAMSON

Title 7.   CAMERA
ERNEST PALMER
SKEETS KELLY
MONTY BERMAN

Title 8.   PRODUCTION STAFF
GERARD BLATTNER
A. SEABOURNE
VERNON C. SEWELL
W. H. FARR
GEORGE BLACK

Title 9.   EDITOR   DEREK TWIST
ASSISTANT EDITOR   BOB WALTERS
SOUND   L. K. TREGELLAS
PROPS   W. OSBORNE
RECORDING ENGINEER
W. H. O. SWEENY

Title 10.   CAST
The Manson Family
PETER   JOHN LAURIE
RUTH, his daughter
                    BELLE CRYSTALL
ROBBIE, her brother ERIC BERRY
JEAN, their grandmother
                    KITTY KIRWAN
The Gray Family
JAMES GRAY   FINLAY CURRIE
ANDREW, his son
          NIALL MACGINNIS

Title 11. THE CATECHIST
          GRANT SUTHERLAND
THE LAIRD
          CAMPBELL ROBSON
THE TRAWLER SKIPPER
          GEORGE SUMMERS

Title 12.   And all the people of the lonely
                    island of
               FOULA
          where this story was made.

In most films the credit titles, no matter how ingeniously presented, are a dull interlude. But behind those sober names lie concealed for me, and for you who read this story, old friends, loyalties and adventures. No one man ever made a film. He can inspire it. He can stamp his personality on it. But in the long run it is good team-work that makes a good film.

Index

★

329

Index

Index

Index

332

Index

Index

Soberlie, 105, 119, 120, 275–6, 282, 311

Souvenir Map, 322 (and frontis-piece)

Sphere, The, 12

Springs, 121

St. Kilda, 11, 12, 15, 16, 17, 40, 46, 47, 48, 49, 50, 75, 94, 95, 230

St. Kilda, The Last Days of, 17

Stack of the Gaads, 121, 208

Stöel, 114, 202, 253

'Storm, The Great,' 312

Stornoway, 46

Streeter, Syd, 8, 76, 77, 78, 86, 87, 104, 121, 130, 131, 134, 143, 144, 148, 153, 154, 177, 188, 189, 190, 196, 199, 201, 202, 203, 220, 221, 243, 252, 261, 265–6, 287–9, 296–8, 306, 313

Sullivan, Tom, 193, 195, 213, 214, 243, 290, 300, 313

Sumburgh Head, 57, 90, 91

Sumburgh Röst, 90

Summers, George, 7, 81, 149, 152, 179, 180, 184, 185, 213

Sunday Graphic, The, 309

Sutherland, Hamish, 7, 10, 80, 81, 130, 149, 195, 213, 217, 220, 243, 256, 261, 264, 290, 296, 298, 299, 300

Sweeny, Bill, 7, 188, 206, 213, 284, 286

Synopsis of Film, 161

Thurso, 86, 149

Tiger Tim, 207, 208

Times, The, 12

Tom o' Gravins, 8, 178, 228, 240, 248

Traill, Mrs., 245–6

'Travelaughs', 14

Trawlers, 93, 94, 95

Tregellas ('Puffin'), 7, 206, 290, 297

Twagoes, 8, 177

Twist, Derek, 234, 235, 281

Tyree, 54

Udal Tenure, 139

Ufshins, The, 114, 117, 253–4

Ultima Thule, 161

Umphray, Andrew, 8, 126

Umphray, Gerald, 247, 261

Umphray, Robbie, 247, 264

Umphray, Scotty, 133, 145, 147

Vaila, 146, 217

Vedra, The
Her habits, 4; at Aberdeen, 6; her problems, 143; arrival at Lerwick, 176, 177; at Ham Voe, 193; her radio, 193, 295; her uses, 204; her drawbacks, 205, 207, 209; her social attractions, 206; Sunday excursions, 283; her unwilling co-operation, 294; at Scalloway, 155, 183, 314; evacuation of Rock City, 323

Veedal, 131, 132, 271

'Vernon,'
His stammer, 3; his professional pride, 5; his adequacy, 25; his trawler film, 27, 93; his numerous friends, 28, 31, 32; Portsmouth fiasco, 28; Highland fling, 29; Success at Sunderland, 30, 149, 150; *** the Dook! 41, 48; retreat from Glasgow, 48–50; at the Coral Island, 152, 155; his Knights-bridge cellar, 169; barratry at Scalloway, 183; friction with Smallie, 199, 209, 210; 'Black Jack', 205, 206, 207; abduction of Peggy, 288; 'Ancient Mariner' stuff, 294, 295, 309, 314; The Flag-Lieutenant, 318, 320

Ve Skerries, 137

Victoria Pier (Lerwick), 177, 179, 185

Walker, Joseph, 172

Walls, 99, 145, 146, 147, 155, 173, 213, 215–22

Walters, Bob, 235, 326

Warner Brothers, 18, 170, 171

'Water Battle, The,' 299

Whirley Knowe, 112

White, Bill, 5, 208, 219, 299–301

White, Bob, 213, 306

Wick Radio, 314–15

Willie of Ham, 271